Inflation, Trade, and Taxes

Inflation,

EDITED BY

David A. Belsley

Edward J. Kane

Paul A. Samuelson

Robert M. Solow

Trade and Taxes

Essays in Honor of Alice Bourneuf

OHIO STATE UNIVERSITY PRESS: COLUMBUS

HG229
I46

Library of Congress Cataloging in Publication Data

Main entry under title:

Inflation, trade and taxes.

Includes index.

Contents: Inflation: Solow, R. M. Down the Phillips curve with gun and camera. Lerner, A. P. Wages, profits, and marginal analysis. Esposito, F. F. and Esposito, L. Industry price changes, market structure, and inflation. Belsley, D. A. United States silver coinage. [etc.]

1. Inflation (Finance)—Addresses, essays, lectures.   2. Commerce—Addresses, essays lectures.   3. Taxation—Addresses, essays, lectures. I. Bourneuf, Alice. II. Belsley, David A.

HG229.I46   332.4'1   75-19099

ISBN 0-8142-0194-6

Contents

Preface

This volume is a testimony to Alice Bourneuf. That cannot be said in the same sense of every Festschrift, for often the continental mode prevails in which a scholar who has a stranglehold on an important university and area of study has tribute exacted from his students: paying such *Danegeld* is like paying taxes, a necessary cost of doing business. Bourneuf commands only our respect.

I count more than nine lives for Alice Bourneuf as a scholar. She was both of the age of Taussig and the age of Schumpeter at Harvard in the 1930s. And for that matter of the age of Hansen. Once when I wrote of how Schumpeter gave only A's to women where Taussig gave them only C's, a friend gently reminded me that Bourneuf's A was a person's A.

To the current generation, idle gossip of that bygone time has the unreality of the Trojan Wars or the medieval era. Was it really the case within the present half-century that Radcliffe females could not discuss Shakespeare in the same room with Harvard males for fear that a six-letter word might occur? (President Emeritus Lowell once asked me indignantly, "Would you want *your* sister to discuss Macbeth with men?" I have no sister, but still. . . .) Economics, at the graduate level, was emancipated already by the 1930s; only at the under-graduate level did the charade persist of having a Mason give his hour class to 60 Harvard men, and then repeat it later to 9.7 Radcliffe women. Also, female dissertations had to be shorter because, although Radcliffe graduate students had stack privileges in Widener Library, they had to leave at 6 P.M.; any midnight oil was to be burned in their own garrets.

All of us in the 1930s were children of the depression. The fact that there were no jobs was liberating: if one had a little, one could pursue the unhurried life on that little. But all good things, and depressions, come to an end.

Bourneuf went to study at Louvain in Belgium just in time to be caught by World War II's outbreak. After a term in Seymour Harris's research galleys, she proceeded to the Office of Price Administration. The late Stephen Enke, in his algebraically sweet manner, once asserted: There are three kinds of economists—competent economists, incompetent economists, and OPA economists. He was more right than he realized. Kenneth Galbraith, Dick

Gilbert, Walter Salant, Victor Perlo, Jacob Mosak, David Lusher, Murray Geissler—the list is long—were alumni of that remarkable wartime group whose names came to be heard of. I can remember a visit in the early 1940s to one of the hot temporaries on the Mall, where every economist I knew was frantically tearing up completed contributions to a treatise on the subject and reversing their contents: Leon Henderson and J. K. Galbraith shifted gears from "no freeze" to a "general freeze." Everyone but Bourneuf, who had time to chat. Why this exception? I asked. I'm alright, Jack, she replied in effect, my chapter is on the *history* of price controls and not even Ken Galbraith can change that.

Again, all good things come to an end, and Alice Bourneuf moved over to the Federal Reserve. Those were great days at the Fed because of the carpetbaggers from the universities: Dick Musgrave, Robert Triffin, Lloyd Metzler, Evsey Domar, Gottfried Haberler, Alex Gerschenkron, Howard Ellis, Agnete (Laursen) Kalckar. A regret of my life is that I never heard Keynes at his two wartime Federal Reserve seminars. Like Moses, it was not given me to enter into the promised land of the 1944 Bretton Woods meetings, where Ajax and Hector—I mean, White and Vinson and Keynes—did mighty battle. But, like Joshua, Bourneuf was there. A muckraker might say she was there to set up the International Monetary Fund, where she proceeded to get a job. It is not documented that she contrived to create the Marshall Plan so that she could go to Norway. But bliss was it in that dawn to be alive and be Dick Bissell's plenipotentiary in the Norway that Brofuss was propelling into the twenty-first century.

Good Americans go to Paris when they die. Lucky Americans go there on a U.S. payroll while they live. Alice Bourneuf moved "down" from Oslo to Paris just when the Marshall Plan was at its zenith. How can you get them back on the Washington farm after that? Moreover, Joseph McCarthy's Washington was no great place to be, even for those who had never signed a petition for the release of Mooney or sold cookies for Spanish Refugee relief. Our victories yet to come, in Indochina and elsewhere, had to be won in the seminars of Mt. Holyoke. The Eisenhower years provided a rich spectacle for the scholar and teacher in macroeconomics. The long academic vacations provided the leisure to write up the Norwegian experience, and investigate the undulations of inventories. From a distance of 100 miles, I can guess that Bourneuf's voice was heard in the Holyoke senior common room. I recall once hearing her indignation when one of her honors students, who had written an original analysis of an accelerator-multiplier model, was asked in her oral examination by an interdisciplinary colleague: "But what is the *sociology* of your model?"

Two years as a visiting professor at the exciting and turbulent Berkeley of the 1950s may have made Bourneuf a loose ion. In any case, when Boston College called, she jumped. Never one to tolerate sexual discrimination, her indignation was unsparing when someone proposed that another woman be appointed to share an office with Bourneuf. And never underestimate the powers of an activist: many a dean at B.C. must have divided time into "Before and After Bourneuf." At AEA conventions, when Father McEwen and Alice Bourneuf appeared, department heads quaked for the ivory they were hoarding. The results are now history.

It is not meet to register in a public place the bonds of affection this remarkable economist has inspired. She is living disproof of the Durocher Theorem that good guys end up last. A female scholar in a Neanderthal age of men, a Catholic in the American university of the first half of the twentieth century when there was a shameful trace of truth in the phrase "Anti-Catholicism is the antisemitism of the intellectual," such a person could be forgiven for becoming abrasive. Not so Bourneuf. The militance I wrote of had no self-pity or resentments in it. She sought excellence, and learned some of the Jesuit arts of persuasion and feasibility in its pursuit. Sharp elbows are not shapely, and people are loved, some sage has said, in inverse relationship to their ability to take care of themselves in the Darwinian struggle for existence. Alice Bourneuf has been much loved. Her friends and colleagues—but I repeat myself—feel honored in presenting these birthday gifts.

Paul A. Samuelson

Inflation, Trade and Taxes

Down the Phillips Curve with Gun and Camera

Robert M. Solow

Any time seems to be the right time for reflections on the Phillips curve. So long as the actuality or threat of inflation remains a current problem, and so long as no clearly better organizing device presents itself, economists will argue about the Phillips curve. I do not intend to provide a complete survey of recent ideas on this subject, but only to comment on a few issues of theory and fact. In particular, I have stayed away from those aspects of the problem that were thoroughly discussed in James Tobin's splendid Presidential Address to the American Economic Association [14].

BEGINNINGS

The idea of a relation between the level of output or employment on the one hand and the rate of change of the money wage rate or the price level on the other is hardly new. There is casual reference to it in the *General Theory*, and a somewhat less casual remark in Joan Robinson's early *Essays in the Theory of Employment*.[1] It is not a very deep or subtle idea, and economics did not begin with Keynes; so it would hardly be surprising if such casual observations could be found in even earlier literature. Still, it fits more comfortably into Keynesian

1. " . . . In any given condition of the labor market there is a certain more or less definite level of employment at which money wages will rise, and a lower level of

and post-Keynesian modes of thought, because the earlier economics tended to divorce real and monetary phenomena and therefore almost had to regard the level of aggregate output and the rate of change of the value of money as essentially independent, except perhaps for ephemeral disequilibria.

In any case, those casual remarks do not earn many brownie points. Really systematic attention to the relation between real tightness in the economy and the rate of inflation dates only from Phillips's paper of 1958. (I think Paul Samuelson and I coined the term "Phillips Curve" in a paper we gave at the 1959 AEA convention [12]). The date is significant. What was in everyone's mind at the time was the experience of 1955–58, the years that gave currency to the phrase "creeping inflation," though by now they begin to look like the good old days. The Phillips curve was one way of making sense of that episode. Compensation per man-hour rose at an annual rate of 5.5% to 6% between 1955 and 1957 when the unemployment rate averaged just a bit over 4%, while compensation per man-hour rose at an annual rate of about 4% between 1957 and 1959 when the unemployment rate averaged something over 6%. Correspondingly, the private non-farm deflator inflated at an annual rate of 3.5% in the earlier two years and 1.5% to 2% in the later two years. Those were not very good years for productivity increase—if we could achieve that kind of wage behavior now, it would probably be accompanied by a somewhat slower rise of the price level. In any case, with that sort of immediate historical backdrop and no great show of econometrics, Samuelson and I hazarded the guess that it would take at least 5.5% unemployment to stabilize the price level, and that 4% unemployment would be accompanied by wage increases of 5% a year and price increases of 2.5% a year. For a while that looked reasonable. Maybe five years is a reasonable lifetime for an educated guess. George Perry soon did a really first-class analysis and confirmed the orders of magnitude [9].

It did not occur to me then that the Phillips curve (or perhaps Phillips surface would be better, to signal that more than the unemployment rate governs the rate of wage increase) needed any subtle theoretical justification. It seemed reasonable in a commonsense way that the change in the money wage, like the

employment at which money wages fall. Between the two critical levels there will be a neutral range within which wages are constant. . . . When employment stands above the critical level, then, if conditions are such that a general rise in money wages sets up no reaction to reduce effective demand there will be a progressive rise in wages with a constant level of employment, for prices and profits will rise with money wages and all the circumstances which led to a first rise in wages will remain in force and lead to a second. But the existence of unemployed workers anxious to find jobs exercises a drag upon trade unions and the rise in money wages will be slight and gradual. An increase in employment, in this situation, will strengthen the trade union position and tend to speed up the rise in money wages, but so long as unemployment remains appreciable the upward movement can not become overwhelmingly powerful" [11, pp. 7–8].

change in any other price, should respond to the demand-supply balance in the labor market. That is the content of the passage from Joan Robinson already quoted. It was fairly obvious that the aggregate unemployment rate was not an ideal measure of the excess demand for labor. In the first place, one would want something like the excess of unfilled vacancies over the number of unemployed. In the second place, the implications of any given difference between vacancies and unemployment must depend on the degree of imperfection of the labor market and on the degree of substitutability of one kind of labor for another; so even if comprehensive data on vacancies existed for the United States (as they did not and do not), one would still not have an unambiguous measure of excess demand for labor. In the third place, even if we were to agree to summarize the state of the labor market by the unemployment rate, it is hard to say what particular unemployment rate "ought" to correspond to wage stability; indeed, since measured unemployment has a component coming from voluntary turnover, new entrants and reentrants to the labor market, and minimal frictions, and since this component could easily change from time to time, the correspondence between the unemployment rate and the demand-supply balance in the labor market might be subject to unpredictable shifts. In spite of these qualifications and others, the unemployment rate seemed like a fair barometer of the pressure of demand in the labor market. I considered it a defensible hypothesis that excess demand for labor should drive its price up; though of course that leaves entirely open the question of the mechanism that determines the equilibrium unemployment rate, if there is one.

Nevertheless, the Phillips curve came under theoretical attack right away. Anti-Keynesians did not like it, although, as I have said, there is little that is specifically Keynesian about it, either historically or analytically. I think the main reason for this alignment is the one I have already mentioned; once upon a time economists had believed that there was no durable (I will not insist on permanent) gearing between real things and monetary things. Keynes had disagreed and apparently carried the day. Now it was argued that there could be no durable gearing between real things and the rate of change of monetary things, and some of the arguments sounded very much like the earlier ones.

Money is a veil; or, to put it more technically, all of the real equations are homogeneous of degree zero in prices so only relative prices matter, and they and only they are what can be determined by the real equations of general equilibrium. (By the way, the real question is not so much whether that argument is true as whether it is relevant in calendar time. It is very important to realize this. Failure to realize it has triggered innumerable wasted words.) Twenty-five years and one derivative later, it is argued that the rate of change of money prices is a veil. Therefore only unexpected inflation can be geared to real things. Events in the real economy will be insulated completely from expected inflation by changes in nominal interest rates, escalation provisions in intertemporal contracts, and eventually by the development of money substitutes. Since any steady rate of wage and price inflation must come to be accurately anticipated if it continues sufficiently long, only accelerating inflation or deflation can have a permanent connection with the real economy. It follows that the Phillips curve is an illusion except for the short run. In the short run, with expectations given, any variation in the rate of inflation is unexpected and can therefore have real causes and real consequences. In the long run, however, the only steady rate of inflation is an accurately expected one; whether it is 1 percent a year or 10 percent a year can have nothing to do with the real economy, which will have compensated for it completely. In a word, the change in the price level is a veil. You might say, the rate of change of a veil is a veil (per unit time).

THE ROLE OF EXPECTATIONS

There is something deeply satisfying—not to say suspicious—about any proposition that seems to deduce important assertions about the real world from abstract principles. Let us look at this one more closely. With particular reference to the behavior of money wages, it seems to say something like this: start with any wage equation or Phillips surface that gives the percentage rate of growth of the money wage as a function of the unemployment rate, the rate of increase of productivity, and perhaps other real economic variables. Then mere economic rationality tells you that you must add the expected rate of price inflation to the right-hand side of the equation. Why? Well, try the following thought experiment. Suppose that the price level had been constant for a long time, long enough for everyone to believe with certainty that it would remain constant. Then suppose that a particular configuration of real variables were consistent with a money wage growing at 1% a year, say. So we have one point on the Phillips surface. Now suppose something happens to convince everyone, with certainty, that from now on the price level will rise at 2% a year. Then "surely" the very same configuration of real variables can be consistent only with a money wage increase of 3% a year—because wages growing at 3% and prices rising at 2% is "essentially" the same thing as wages rising at 1% and prices not rising at all. This is just an elaborate way of saying that the rate of change of nominal magnitudes is a veil; but at least now we know that this belief (a definition of economic rationality combined with the judgment that the world behaves rationally) boils down to the statement that the expected rate of inflation appears additively, with a coefficient of one, in the wage equation.

We can keep things simple by assuming that the ratio of price level to unit labor cost (the "mark-up") is itself either constant or a function of real economic variables like the rate of growth of output, or the pressure of demand on capacity. Then it will turn out that an equation for the rate of change of the general price level will also have the expected rate of change of the general price level on the right-hand side, appearing additively, with a coefficient of one.

This arrangement has an important consequence. Go back to the situation I described earlier, in which the price level is constant, and has been constant long enough for the expected rate of inflation to be zero. Suppose again that real configuration is such that the money wage is rising 1% a year, and that this is fully consistent with a stable price level because productivity is rising at 1% a year and unit labor costs are thus constant. Now let something happen to change the real configuration suddenly—a sustained rise in exports, say, that reduces the unemployment rate. For a while, expectations are sluggish, so the expected rate of inflation will remain at or near zero. Since that term on the right-hand side of the wage equation is constant, the lowered unemployment rate will be translated into a faster rise in money wages, and therefore into a rising price level. So far this looks like a Phillips-curve story.

But, of course, if prices continue to rise, the expected rate of inflation can hardly stay at zero. It will start to catch up on the actual rate of inflation. If the actual rate of inflation should level off at some maintained figure, then eventually the expected rate of inflation would become equal to the actual maintained rate. But then, because of the structure of the price equation, the actual rate of inflation on the left and the expected rate of inflation on the right would just cancel each other off, and it would all be exactly as it was when both were zero. That is to say, the only real configuration compatible with steady inflation of x percent a year is the same one that is compatible with steady inflation at any rate. (There may be a family of equivalent real configurations instead of just one, but in the literature it is customary to speak of just one real variable, the unemployment rate, and to speak of the "natural rate of unemployment.")

Alternatively one can say that to maintain the new lower unemployment rate forever, it will be necessary to preserve forever the initial difference between the actual and expected rates of inflation, and the only way to do this, apart from mass hypnosis, is to have accelerating inflation, just fast enough so that expectations lag behind actuality by a fixed amount. For this reason, believers in this argument and in the existence of a natural rate of unemployment are often labeled "accelerationists." If the argument is right, then indeed the downward-sloping Phillips curve is a short-run phenomenon that is necessarily shifting whenever the economy is observed to be on it. The only permanent long-run Phillips curve, compatible with correct expectations, is vertical at the natural rate of unemployment.

TESTS OF THE ACCELERATIONIST HYPOTHESIS

Even propositions that are self-evidently true ought to be tested occasionally. In this case we need only check that the expected rate of inflation enters the wage equation additively with a coefficient of one. There is, however, a small problem: nobody knows what the expected rate of inflation actually is.

The earliest attempts to measure Phillips surfaces usually introduced a lagged rate of price increase as an independent variable. The reasoning was not so sophisticated as what I have just sketched; the idea was simply that a recent history of rapid price increase would make workers pushful and employers yielding, other things equal. Nevertheless, one could imagine a lagged rate of price increase serving as a proxy for the expected rate of inflation, on the overly restrictive hypothesis of static expectations. That is hardly convincing, and we shall have to do better. But it must be recorded that whenever and wherever the lagged rate of price increase appears as an independent variable in a wage equation, it appears to have a coefficient of roughly one-half, more often slightly less. This is significantly less than the accelerationists' theoretical value of unity, both in the statistical and analytical sense. If there were static expectations, and if the true coefficient were really one-half, then the long-run Phillips curve would be twice as steep as the short-run curve, but that is a long way from being vertical. And the world would behave not quite rationally.

Of course, one ought to be able to do better than static expectations, and anyhow you cannot kill a theory with a fact. There have been a few recent attempts to get at this question with a more sophisticated apparatus, notably by the Saint Louis Federal Reserve Bank [1], by Robert J. Gordon [5,6], and by Otto Eckstein and Roger Brinner [4]. They have succeeded in getting that crucial coefficient much closer to unity. I want to discuss these attempts at some length, for two reasons. The first is that the question itself is intrinsically interesting. The second reason is that these studies—and some other current research on the Phillips surface that I shall also mention—raise some difficult general questions about the relation of theory to practice in our econometric age.

The analysis by the Saint Louis Federal Reserve Bank comes very close to verifying the accelerationist hypothesis. Gordon rejects it, but he produces a steeper Phillips curve than most—and in some variants is unable to reject the strict accelerationist hypothesis. Although they are in other respects quite different, these two analyses are rather similar in the way they try to measure "the expected rate of inflation." A natural step beyond the assumption of static expectations is the notion of representing the expected rate of price increase. The mechanism of adaptive expectations represents the expected rate of inflation as an infinite weighted sum of past observed rates of price increase, with the weights decaying geometrically toward zero as one goes further back into the past. There are various generalizations of this idea. An alternative is to take only a finite weighted sum of past rates of increase, with the weights constrained only to change smoothly and to go to zero at the end. Both Gordon and the Saint Louis economists choose this latter option. They both end by measuring the expected rate of inflation through a very long distributed lag on past rates of inflation, with weights whose center of gravity lies rather far in the past. And they both draw their weights from regressions relating nominal interest rates on Treasury securities to past rates of price increase and other variables.

In Gordon's most recent paper his preferred series of weights comes from a regression on the Treasury bill rate: the mean lag of expected behind actual price increases is about five quarters; more significantly, the weight attributed to the actual price change twelve quarters ago is still about one-fifth the size of the weight attributed to the current rate of inflation. (When the same process is applied to the rate of interest on three-to-five-year Treasury bonds, the mean lag is more than six quarters, and the weight for twelve quarters back is still more than half the weight on current price changes.)

In the case of the Saint Louis economists, the weights for price expectations come from a regression to explain the corporate Aaa bond rate, and the lag is even longer. The center of gravity of the lag distribution comes nine quarters in the past, and, since the weights are symmetric, fully half of the explanation of the currently expected rate of inflation rests on observed price changes between nine and seventeen quarters in the past.

INDIRECT MEASUREMENT OF INFLATIONARY EXPECTATIONS

I do not intend to criticize the use of mechanical models per se to measure the effects of expectations. I might do so if I had a better alternative to suggest, but I know of none. But I do think there are some dubious aspects of this particular device.

The most important preliminary is to understand *why* these long lags seem to be needed to make wage equations work; that is a matter of fact, not theory. The problem is this: why did wages (and unit labor costs and prices) rise more moderately in 1968 and 1969 when the unemployment rate was 3.5% than in 1970 and 1971 when the unemployment rate was first 5% and then 6% for months at a time? This is hardly an idle question. If we knew the answer to it, we would know why those early guesses that 4% unemployment would be accompanied by price increases of 2.5% a year have now given way to the much more pessimistic guess that prolonged 4% unemployment would be accompanied by inflation of the price level at a 5% annual rate, or perhaps even at a perpetually accelerating rate. More topically, we would understand why Mr. Nixon, who came into office in 1969 to set the economy free, was engaged in wage and price control by 1971.

The accelerationist hypothesis, combined with long lags in the formation of price expectations, has an answer to the puzzle. That is why it works in regressions. It says: wages rose so moderately in 1968 and 1969 because the 1% and 2% price increases of 1965 and 1966 were still holding down the expected rate of inflation. In effect, the momentary Phillips curve was unsustainably flat because some of the inflation was unanticipated. Symmetrically, wages rose so rapidly in 1970 and 1971, despite the recession, because the rapid price increases of 1968 and 1969 were still holding up the expected rate of inflation; it will take a long time to break down the inflationary expectations just as it took a long time to build them up. (This sounds contradictory, but it is not: prices were rising substantially in 1968 and 1969, just less than the tightness of the economy might have suggested.) The accelerationist and near-accelerationist models account for the puzzle by having expectations lag substantially behind facts, and by attributing an important effect to expectations. This is important because anyone who would like to do without the accelerationist hypothesis will have to find another way to explain the critical facts. I will come to some alternatives later.

I am, in fact, suspicious of that long lag, and only partly because I have a sneaking feeling that long lags provide too much leeway for the econometrician. Given enough flexibility in lag structure, you can explain anything; and what can explain anything explains nothing. A more important *a priori* reason for suspecting the long lag is this. The logic of the models says that the expected rate of inflation needs to be in there because wage bargains and wage decisions are real decisions, and money-wage changes can be converted to real changes only through the implicit intervention of expectations about the future of the price level. But most wage decisions are decisions for a year or even less. Obviously the highly visible heavy-industry collective bargaining contracts are two-year and even three-year decisions, but they cover only a fraction of the labor force, most of which is not even organized. Now if you want to form expectations about the price level in the next year or two, it is doubtful that events three years ago contain much useful information. The very distant behavior of the price level is what really matters for the extrapolation relevant to the purchase of a life insurance policy, but not to the setting of a wage rate that can be changed again soon.

When you think about it, Gordon's regression on the bill rate is very difficult to understand. A Treasury bill is at most a ninety-day commitment; what matters is mostly the behavior of the price level in the next 90 days, and I find it hard to believe that the behavior of the price level between seven quarters ago and eight quarters ago contains any useful information not contained in much more recent data. In this regard, it is interesting that a regression using the three-to-five-year bond rate estimates a considerably longer lag, which is consistent with the fact that what is wanted is a longer extrapolation. And the Saint Louis economists, who use a long-term rate, estimate the longest lags of all. It may be, however, that the whole maturity structure is too closely knit together to permit this kind of discrimination. I continue to think that the long-lag sluggish-expectations variables are inappropriate measures of anything but rather long-run expectations about the price level, and what is relevant for wage behavior is something more sensitive to what has happened to prices in the immediate past.

DIRECT MEASUREMENT OF INFLATIONARY EXPECTATIONS

One could see more clearly what is happening if there were some usable direct measures of price expectations. In fact, there are at least two such, but neither is quite appropriate in the circumstances. J. A. Livingston, formerly financial editor of the *Philadelphia Bulletin*, has for years collected expectations about the change in consumer prices from a panel of about fifty business economists. When Gordon substituted this series for his own estimates of the expected rate of inflation, the over-all fit deteriorated slightly but the coefficient of the "expected rate of inflation" was very small—small enough to reject the accelerationist hypothesis out of hand, small enough, even, to give a fairly flat Phillips curve. Of course, the smallness of the regression coefficient may simply reflect the fact that the Livingston series is a very noisy proxy for the expected rate of inflation. (This might be so even if the business economists were accurate; it is the expectations of workers and employers that we really need.)

The Survey of Consumer Finances of the Survey Research Center at Ann Arbor, Michigan, has long asked questions about the price expectations held by its sample of respondents. Mere inspection at the results, however, raises questions in my mind about the interpretation of such survey results. In the first place, one wonders about the 10 to 20% of the sample that expected (or said it expected) prices not to rise at all in the next year, and said this steadily through 1966–69. One wonders how they differed from the smaller group, some 4–8% of the total, who expect prices to rise by 10% a year during that same period. The largest subgroup, about a third of the sample, was that predicting a price rise of 1–2% a year; about a quarter, each time, predicted that prices would rise by 5% in the coming year. The dispersion of replies is consistently so great—and the attraction of round numbers like 5 or 10% so strong—that one despairs of tracing any single "expected rate of inflation." It is true, partly because of this wide dispersion, that a crude average of these expectations changes sluggishly; but that is not the same thing as saying that the average responds with a long lag.

The most devastating direct commentary on the long-expectations-lag hypothesis comes from the survey results for 1969 and 1970. The theory gets its explanatory power by saying that inflationary expectations were much stronger in 1970–71 than in 1968–69. But in fact, the survey results suggest no stronger or more widespread expectations of rising prices in 1970 than there were one or two years earlier. In one way, just the opposite happened. In each of the four quarterly surveys in 1970, between 25% and 30% of the sample said they expected faster price increases in the next twelve months than in the past twelve months. In the fourth quarter of 1969 the figure was about the same; but in the second and third quarters, 45% and 39% of the sample said they expected accelerating inflation. In the last quarter of 1969 and all quarters of 1970, 20% and 26% of the sample said, "Prices will not go up; not ascertained if will." In the second and third quarters of 1969 only 10% and 14% gave that answer. In other words, this direct evidence, for what it is worth, says that inflationary expectations were weakening, not strengthening, in 1970, when the theory requires just the opposite. The survey figures do not show the sort of steady build-up of inflationary expectations between 1966 and 1970 that the new-style accelerationist story needs.

These impressions are confirmed and extended by a more systematic analysis of the survey data by George de Menil and Surjit Bhalla [2]. They code the sample responses in a reasonable but complicated way that I need not specify here. The result is a quarterly series for the expected rate of inflation in the forthcoming year. This series controverts the accelerationist story in more or less the way I have just described. There is no drastic build-up of inflationary expectations from 1966 to 1970. In fact, the constructed series shows very little change in that period, apart from irregular fluctuations. One can perhaps see a slight rise from 1966, but it peaks in mid-1969; by early 1971 the expected rate of inflation is as low as it had been in the previous ten years.

When de Menil and Bhalla use their constructed series as an independent variable in Phillips-curve estimations, they find that it performs just about as well as the more-popular indirect measurements. But always it attracts a coefficient considerably smaller than one, in fact, near one-half.

This is perhaps the place to comment on the work of Eckstein and Brinner[4]. Their mechanism for capturing expectational effects is a bit different from the usual. It comes in two parts. The first is a conventional moving average of past-observed rates of inflation, but with a considerably shorter lag than that used by Gordon and Saint Louis. What the others accomplish through the long lag, Eckstein and Brinner do with a nonlinear threshold effect. They include a new variable whose value is defined to be the average annual rate of inflation in the past two years, provided that average exceeds 2.5%, and zero otherwise.

With this machinery Eckstein and Brinner conclude that the long-run Phillips curve is not wholly vertical, but that it essentially turns vertical at a critical lower rate of unemployment, estimated to be about 4%, perhaps a trifle higher.

I am suspicious of this mechanism, too, for a different reason. It seems to be too ad hoc, too much invented to explain precisely the 1968–71 episode. Indeed, de Menil and Bhalla report that the threshold variable is statistically insignificant if the sample period ends before 1969. It can legitimately be said that the threshold is only crossed after 1968, so that one would hardly expect the variable to cut any ice in the earlier period. But then, in effect, we have no test of significance at all for the full period: the threshold variable is a dummy variable introduced to explain the single episode from 1969 to 1971. The data have been mined; the confession has been extracted by torture, and the case will not stand up in court. This raises a general point to which I want to return at the end of this essay.

I am far from sold, then, on either leg of the accelerationist position. The long lag of price expectations behind reality is dubious at best. Nor am I ready to believe for practical purposes that the expected rate of inflation—if it is a permissible abstraction at all—enters the wage equation with a coefficient of unity as "economic rationality" requires. There is nothing in the Survey Research Center data to suggest that one ought to impute economic rationality to the respondents in this subtle matter.

As a theorist, I feel it would be prudent to hedge a little. For some purposes it is sensible and natural to assume that economic behavior is rational; for some purposes I would still assume that the expected rate of inflation enters the wage equation with a coefficient of one, at least in the very longest of runs, in the very stablest of conditions. In the very longest of runs under the very stablest of conditions, the Phillips curve may therefore be vertical. In the light of the evidence, however, I think it is folly to suppose *as a matter of logic* that twenty or thirty or fifty years of data culled from the real world will permit you to see the Phillips curve becoming vertical. For any span of years meaningful for the formulation and execution of economic policy, it may still be right and necessary to imagine the economy as trading off real output for price stability.

I do not think one can dismiss the explanations of recent wage and price behavior based on expectations, but I have tried to say why I am still in the market for something better. George Perry, who was one of the earliest quantifiers of the Phillips surface, has recently produced an alternative explanation of great interest [10].

LABOR-MARKET EXPLANATIONS

Perry's basic insight is that the aggregate unemployment rate may be an ambiguous measure of pressure in the labor market when the composition of the labor force and of the group of unemployed is changing. For example, it is plausible that an unemployed part-time worker should exercise less downward pressure on the money wage than an unemployed full-time worker. If, then, at a *given* over-all unemployment rate there would now be relatively more unemployed part-timers and relatively fewer unemployed full-timers than there would have been ten years ago at the *same* over-all unemployment rate, there would now be less downward pressure on the money wage. Therefore, money wages would rise more rapidly now at any given unemployment rate than they would have done ten years ago, at that unemployment rate. In other words, the Phillips curve would have shifted upward. Perry argues that such a change has indeed taken place.

The age distribution of the population has changed in response to the high birth rates of the forties and fifties; in addition, the participation rate of women in the labor force has increased. So today's labor force is more heavily weighted with the young and the female than the labor force of a decade ago. Moreover, as anyone knows who has looked at the statistics, the labor-market experience of the young and the female has worsened relatively; even in recessions, unemployment falls more heavily on them, whereas the unemployment rate for adult males stays remarkably low. Perry quantifies this observation by making the plausible assumption that an unemployed body generates downward pressure on the wage level proportional to the amount of "unemployed labor" he or she represents. In turn, the amount of unemployed labor can be measured by the number of dollars of wages it represents. This allows both for differences in hours normally worked and for differences in wage rates as well: thus an unemployed person who normally worked 40 hours a week at $4.00 an hour represents $160.00 worth of unemployment a week, more than twice as much as an unemployed person who normally worked 30 hours a week at $2.50 an hour—though each counts for one in the monthly tally of unemployment. By using average-hours-worked and average-hourly-earnings for a breakdown of the unemployed by age and sex, Perry is able to construct a weighted unemployment rate to use as an independent variable in his wage equation.

In addition, if the Phillips curve is nonlinear, a given weighted unemployment rate will have different effects on wages according as it represents the average of widely different age-sex specific unemployment rates, or the common experience of nearly all groups. To catch this effect, Perry calculates a dispersion index for his breakdown of the labor force.

This idea—that dispersion of experience among separate labor markets combined with a nonlinear wage response can have important substantive effects on the location of the Phillips curve—goes back to Lipsey's [7] early commentary on Phillips. It has been developed further by Tobin [14]. If wages are more flexible upward than they are downward with respect to excess demand for labor, and if mobility between labor markets is less than perfect, then even if the labor market is in aggregate balance—with unemployment here being offset by an equal number of vacancies there—wages will rise on the average. Moreover, with the aggregate pressure of demand held constant, increased dispersion will increase the rate at which wages will rise, and decreased dispersion will reduce it. Lipsey had in mind regional, industrial, and occupational labor markets; Perry applies the same thought to age-sex categories. Now occupations and industries exhibit systematic differences in the demographic composition of employment, so Perry is not so far from Lipsey. There is one interesting difference, however: direct mobility is possible between regions, industries, and occupations, but not between age-sex groups (except with the slow passage of birthdays and occasional major surgery). Although changes in relative wages can substitute for direct mobility in narrowing the differences among age-sex–specific unemployment rates, it may be a slower process. If it is, then changes of the kind that Perry finds in the age-sex make-up of the labor force and in the dispersion of unemployment rates by age-sex group can generate long-lasting shifts in the conventional Phillips curve.

As Laplace found that he could explain the universe without invoking God as a hypothesis, Perry finds that he can explain recent history without invoking expectations. He finds that a short-lagged single rate of past price increase does as much for his wage equation as Gordon's long-lagged weighted-average proxy for price expectations. He finds also that whichever lagged price-increase variable he introduces, it enters with a coefficient well away from unity, and in the customary neighborhood of four-tenths. And finally he finds that he can explain both the 1970 experience and the earlier period in a unified way. Perry's model says something straightforward, if true: it says that right now the labor market is as tight with a 5.5% unemployment rate as it used to be, ten or fifteen years ago, with a 4% unemployment rate. That is to say, nowadays when the conventional body-count unemployment rate is 5.5%, the situation differs in two ways from a time ten years ago with the same conventional unemployment rate. In the first place, relatively more of the unemployed bodies are young and female, and relatively fewer are adult males. Thus relatively more are low-wage part-timers, and relatively fewer are high-wage full-timers. Measured Perry's way, there is less unemployment now than there used to be with the same measured unemployment rate. In the second place, there is more dispersion in the unemployment rates of different age-sex groups, with adult males having unusually low unemployment rates and women and youth having unusually high unemployment rates. For both reasons, a 5.5% unemployment rate now represents more upward push on wage rates than it used to. In fact, as I mentioned, Perry estimates that 5 or 5.5% unemployment now produces a push on wages about as strong as 4% unemployment used to do. Another way to put it is that the Phillips curve has shifted upward, so that any measured unemployment rate in the moderate range generates a rate of wage-increase about 1.5% per year higher than it used to. The main shift appears to have happened about 1962–63.

It should be kept in mind that when Perry says that 5% unemployment now is like 4% unemployment ten years ago, that is a statement about implications for wage inflation. It does not say that 5% unemployment now is just as bad as 4% unemployment used to be, so that if 4% was a proper target then, 5% is a proper target now. That would follow if the only consequence of unemployment that mattered was its effect on money wages. But if you think that the unemployment of young, female, and black people is worse (or, for that matter, better) than the unemployment of adult white males, then you have to make the welfare judgment in those terms. The proper target for you depends on your weighting of the consequences of different amounts of unemployment for social peace, equity, real output, and inflation.

I must say that I find Perry's results rather impressive. I think some caution is in order, however, for a simple methodological reason. One must always be wary of econometric results about the causal importance of some variable that has so far always moved in one direction through time. We are really after reversible relations; and I will feel happier about Perry's results if we should ever have a reduction in dispersion or in the proportion of women and the young in the labor force, and if, when that happens, the Phillips curve crawls back down along Perry's regression equations. Until then, I guess I believe those equations tentatively, but I would be prepared to punt at a moment's notice.

Next I would like to mention some very recent experiments of Charles Schultze [13], because they make a logical bridge from Perry's work to another way of looking at the problem. Schultze begins by suggesting that the voluntary quit rate may be a better indicator of labor-market tightness than the unemployment rate itself, because the quit rate should also contain information about the availability of unfilled jobs, on which no direct observations are available. Schultze finds that the quit rate performs just about as well as the unemployment rate as an independent variable in wage equations like Perry's.

But the most interesting thing he finds is this: from 1952 to 1965 there is a fairly close relationship between the quarterly quit rate (in manufacturing) and the quarterly rate of general unemployment. From 1966 to 1970, however, that relation consistently underpredicts the quit rate by a substantial amount. In other words, the quit-rate/unemployment-rate curve seems to have shifted upward, perhaps permanently, in 1966, in such a way that the quit rate is now higher for any given unemployment rate than it was before. (It is only fair to remark that Schultze's equation, like Perry's, tends to over-predict the rate of wage inflation in 1969, though they both track well in 1970. One of the advantages of the Gordon expectations formulation is that it can handle both 1969 and 1970, because it doesn't depend on a one-way shift in the demographic composition of the labor force, or in dispersion, or in the behavior of voluntary quits.)

Now if Schultze is right that the quit rate is a better indicator of excess demand in the labor market than the unemployment rate, then a shift in the quit-rate/unemployment-rate relation is equivalent to a shift in the Phillips curve. It signals that a given measured unemployment rate is now associated with a tighter labor market than used to be the case, and therefore that wages will increase faster at any unemployment rate than they used to. Schultze estimates about the same sort of shift in the Phillips curve as Perry did—from 3% inflation at 4% unemployment to 4.5% inflation at 4% unemployment (and 3% inflation at 5% unemployment).

It remains to wonder what is at the bottom of the shift to higher quit rates. Schultze does not offer any explanation. It is not hard to imagine logical possibilities, but none of them is easily verified. The upward shift in voluntary quits could come about from an outward shift in the (Beveridge) curve relating unfilled vacancies to unemployment. This in turn could be symptomatic of any kind of worsening of "structural unemployment" broadly interpreted: a poorer match of skills supplied to skills demanded, lessened intermarket mobility of labor, more uneven development of demand in different industries or regions. It is certainly possible that events have at last caught up with the prophets of structural unemployment, that what in 1961 they were saying had happened in 1957 did at last happen in 1967! Alternatively, one might adopt a more "voluntaristic" explanation. Changes in attitudes toward work and wages provide a kind of all-purpose independent variable, much like changes in expectations. Here, as with the demographic explanation, I will feel better when the new approach succeeds in explaining a sequence of events other than the one that called attention to it in the first place.

TACTICS IN ECONOMETRIC RESEARCH

It is useful to remember what started all this. An econometric relationship went sour; wage equations that seemed to work for the period from the end of the Korean War to the late 1960s began to fail. Under such circumstances, what can an econometrician do?

One reaction is to rethink the underlying relation and perhaps conclude that it has been mis-specified initially. That is what the expectations theorists have done.

A different tactical reaction is to ask if the original relationship, though fundamentally sound, may have shifted. Perry attributes such a systematic shift to a change in the demographic composition of labor force and employment, Schultze to a change in the relation between the quit rate and unemployment.

Another possible response for the econometrician is to stand pat and do the best he can with minor refinements and reestimations of the old model. This is more or less what the Fed-MIT-Penn Model has done, as reported by George de Menil and Jared Enzler [3]. The wage equation in that model is still a more-or-less standard Phillips surface. Unlike some others, it finds a significant effect of the rate of change of the unemployment rate. Its only other special feature is that it gets a slightly higher coefficient on the (lagged) price-change variable than some others, 0.6 instead of, say, 0.4, but still quite far enough from unity to be evidence against the accelerationist view.

Price change is represented in the wage equation by a simple rate of change of the consumption deflator, lagged six months. De Menil reports the following test of the accelerationist hypothesis. He adds to the equation, along with this price-change variable, a long-lagged geometric-weighted average of past rates of price change. When that is done, the short-lag measure of price change continues to enter positively and the long-lag measure picks up a significantly negative coefficient. Moreover, the negative coefficient is absolutely larger than the positive one, which would have the unacceptable implication that the faster prices are rising, so long as they are rising steadily, the slower nominal wages will be rising. De Menil concludes that the long-lag variable does not belong to the wage equation.

This equation was estimated from a sample period that includes 1968, so it is perhaps pointless to look at its performance in 1968 (actually, it underestimates the rate of change of compensation per man-hour). In 1969, which was approximately as tight a year as 1968, the model tends to overestimate the rate of wage inflation, and then in the first quarter of 1970 it slips over into underestimation. I have not seen any report on the model's behavior since then. But since in simulations it tends to transmit changes in unemployment into wages fairly promptly—with over half the ultimate inflationary effect coming within six months—it seems very likely that it must have underestimated substantially the rate at which wages were rising from the spring of 1970 until the summer of 1971.

I want to record for future reference one other fact about the Fed-MIT-Penn equation. De Menil reports that it quite substantially underestimates the rate of wage increase in 1956. That is important, if only because it was the 1956 episode that marked the beginning of talk about "creeping inflation" as a possibly endemic disease in our economy.

Now I come to the hard question and the point of it all: What is a reasonable man—with something more than mere skepticism and something less than blind faith in econometrics—what is he to believe? Here are some important facts that used to seem orderly, and now act up. Should one accept an amended Phillips surface—and if so, which amendment seems best—or should one retreat into skepticism pure and simple?

As a practical matter, I am prepared to reject simple skepticism. It is not that economists ought to resist saying that they do not know when in fact they do not know—that is mere honesty and should override anything else. But it seems to me mistaken to conclude from the breakdown of an established regularity that it was nonsense all along. One ought to try to improve the toolbox, and in the meantime to attach greater uncertainty to the best predictions one can make. To pretend utter ignorance, however, is just that—a pretense.

Is it possible that the whole Phillips business is mistaken, and that a better explanation of money wages will be found along some quite different train of thought? That is certainly conceivable, but I think it is methodologically wrong to concede more than that without some indication of what the alternative train of thought may be. It is not only a true fact, but a useful principle, that you cannot lick something with nothing. And I have yet to see something.

Suppose the sensible alternative right now is to try to improve on the Phillips family of wage equations: the ingenuity of econometricians is bound to produce several ways to do that. The risky thing about empirical macroeconomics is not that it is too hard to find relationships that fit but that it is too easy. I have just finished describing—and criticizing—several variations, any one of which you could live with, so far as the data are concerned. Which one should a reasonable man adopt? And how can a reasonable man deny that there is likely to be some truth in all of them?

One of the reasons this is a hard sort of decision to make is that we have no clear idea about how good an explanation we are entitled to. That may sound like a peculiar thing to say: are we not entitled to a complete explanation? I have no wish to get hung up on deep philosophical questions about whether human or social behavior is causally determinate. My point is a much more pragmatic one. For as far ahead as one can imagine, there will be unexplained noise in econometric relations, and not simply white noise of constant variance—there will be occasionally large deviations that can only be explained away after the event, if then. In that case, given that economic knowledge is based not on controlled experiment but on *ex post facto* observation of history's single experimental run, there is always danger of over-fitting, of explaining those inexplicable deviations by mining the data of the recent past. There is little harm in that unless the process produces new econometric relations that are more likely, not less likely, to go sour when that big deviation goes away.

That is why I was intrigued by the fact that the Fed-MIT-Penn equation underpredicted the bulge of wage increases in 1956 and then apparently settled down to do rather well for the next twelve or thirteen years. It is possible—though this is not my favorite guess—that 1970–71 will in the end turn out to be like 1956: a deviation that went away.

Another possibility—and this intrigues me more—is that 1970–71 will turn out to mark a permanent shift in wage behavior, not a transitory residual, and not something that can properly be accounted for by the exchange of one independent variable for a slightly different one. Schultze's observation that the relation of the voluntary quit rate to the unemployment rate shifted sometime around 1966 fits in with this line of thought. And so does a very important fact that I have not mentioned until now. Money wages have been behaving anomalously almost everywhere! It is not only in the United States that 1970 and 1971 appear to have climbed off the Phillips surface that explained earlier years. The outstanding other case is Great Britain, which has had several years of extraordinarily high unemployment (by their standards) and still faced a wage explosion of the order of 12% or 14% a year in 1970–71, which has not abated since. I am told that the London Business School econometric model is now treating the money wage as exogenous in its forecasting work, having abandoned its earlier wage equation. But the coincidence is far more widespread than that. The same thing has happened in Italy, in France, and in the Scandinavian countries, all of which had resorted to wage and price control a year before President Nixon's decision of August 1971. It is fair to say that in the last few years there has been inflation in all major industrial countries, and only in some of them can tight demand have been the sole explanation. For an interesting survey, see the paper by Nordhaus [8].

Now it does not follow logically from the fact that wages have been rising unusually rapidly—given the other circumstances—in many or all industrial countries that the explanation has to be the same in all of them. But it is natural to ask of any explanation proposed for the United States whether it can generalize to other places.

One possibility is that everywhere workers—and employers—have learned to form expectations in real terms; and when their expectations for real wages are frustrated by rising prices, they try to make good the deficiency in later years. This notion is very closely related to the accelerationist hypothesis I discussed earlier. The difference is that this hypothetical upsurge of consciousness of real changes need not be related to any long-lag weighted-average representation of expected price changes; and, indeed, it need not have been effective at all in the years from 1950 to, say, 1969 or 1970. If there is anything to this idea at all, it raises two very interesting questions. The first is, Is it temporary or is it, as with Eve's apple, a permanent loss of innocence? The second question follows on: What becomes of the theory of income and employment, quite apart from the theory of inflation, if labor can and does after all "bargain for the real wage?"

Finally I want to suggest one other possible explanation that does pay some attention to the worldwide character of the thing it is trying to explain. One expects unemployment to exert downward pressure on the money wage in roughly the same way that one expects excess supply of any commodity to put downward pressure on its price. If excess supply is known or expected to be temporary and limited, it is likely to have less effect on prices than if it is half-expected to be prolonged and severe. The same is true in the labor market, on both sides of the labor contract. Organized and unorganized workers are more likely to continue to press for higher wages at some moderate unemployment rate if they are confident that the unemployment rate will soon fall, or will not rise. Employers are less likely to resist wage increases, or even to chance substantial layoffs, if they expect that markets will soon improve and experienced labor will become fairly hard to get.

It would be the most natural thing in the world if such expectations should seize workers and employers in the main industrial countries of the world, for the simple reason that they are probably true. (Those words were written before the recession of 1974-75. Now the question is open again.) If this is any part of the explanation—and I am inclined to think it represents a good part although not all of the explanation—then we are seeing a permanent shift in the wage equation, and the 1950s and 1960s will not come this way again. The awful thing is that I do not see how we can possibly know until some years have passed.

That leaves me in an uncomfortable but not impossible position. We have a modest grip on wage behavior, but it is obviously imperfect and uncertain. There are several plausible competing candidates for an improved version, or at least a version more descriptive of current conditions. One or more of these might turn out to be what we need, but it will take careful observation to decide among them. In time, we may have an improved grip on wage behavior; although in time we may also have more surprises and have to go back to the old drawing board. I said this is an uncomfortable position to be in, but in a way it is no more uncomfortable than the position of any nonexperimental scientist, which indeed it closely resembles.

References

1. L. C. Andersen and K. M. Carlson, "An Econometric Analysis of the Relation of Monetary Variables to the Behavior of Prices and Unemployment," in *The Econometrics of Price Determination*, ed. O. Eckstein (Washington, D.C.: Federal Reserve System, 1972).

2. G. de Menil and S. Bhalla, "Popular Price Expectations," unpublished paper, Princeton University, 1973.

3. G. de Menil and J. Engler, "Prices and Wages in the FR-MIT-Penn Econometric Model," in Eckstein, ed., *The Econometrics of Price Determination*.

4. O. Eckstein and R. Brinner, *The Inflation Process in the United States*, 92d Cong., 2d sess., 1972.

5. R. J. Gordon, "Inflation in Recession and Recovery," *Brookings Papers on Economic Activity*, 1971, no. 1.

6. ———, "Wage-Price Controls on the Shifting Phillips Curve," *Brookings Papers on Economic Activity*, 1972, no. 2.

7. R. G. Lipsey, "The Relation between Unemployment and the Rate of Change of Money Wage Rates in the United Kingdom, 1862–1957: A Further Analysis," *Economica*, February 1960.

8. W. D. Nordhaus, "The Worldwide Wage Explosion," *Brookings Papers on Economic Activity*, 1972, no. 2.

9. G. L. Perry, *Unemployment, Money Wage Rates, and Inflation* (Cambridge: MIT Press, 1966).

10. ———, "Changing Labor Markets and Inflation," *Brookings Papers on Economic Activity*, 1970, no. 3.

11. J. Robinson, *Essays in the Theory of Employment* (New York: Macmillan, 1937).

12. P. A. Samuelson and R. Solow, "Analytical Aspects of Anti-Inflation Policy," *American Economic Review*, May 1960.

13. C. Schultze, "Note on Recent Wage Behavior," *Brookings Papers on Economic Activity*, 1971, no. 2.

14. J. Tobin, "Inflation and Unemployment," *American Economic Review*, March 1972.

Wages, Profits, and Marginal Analysis

Abba P. Lerner

1. Joan Robinson is perhaps the most prominent of a group of economists, centered in Cambridge, England, who have been claiming, as a part of a general attack on "marginalism," that the level of profits is determined not by the marginal productivity of capital, which is meaningless, but by how much business spends (on investment and consumption) minus how much workers save.

This must be so because everybody taken together must receive (earn) in total exactly what they spend. There is nobody else to receive any of the spending. If we divide the economy into two sectors, and if one of the two sectors *spends less* than it receives, the other sector must be *receiving just that much less* than it spends.

Let the two sectors be business and workers. Then to the degree that workers save, i.e., spend less than they earn, business must be earning (as profits) that much less than it spends. "Profits equals spending out of profits minus saving out of wages." Michal Kalecki, neglecting saving out of wages, concludes that "capital (i.e., business) gets what it spends and workers spend what they get."*

---

*Let Y, E, and S stand for income, spending, and saving, and subscripts b and w for business and workers. Then

$$Y = E = Y_b + Y_w = E_b + E_w \; , \; Y_b = E_b + E_w - Y_w = E_b - (Y_w - E_w)$$
$$= E_b - S_w \; .$$

Is this an explanation of what determines profits? The arithmetic is perfect, but arithmetic is symmetrical and equations are reversible. The equations are very close relatives to the famous equality between total actual investment and total actual saving. It is just as true, neglecting savings out of wages, that "workers earn what they spend and business spends what it earns." The significance of the equalities lies only in the dynamics behind them. The difference between workers and business is that spending by workers is pretty closely determined by what they find themselves earning, whereas business spending is influenced by unpredictable optimism and pessimism—what Keynes called "animal spirits"—given scope in actual spending by reserve funds and access to credit.

When we examine the effects of changes in business spending on profits and wages, we find that the arithmetical equalities are not helpful. We get quite different results in conditions of unemployment and in conditions of full employment.

2. In the unemployment situation increased spending by business increases employment, output, real wages, and real profits, but it increases net profits in a greater proportion than wages. This is because there is an element of fixed costs, which includes some fixed-wage income to such labor as does not vary with output.

With a given rate of markup of price over average variable cost, and with constant average variable cost, total gross profits moves in the same proportion as output. The total wage bill, because of the fixed-wage income included in it, increases in a smaller proportion than output. On the other hand, net profits (what is left over when fixed costs are subtracted from gross profits) increase in a greater proportion than output. (The converse would hold, of course, for decreases in output. Employment and the wage bill contract in a smaller proportion than output, whereas net profits decrease in a greater proportion, and may even become negative.)

With both profits and wages increased, there is increased spending on consumption out of profits as well as out of wages, and we have a complex "multiplier" depending on the ratio of profits to wages and the different marginal propensities to consume out of profits and out of wages. Equilibrium is reached when total saving (which is always equal to total investment) is no more than seems appropriate at the higher levels of profits and wages (i.e., when actual saving is equal to desired saving).

3. In the case of full employment, the increase in business spending cannot

---

If $S_w = 0$, then $Y_b = E_b$ and $E_w = Y_w$. (I am indebted to my colleague Dean Albert Levenson for some suggestions that have simplified the text and for persuading me to add this algebraic footnote.)

lead to an increase in employment or output or total real income. It can only lead to inflation of prices and of money incomes. It may, however, affect the division of the output between investment and consumption and the division of the real income between wages and profits.

If total money wages and total money spending out of wages stay the same, additional business spending all becomes additional profits since it is received by business as additional revenue and there is no increase in costs. (Any bidding up of the prices of materials does not affect this since it increases both costs and revenues by the same amount.) Business "gets what it spends."

This is in money terms. What business gets in real terms depends on how much is bid away from the workers by the higher prices setting free resources to be used for producing either more investment goods or more consumption for capitalists. Real income is shifted from wages to profits up to the point where the increase in saving (equal to the increased investment) no longer seems excessive but appropriate because of the shift of income from less-thrifty wage-earners to more-thrifty profit-earners. The rate of investment and the different degrees of thrift together determine how the real income is divided between wages and profits. The more thrifty the capitalists as compared to the workers, the smaller the amount of real income that has to be shifted from wages to profits to bring the desired saving up to equality with the investment. If there should be the same marginal propensity to consume out of profits as out of wages, the increase in desired saving could not be generated; and the inflation, with the continuing shift of real income from wages to profits, would go on until something else gave way.

4. If money wages are raised but not as much as prices, there is a similar shift to profits and a similar equilibrium is reached where the increased level of real saving out of the same total of real income is equal to the increased level of real investment. Some of the increased spending by business becomes increased (money) income for workers, but if the workers "spend what they get" (increasing their money spending by as much as their money income is increased), the increase comes back to business, which still "gets what it spends." If the workers increase their spending by more or by less than the increase in their income, so much more or so much less will come back to business.

5. It used to be assumed that in inflations money wages lagged behind prices, and "forced saving" or "forced abstinence" was imposed on the workers. Elaborate theories of business cycles were built on this basis. But if the workers resist such impoverishment and insist on higher money wages sufficient to meet the higher cost of living, these structures collapse. If wages rise parallel with prices, nothing happens in real terms. There is no increase in real investment, or in real profit, or in consumption out of profits, and there is

no reduction in the real wage. There is instead a general inflation of all prices and all incomes.

If money wages were to rise more than prices, there would be a shift in the opposite direction, from real profits to real wages. However, it is even less likely that business would allow prices to lag behind wages than that workers would allow wages to lag behind prices. Business would raise prices further to restore the established rate of markup, and we are back again in the original situation in real terms, except that an inflation is under way.

6. The inflation, and/or the measures taken to check the inflationary excess demand, will raise interest rates, and that will tame the animal spirits that caused the increase in business spending. It will reduce real investment to the level of desired real saving, i.e., to the degree to which consumption out of full-employment income leaves resources for investment.

With income maintained at full employment, any change in the demand for money must be met by corresponding changes in the supply of money. This leaves only the willingness of workers and capitalists to save in conjunction with the eagerness of investors to determine the supply and the demand for loans and the rate of interest at which these are equal to each other. If thrift is insensitive to changes in the rate of interest, the direction of influence will be entirely from saving to investment. An increase in thrift, since it is not permitted to produce a depression, lowers the rate of interest (either through downward wage and price flexibility or through functional finance—a full-employment monetary and fiscal policy) until investment is raised to equality with the higher rate of desired saving at full employment. An increase in desired investment (animal spirits) raises the rate of interest (either through validated inflation or through functional finance) until desired investment is brought down again to equality with desired real full-employment saving.

The direction of influence will be entirely from investment to saving only if (a) investment is governed only by "animal spirits" and is insensitive to the rate of interest as well as to the level of income and to changes in it, or if the rate of interest is pegged in a liquidity trap; and (b) saving is fully adjustable, via the response of the propensity to save to interest changes or via adjustments in the total volume of real income (through changes in the rate of employment) or via inflation-induced changes in the distribution of income between sectors with different marginal propensities to save. This is not a general "Keynesian" condition.

7. That "business gets what it spends (minus saving out of wages)" (in the significant sense that an autonomous increase in "animal spirits," or in the marginal propensity to consume, will increase the share of profits in total income to the degree required to bring the volume of desired savings into equality with the maintained volume of investment) is true only:

a. in the "upside-down economy" of unemployed resources, where the general principle of scarcity on which all economics is built becomes dubious, and where total income adjusts to investment by a multiplier that depends on an *aggregate* marginal propensity to save based on how the income is shared, after any redistributions, among sectors with different propensities to save; and

b. where, in spite of full employment, money wages remain constant, or persistently lag behind prices, while inflation is in progress, such an "equilibrium" requires that the inflation continue, and if necessary escalate, so as to keep prices sufficiently ahead of wages (and the wage sufficiently below the initial relationship to its marginal product) to maintain the required increase in the share of profits. The required inflation would be fueled by the high marginal profits, and would have to be validated by an appropriately expansionary monetary and fiscal policy.

8. The owners of property or capital goods (including money) get as income the earnings of the capital goods—what the hirers of the capital goods pay for their hire. The values of the capital goods are determined by their expected future earnings discounted at the appropriate rates of interest for the different periods. The rates of interest are affected by the willingness to save (thrift), the eagerness to invest (animal spirits), the supply of money and money substitutes, and the demand for money and money substitutes to hold. On top of this are, of course, all sorts of monopolies and other rackets.

9. This analysis is not invalidated by the nonexistence of a homogeneous stock of capital with a marginal productivity or marginal efficiency independent of the rate of investment or disinvestment and therefore equal to the marginal efficiency of investment (like Frank Knight's "Crusonia"). Nor is it affected by the questionable fruitfulness of elaborating mathematical models of steady states or "golden ages" in terms of clay or putty or putty-clay abstractions from the complex sets of instruments that are part of a modern economy.

There is no "marginal productivity of capital" that directly determines the division of the national income between profits and wages. But the accumulated stock of capital equipment and of know-how (human capital) together with the state of the arts and of the exhaustible resources (including the newly discovered pollutable resources) determine the shape and position of the schedules of the marginal efficiency of investment for different periods. These schedules play their part in determining the rates of interest at their intersections with the margins of thrift and liquidity. The rates of interest, together with the expected future earnings of the capital goods determine the present values of the capital goods. The current rate of interest multiplied into the sum of these values shows the current income accrual from the ownership of property. It is perhaps not overgenerous to suppose that something like this is intended by the statement that profit is determined by the marginal productivity or marginal efficiency of capital. This is less wrong than to deny, or even to seem to deny, that lower rates of interest, by stimulating investment, will increase or improve the stock of capital goods (though not necessarily its aggregate value) and that this will increase potential future output; or that (in full employment) an increase in thrift, by reducing interest rates, will increase investment, the stock of useful capital goods, and potential future output.

Industry Price Changes, Market Structure And Inflation

Frances Ferguson Esposito and Louis Esposito

Between January 1970 and January 1971 the unemployment rate in the United States increased from 3.9% to 6.0%. At the same time consumer prices rose by 5.2%.[1] The phenomenon of jointly rising unemployment and prices increased interest in the pricing policies of American industry and, in particular, in the effect of market structure on these policies. Indeed, in a recent study Eckstein and Wyss (1972), using quarterly data for the period 1950–69, investigated the responsiveness of industry price changes to supply-and-demand conditions in sixteen U.S. manufacturing industries defined at the SIC two-digit level.[2] They

The authors are indebted to David A. Belsley, Edward J. Kane, and Otto Eckstein for helpful comments and suggestions on an earlier draft of this paper and to William Hogan, Daniel Primont, and Jack J. Gottsegen for useful discussions during its preparation.

1. *Economic Report of the President,* January 1972, tables B-24 and B-45.

2. Recent investigations into the pricing behavior of American industry focus primarily on the estimation of aggregate price equations. Eckstein and Fromm (1968), employing quarterly data for the period 1954–65, fitted price equations for all of U.S. manufacturing and for durables and non-durables. Their results suggested that an equation incorporating elements of both the competitive and oligopolistic price mechanisms provided the best explanation of price changes for all manufacturing. Equations employing variables suggested by the oligopolistic pricing model gave the best explanation of price changes in the durables sector. In the non-durables sector,

concluded that industries with low concentration ratios generally followed a pricing pattern suggested by the competitive pricing model. Highly concentrated industries followed a pricing pattern suggested by the oligopolistic target-rate-of-return model.

This paper reports the results of a similar investigation employing cross-section data for a sample of 321 U.S. manufacturing industries defined at the SIC four-digit level. Industries are classified into three groups according to the degree of seller concentration, and separate price equations are fitted for each industry group for the two time periods 1963–66 and 1966–69.[3]

Section 1 of the paper presents the price models and briefly discusses the theoretical rationale for differential responses to changes in cost-and-demand conditions by competitive and oligopolistic industries. Section 2 describes the empirical analysis. Section 3 summarizes the main findings of the paper.

1. THE PRICE MODELS[4]

Three basic equations are estimated for the periods 1963–66 and 1966–69. The equations differ only with respect to the specification of the labor-cost variable. They are:

$$\frac{P_{t+3}}{P_t} = \alpha + \beta_1 \frac{ULC_{t+3}}{ULC_t} + \beta_2 \frac{UMC_{t+3}}{UMC_t} + \beta_3 \frac{UKC_{t+3}}{UKC_t} + \beta_4 \frac{(I/S)_{t+3}}{(I/S)_t} \quad \text{(a)}$$

---

equations based on either pricing model appeared to perform equally as well. Laden (1972), using quarterly data for the period 1954–66, fitted price equations for U.S. manufacturing. The price equation was specified so as to test the comparative explanatory power of the competitive and oligopolistic pricing models. The results suggested that the manufacturing sector conformed to oligopolistic pricing behavior.

3. Several studies, most notably those of Weiss (1966, 1970), also analyzed industry price changes using cross-section data. Weiss, however, used considerably smallei samples and combined both competitive and oligopolistic industries in one sample. Using cost and demand variables and the four-firm concentration ratio as a measure of market structure, Weiss found the concentration variable to be significant in the equation estimated for the 1953–1959 period. The significance of the concentration variable was attributed to oligopolistic industries finally catching up with post-war cost changes. The method employed by Weiss assumes no differential responses by competitive and oligopolistic industries to changes in current cost and demand conditions during the 1953–1959 period. The method employed in this study allows us to investigate directly whether competitive and oligopolistic industries respond differently to changes in current market conditions.

4. For a more extensive discussion of the pricing models described in this Section, see Eckstein and Fromm (1968), pp. 1159–66.

$$\frac{P_{t+3}}{P_t} = \alpha + \beta_1 \frac{AHE_{t+3}}{AHE_t} + \beta_2 \frac{Prod_{t+3}}{Prod_t} + \beta_3 \frac{UMC_{t+3}}{UMC_t} + \beta_4 \frac{UKC_{t+3}}{UKC_t}$$

$$+ \beta_5 \frac{(I/S)_{t+3}}{(I/S)_t} \tag{b}$$

$$\frac{P_{t+3}}{P_t} = \alpha + \beta_1 \frac{ULC^*_{t+3}}{ULC^*_t} + \beta_2 \frac{UMC_{t+3}}{UMC_t} + \beta_3 \frac{UKC_{t+3}}{UKC_t} + \beta_4 \frac{(I/S)_{t+3}}{(I/S)_t} \tag{c}$$

where

P_t	is the industry price in period t;
ULC_t	is unit labor cost (production workers only) in period t;
ULC^*_t	is unit labor cost (production-worker wages plus nonproduction-worker salaries) in period t;
AHE_t	is average hourly earnings (production workers only) in period t;
$Prod_t$	is labor productivity (production workers only) in period t;
UMC_t	is unit material cost in period t;
UKC_t	is unit capital cost in period t;
$(I/S)_t$	is the ratio of finished-product inventories to sales in period t;
t	is 1963 or 1966.

Competitive Model

The specification of equations (a) and (c) is suggested by the competitive pricing model. In perfectly competitive markets changes in demand or supply conditions are reflected in instantaneous adjustments in equilibrium prices and production. If we assume that the firm maximizes its short-run gross return to capital, the change in price equals the change in marginal cost. If one assumes that the change in marginal cost equals the change in unit variable cost, then the change in price equals the change in unit labor cost plus the change in unit material cost.[5] Thus, given instantaneous adjustments in price and production *ULC* (*ULC**) and *UMC* determine price changes in competitive markets.

However, a realistic model of competitive behavior recognizes disequilibrium as the common situation and that prices need not immediately adjust to changes in market conditions. For example, should demand increase, several responses other than a price increase are possible in the short run (Eckstein and Fromm, 1968, pp. 1160–62): (1) suppliers may decrease inventories below

5. This assumption is necessary because it is not possible to obtain a measure of marginal cost. However, the longer the time period over which a price change is measured, the more likely the price change will approximate the change in unit costs.

desired levels; (2) orders may be backlogged if buyers agree to accept delivery at a later date; (3) orders may be abandoned if buyers refuse to accept delayed deliveries. Short-run disequilibrium could therefore be reflected in changes in such variables as unfilled orders or deviations in the actual ratio of inventory to sales from the desired ratio. In the very short run, data on unfilled orders and inventory deviations are unlikely to follow price changes since they fluctuate in place of price.[6] However, as these variables persistently increase or decrease, pressure on price builds until price changes will be inevitable.

It is not possible to obtain either desired inventory/sales ratios or unfilled orders for the SIC four-digit industries used in this study. The proxy measure of demand employed is the change in the actual inventory/sales ratio (I/S). To the extent that the desired inventory/sales ratio does not change in each industry during the sample period, significant changes in the actual inventory/sales ratio reflect changes in industry demand.[7]

Since the time periods utilized in this study are each of a three-year duration, a measure reflecting changes in unit capital cost (UKC) is included in equations (a) and (c). Three years is likely to be a period long enough for some industries to alter or to replace their plant and equipment. Clearly, over the longer run, changes in prices reflect changes in unit capital costs as well as changes in unit material costs and unit labor costs.

Oligopoly Model

Equation (b), which utilizes average hourly earnings and productivity (AHE and $Prod$) rather than unit labor cost (ULC), is suggested by a standard-cost pricing model. Unlike firms in competitive industries, large firms in oligopolistic industries are likely to follow some form of standard-cost rather than actual-cost pricing. The most common form of standard-cost pricing is target-rate-of-return pricing (Kaplan, Dirlam, and Lanzilotti, 1958).[8] Prices are set to yield a target return on capital at some standard sales volume.[9]

6. Another variable that signals pressure on price is the industrial operating rate. Clearly, declining utilization rates indicate a weakening demand and prices fall if low utilization rates persist; high utilization rates push prices upward. Since in the real world even competitive firms operate under conditions of uncertainty, firms feel more confident about raising prices when high utilization rates persist since the likelihood of buyers finding alternative sources of supply decreases.

In the short run, the utilization rate may also reflect disequilibrium conditions in the market. High utilization rates are likely to be associated with delivery delays, inventory reduction, etc.

7. Expectations with respect to strikes, defense activities, etc., may cause industries to produce temporarily to stock rather than current demand. Under these conditions the change in the actual inventory-sales ratio is a less useful measure of demand.

8. The particular target rate of return depends on the structural characteristics of the market: seller concentration, barriers to entry, foreign competition, and so on.

Under target-return pricing

$$P = \frac{\Pi K}{q^s} + ULC^s + UMC^s$$

where

Π is the target rate of return;
K is the capital stock;
q^s is standard output;
ULC^s is standard unit labor cost;
UMC^s is standard unit material cost.

Under target-rate-of-return pricing, prices change in response to changes in input prices but not to cost changes resulting from changes in utilization rates.[10] Additionally prices do not change in response to changes in demand.

Standard-cost pricing is advantageous to oligopolistic firms in general because it is internally consistent with target-rate-of-return pricing. In tight oligopolies, where seller concentration is high and therefore the likelihood of collective activity is great, standard-cost pricing allows for effective collusion through price leadership. The price leader can set prices using some commonly accepted method of standard-cost calculation.

In partial oligopolies standard-cost pricing is desirable because it results in less frequent price changes. Partial oligopolies have moderate seller concentration and the likelihood of disciplined collusion is lower than in tight oligopolies. Individual firms are less certain as to their rivals' reactions to price changes and the effect of these reactions on the firm's market share and profits. Consequently, partial oligopolists are apprehensive about frequent price changes in response to changing supply-and-demand conditions. Partial oligopolists producing intermediate goods are even more likely to prefer infrequent price changes because stable prices help to secure their large-customer relationships. Indeed, the loss of a large buyer is likely to have a significant impact on profits and market share.[11]

9. An alternative standard-cost pricing hypothesis is "mark up" or "average cost" pricing:
$$P = (1 - \alpha) (ULC^s + UMC^s)$$
where α is the standard mark-up.

10. Prices can also change if technology changes production costs at the standard volume of output.

11. Tightly oligopolistic intermediate-goods producers that successfully collude have less concern with buyer relationships since they presumably raise prices together or have clearly delineated buyers for each seller. To the extent that tightly oligopolistic intermediate-goods producers are less successful in colluding, the avoidance of frequent price changes becomes more important.

In equation (b) changes in average hourly earnings (*AHE*) serve as a proxy for changes in standard unit labor costs since, unlike actual unit labor costs, they are unaffected by short-run productivity changes. Because short-run productivity changes may exert an independent influence on price, the inclusion of a productivity measure (*Prod*) in a standard-cost pricing model is also appropriate. Short-run productivity swings result in deviations between standard unit labor costs and actual unit labor costs. If these deviations are sufficiently large, prices are likely to be affected (Eckstein and Brinner, 1972, p. 21).

With respect to standard unit material costs, differences in standard and actual unit material costs tend to be minimal since short-run changes in productivity and output do not significantly alter material inputs per unit of output. Thus changes in actual unit material costs reflect, more or less, changes in standard unit material costs.

As suggested earlier, oligopolists tend to view price changes as relatively long-term decisions. Attempts to equate supply and demand in the short run are likely to take the form of inventory changes, backlogging of orders, and so on, rather than price changes. Thus equation (b) also includes the inventory/sales ratio.

Since the time periods under investigation are each of a three-year duration, some industries may have incurred increased capital costs per unit of output. Therefore, the unit capital-cost (*UKC*) variable included in equations (a) and (c) is also included in equation (b).[12]

2. EMPIRICAL ANALYSIS

Industry Groupings

The empirical investigation of industry pricing responses to changes in market conditions employs multiple-regression analysis. The study includes 321 SIC four-digit industries, grouped according to their degree of seller concentration.[13] Three groupings are distinguished: (1) high-concentration, (2)

12. Preferably the capital-cost variable included in equation (b) should measure changes in unit capital costs at the standard output level. However, since these data are not available, a measure of changes in actual unit capital costs is employed.

13. The 1963 *Census of Manufactures* reports data for 415 SIC four-digit industries. Thirty-six of the 415 industries are eliminated from this study because the price indices of the Bureau of Economic Analysis (BEA) are based primarily on input-cost indices and 17 because applicable price indices are not available and BEA uses a proxy output deflator. Of the remaining 362 industries, 27 are eliminated because data on the gross book value of depreciable assets are not available, 3 because they are combined in the *Annual Survey of Manufactures,* and 3 because the 1963 four-firm concentration ratios are not available. Eight ordnance industries are also eliminated. Because ordnance

moderate-concentration, and (3) low-concentration industries. Forty industries fall into the high-concentration group, 128 into the moderate-concentration group, and 153 into the low-concentration group.

Industries possessing four-firm concentration ratios of 70 and above are classified as having high seller concentration; those between 40 and 69 as having moderate seller concentration, and those below 40 as having low seller concentration.[14] This classification scheme grows out of a prior study on the relationship between excess capacity and market structure (Esposito and Esposito, 1974). Industries with four-firm concentration ratios between 40 and 69 were found to experience significantly more excess capacity in periods of increasing demand then did industries with higher and lower concentration ratios. There is reason to suppose that these same limits would capture differential price responses among industries.

Industries in the high-concentration and moderate-concentration groups are identified as tight and partial oligopolies, respectively; those in the low-concentration group, as competitive or atomistic industries.[15] Both the high- and moderate-concentration groups are expected to follow the standard-cost pricing model. Therefore, one expects equation (b) to perform better than equation (a) for these industries. Low-concentration industries are expected to conform more closely to the competitive model (equation [a]).[16]

Sample Time Periods

Industry price changes are analyzed for two time periods: 1963–66 and 1966–69. The 1963–66 period was characterized by steady noninflationary economic expansion. In the U.S. manufacturing sector unit labor costs and the implicit price deflator rose at an annual average rate of 0.5 percent and 0.8 percent, respectively. During this period cost changes (both actual and standard) were small and probably infrequent. The 1966–69 period was charac-

---

industries rely primarily on government contracts, their prices are generally set on a cost-plus basis.

14. The concentration ratio used for identifying each four-digit industry according to its degree of seller concentration is the average of the 1963 and 1967 four-firm concentration ratios reported in the 1963 and 1967 *Census of Manufactures*. Forty-three of the 321 sample industries have regional markets. Estimates for the average four-firm regional concentration ratio for these industries were obtained from Shepherd (1970, Appendix, Table 8) and Schwartzman and Bodoff (1971).

15. Atomistic industries have low seller concentration but are not perfectly competitive in the theoretical sense. However, one expects firms in these industries to act independently, and therefore price and production outcomes should approximate those in perfectly competitive markets.

16. These same comparisons cannot be made with respect to equation (c) because labor costs are measured differently than in equation (a) or equation (b).

terized by increasing inflation as the economy neared full employment. Unit labor costs and the implicit price deflator increased at an annual average rate of 3.8 percent and 2.1 percent, respectively.[17] During this period cost changes (both actual and standard) were relatively large and probably more frequent.

By subdividing the 1963–69 period, one is also able to investigate whether general economic conditions affect price responses in different industry market structures. General economic conditions should not significantly affect pricing behavior in tight oligopolies and atomistic industries. In tight oligopolies one expects pricing decisions to be well-coordinated among the largest firms. Therefore, cost increases will tend to be passed on rapidly and fully. Since pricing decisions are independent in atomistic industries, the same behavior is expected.

In partial oligopolies, however, general economic conditions may affect price behavior. When cost changes are small and infrequent, the partial oligopolist is likely to pass on costs rapidly and fully. He is not likely to be concerned about his rivals' reactions to small and infrequent price increases since, in the absence of corresponding price increases, only small losses in market share result. However, during inflationary periods when cost changes are large and frequent, costs will be passed on less rapidly and less fully. Price adjustments will be relatively small since failure of rivals to respond to large and frequent price increases will result in a significant decrease in the firm's market share.

Variables

Data for industry prices are the U.S. Department of Commerce, Bureau of Economic Analysis, unpublished SIC four-digit implicit price deflators.[18] With one exception, data for all independent variables are found in the 1963 *Census of Manufactures* and the 1966 and 1969 *Annual Survey of Manufactures*.[19]

17. See the *Economic Report of the President,* January 1972, Table B-34, for data on changes in the implicit price deflator and unit labor-cost index.

18. The BEA's SIC four-digit implicit price deflators are constructed primarily from SIC five-digit (product classes) wholesale price indices supplied by the Bureau of Labor Statistics. The BLS product-class deflators are grouped into SIC four-digit industries using current-year product-class weights. A major criticism of BLS wholesale price indices is that they do not adequately reflect price changes, since they are list prices and not transaction prices (Stigler and Kindahl, 1970). However, whereas this may create a serious problem when BLS prices are used in quarterly time-series studies, the problem should be reduced when price changes are analyzed over a three-year period as in this study.

19. Gross book value of depreciable assets are not available for 1965, 1966, or 1969, but are available for 1964 (1964–65 *Annual Survey of Manufactures*) and 1967 and 1968 (1968 *Annual Survey of Manufactures*). Gross book value of depreciable assets for 1966 are obtained by interpolating between 1964 and 1967 gross book value of depreciable

Prices[20]

The industry price variable is:

$$\frac{P_{t+3}}{P_t}$$

where P is the industry's implicit price deflator and t is 1963 or 1966.

Unit Labor Cost

The unit labor-cost (ULC) variable is:

$$\frac{\dfrac{W_{t+3}}{W_t}}{\dfrac{Q_{t+3}}{Q_t}}$$

where W is total production-worker wages and

$$\frac{Q_{t+3}}{Q_t} = \frac{\dfrac{S_{t+3}}{S_t}}{\dfrac{P_{t+3}}{P_t}}$$

and S is industry value of shipments. A variant of the unit labor-cost variable that includes nonproduction-worker salaries as well as production-worker wages is ULC^*. This unit labor-cost (ULC^*) variable is:

$$\frac{\dfrac{EP_{t+3}}{EP_t}}{\dfrac{Q_{t+3}}{Q_t}}$$

where EP is all employees payroll.

---

assets. The 1966–69 percentage change in unit capital cost is approximated by the 1966–68 percentage change in unit capital cost.

20. For ease of computation, all variables used in the regression analysis are expressed as one plus the percentage change over the particular time period. The estimated regression coefficients are identical to those that would be obtained if the variables were entered as percentage changes. However, the intercepts presented in tables 1 and 2 should be interpreted as the stated value minus one.

Wages and Productivity

Since unit labor cost (*ULC*) equals the ratio of average hourly earnings to output per man hour, a wage rate and a labor-productivity variable can be substituted for the unit labor-cost variable in the estimated equations. The percentage change in unit labor costs is approximately equal to the percentage change in average hourly earnings minus the percentage change in labor productivity.

The average hourly earnings (*AHE*) variable is:

$$\frac{\dfrac{W_{t+3}}{W_t}}{\dfrac{MH_{t+3}}{MH_t}}$$

where *MH* is production-worker manhours.

The labor-productivity (*Prod*) variable is:[21]

$$\frac{\dfrac{Q_{t+3}}{Q_t}}{\dfrac{MH_{t+3}}{MH_t}}$$

Unit Material Cost

The unit material-cost (*UMC*) variable is:

$$\frac{\dfrac{M_{t+3}}{M_t}}{\dfrac{Q_{t+3}}{Q_t}}$$

where *M* is industry value of shipments minus industry value added.

Unit Capital Cost

It is not possible to calculate a unit capital-cost variable from *Census* and *Survey* data. However, it is possible to calculate the ratio of gross book value of depreciable assets to output. Changes in this ratio are used as a proxy measure

---

21. A productivity and wage rate variable for all employees (*EP*) cannot be calculated because manhours for nonproduction workers are not available in the *Census* or *Annual Survey*.

for changes in unit capital cost. The unit capital-cost (*UKC*) variable is:

$$\frac{\dfrac{DA_{t+3}}{DA_t}}{\dfrac{Q_{t+3}}{Q_t}}$$

where *DA* is gross book value of depreciable assets.

Inventory/Sales Ratio

The measure of demand employed is the change in the inventory/sales ratio. The inventory/sales ratio (*I/S*) variable is:

$$\frac{\dfrac{I_{t+3}}{I_t}}{\dfrac{S_{t+3}}{S_t}}$$

where *I* is value of finished product inventories (end of year).

Weighting Procedure

Since the percentage change in price given a percentage change in unit cost depends on the proportion each cost constitutes of the value of output, the average hourly earnings, productivity, and unit-cost variables entered in the estimated equations are weighted by the ratio of the particular cost to value of shipments.[22] As a result of the weighting procedure, a regression coefficient of

22. The weights are calculated using 1963 data and are as follows:

Variable	Weight
UMC	$\dfrac{M}{S}$
ULC*	$\dfrac{EP}{S}$
ULC	$\dfrac{W}{S}$
AHE	$\dfrac{W}{S}$
Prod	$\dfrac{W}{S}$
UKC	$1 - \left(\dfrac{M+EP}{S}\right)$

Since it is not possible to calculate from *Census* data the ratio of capital costs to value of shipments, it was necessary to use $1 - (M+EP/S)$ as an approximation of that ratio.

one on the weighted variables will, in general, represent a full pass-through of costs.[23]

Empirical Results

Table 1 presents the price equations estimated for the 1963–66 period. The standard-cost pricing model (equation b) performs better than the competitive

TABLE 1

REGRESSION EQUATIONS FOR INDUSTRY PRICE CHANGES, 1963–1966

Eq. No.	Degree of Concentration	Sample Size	Intercept	$\frac{ULC_{t+3}}{ULC_t}$	$\frac{ULC^*_{t+3}}{ULC^*_t}$	$\frac{AHE_{t+3}}{AHE_t}$	$\frac{Prod_{t+3}}{Prod_t}$	$\frac{UMC_{t+3}}{UMC_t}$	$\frac{UKC_{t+3}}{UKC_t}$	$\frac{(I/S)_{t+3}}{(I/S)_t}$	$\bar{R}^2$
					Equation a						
1a	High	40	.4934	.8955 (4.48)*				.5869 (6.62)	.3366 (3.93)	−.0032 (.13)	.5082
2a	Moderate	128	.6079	.5552 (6.20)				.5065 (10.28)	.3590 (5.57)	−.0229 (.95)	.4704
3a	Low	153	.7388	.4593 (5.88)				.4183 (9.21)	.2412 (3.73)	−.0591 (2.50)	.3926
					Equation b						
1b	High	40	.7320			2.0610 (4.94)	−1.6057 (3.48)	.3716 (3.19)	.1563 (1.49)	−.0116 (.51)	.5587
2b	Moderate	128	.6755			1.7182 (6.22)	−1.3062 (4.90)	.4422 (8.89)	.2868 (4.40)	−.0191 (.82)	.5030
3b	Low	153	.7706			1.0983 (4.21)	−.7262 (2.61)	.3934 (7.42)	.2092 (2.83)	−.0602 (2.54)	.3590
					Equation c						
1c	High	40	.4177		.7747 (5.76)			.6798 (7.91)	.3853 (4.89)	−.0171 (.79)	.6026
2c	Moderate	128	.5390		.5227 (7.14)			.5704 (11.05)	.3794 (6.12)	−.0254 (1.10)	.5087
3c	Low	153	.5628		.6039 (9.47)			.5749 (12.44)	.3178 (5.56)	−.0604 (2.93)	.5333

*Figures in parentheses are t-statistics.

23. The two exceptions are the unit capital-cost variable and the labor-productivity variable. Since the weight applied to the capital-cost variable overstates the ratio of capital costs to value of output, a regression coefficient of somewhat less than one represents a full pass-through of costs. This is also true with respect to the labor-productivity variable and occurs because the influence of productivity is felt through unit labor cost. Since unit labor cost is the ratio of average hourly earnings to labor productivity, a given (weighted) percentage change in productivity results in a smaller percentage change in price if all costs are passed through. Thus, a regression coefficient of less than one on the productivity variable represents a full pass-through of costs. The deviation from one is a function of the size of the productivity changes. For small changes in productivity, a regression coefficient of one approximates a full pass-through of costs.

model (equation a) in the high- and moderate-concentration groups. The average hourly earnings variable (*AHE*), the proxy for standard unit labor costs, has the same level of significance as the unit labor-cost variable (*ULC*) in high- and moderate-concentration industries and a lower level of significance than *ULC* in low-concentration industries. The productivity variable is least significant in low-concentration industries, suggesting that the effects of productivity on price are felt through the *ULC* variable in these industries. The relatively higher significance of productivity in the high and moderate groups suggests that productivity exerts an independent influence in these industries. The demand variable (*I/S*) is significant in the equations estimated for the low-concentration group but never in those estimated for the high and moderate groups. These results suggest that high- and moderate-concentration industries appear to use standard-cost pricing and low-concentration industries conform more closely to the competitive supply/demand pricing model. Since, however, the competitive model (equation [a]) does not explain more variation in low-concentration industries as compared with high- and moderate-concentration industries, this conclusion is tentative.

With two exceptions, the regression coefficients for the individual variables are not significantly different at the .05 level between industry groups.[24] The coefficients on *ULC* and *AHE* are significantly different between the high and low industry groups. The coefficient on *ULC* in the high-concentration group is fairly close to one. The coefficients suggest that high-concentration industries fully pass on increases in production-worker unit labor costs whereas low-concentration industries passed on only about half their increased unit labor costs. The coefficient on *AHE* is approximately one in low-concentration industries, suggesting a full pass-through of wage increases. However, the coefficient on *AHE* is significantly greater than one (at the .05 level) in both the

24. Analysis of covariance is used to test whether the regression coefficients for the individual variables for each basic equation are significantly different across industry groups for the period 1963–66 (Beals, 1972, pp. 329–30). The *t*-statistics for the dummy variates are:

Equations	ULC	ULC*	AHE	Prod	UMC	UKC	I/S
1a and 2a	1.63				.82	.21	.59
1a and 3a	2.21*				1.82	.93	1.73
2a and 3a	.81				1.32	1.29	1.07
1b and 2b			.70	.57	.57	1.09	.23
1b and 3b			2.04*	1.70	.17	.42	1.51
2b and 3b			1.63	1.50	.67	.78	1.24
1c and 2c		1.65			1.09	.05	.26
1c and 3c		1.25			1.17	.74	1.51
2c and 3c		.84			.06	.73	1.13

*Indicates regression coefficients are significantly different at the .05 level or higher using a two-tail test.

high and moderate groups. This suggests that high- and moderate-concentration industries key their price increases to wage increases and pass on changes in other costs at that time.

The analysis of industry price changes for the period 1963–66 suggests that market structure influences pricing behavior in two important respects. First, tight and partial oligopolies appear to use some form of standard-cost pricing, and atomistic industries appear to conform to the supply/demand pricing model. Second, oligopolists key price increases to wage increases, whereas in competitive industries changes in individual cost components trigger price responses. Keying price increases to wage increases reults in less-frequent price changes in oligopolistic industries. This form of pricing behavior is especially important in partial oligopolies, where the likelihood of misunderstanding is rather high.

Although the empirical results suggest that market structure does influence industry pricing behavior, the sets of regression coefficients estimated for each basic equation are not significantly different at the .05 level across industry groups.[25] This suggests that the effect on industry prices of all changes in cost and demand conditions taken together was not significantly different between high, moderate and low groups.

Table 2 presents the price equations estimated for the period 1966–69. The equations estimated for the low-concentration industries explain almost twice as much of the variation in industry price changes as those estimated for both the high and moderate groups. This is in contrast with the period 1963–66, when the price equations for the three industry groups had similar explanatory power. In both time periods, equation (c), which employs ULC^* (the production- and nonproduction-worker labor-cost variable) achieves the highest explanatory power within each industry group. This suggests that nonproduction-worker wages are an important component of labor costs and affect industry prices in the short run.

In low-concentration industries the competitive pricing model (equation a)

---

25. The Chow test (Chow, 1960) is used to determine whether the sets of regression coefficients estimated for each basic equation are significantly different across industry groups. The computed F-statistics for the sample period 1963–66 are:

Equations	F	Equations	F
1a and 2a	1.09	2b and 3b	1.05
1a and 3a	1.90	1c and 2c	.77
2a and 3a	.77	1c and 3c	1.06
1b and 2b	.50	2c and 3c	.96
1b and 3b	1.27		

None of the computed F-statistics exceed its respective critical $F_{.05}$ value.

TABLE 2

REGRESSION EQUATIONS FOR INDUSTRY PRICE CHANGES, 1966–1969

Eq. No.	Degree of Concentration	Sample Size	Intercept	$\frac{ULC_{t+3}}{ULC_t}$	$\frac{ULC^*_{t+3}}{ULC^*_t}$	$\frac{AHE_{t+3}}{AHE_t}$	$\frac{Prod_{t+3}}{Prod_t}$	$\frac{UMC_{t+3}}{UMC_t}$	$\frac{UKC_{t+3}}{UKC_t}$	$\frac{(I/S)_{t+3}}{(I/S)_t}$	$\bar{R}^2$
						Equation a					
1a	High	40	.5018	.8153 (3.08)*				.5442 (3.76)	.5476 (2.64)	−.0222 (.51)	.2214
2a	Moderate	128	.9555	.3663 (5.36)				.0405 (3.97)	.0708 (1.13)	.0120 (.43)	.2313
3a	Low	153	.5404	.8727 (12.76)				.4736 (9.24)	.5035 (7.30)	−.0070 (.70)	.5507
						Equation b					
1b	High	40	.4912			1.3396 (1.76)	−.6420 (.88)	.5560 (3.39)	.5564 (2.48)	−.0178 (.39)	.1739
2b	Moderate	128	.9891			1.2384 (5.06)	−1.0537 (3.97)	.0375 (3.74)	.0721 (1.18)	−.0040 (.14)	.2681
3b	Low	153	.5407			1.2902 (8.77)	−.5431 (3.69)	.4731 (7.68)	.5275 (6.46)	−.0076 (.73)	.5090
						Equation c					
1c	High	40	.4483		.6421 (3.76)			.6302 (4.36)	.5958 (3.03)	−.0480 (1.15)	.2951
2c	Moderate	128	.9465		.3028 (5.69)			.0435 (4.30)	.0483 (.78)	.0123 (.45)	.2494
3c	Low	153	.4539		.7856 (14.32)			.5779 (11.35)	.4254 (6.69)	−.0075 (.80)	.6042

*Figures in parentheses are t-statistics.

has a slightly higher explanatory power than the standard-cost pricing model (equation b). Additionally, ULC has a higher level of significance than AHE. In the moderate-concentration industries, the standard-cost pricing model has a slightly higher explanatory power than the competitive pricing model. AHE enters the price equation at about the same level of significance as ULC. These results again suggest that low-concentration industries conform to the competitive pricing model and that the moderate group follows standard-cost pricing. For the high concentration group the results for the 1966–69 period offer no evidence of standard-cost pricing.[26]

Significance tests on the estimated regressions as a whole indicate that the price responses to cost-and-demand changes of the moderate-concentration industry group differ significantly at the .05 level from both the high and low

26. The AHE variable and the productivity variable are not even significant at the .05 level.

groups.[27] No such significant difference is found between the low and high groups.

With respect to the stability across industry groups of the regression coefficients of the individual variables, UMC, UKC, ULC^* are significantly lower in the moderate-concentration industries.[28] The sum of the unit-cost coefficients for the moderate, high, and low groups are respectively .39, 1.86 and 1.78. Thus, during the period 1966–69, moderate-concentration industries passed on significantly less of the unit-cost increases than either high- or low-concentration industries. This difference is in contrast to the 1963–66 period when unit-cost changes were passed on at about the same rate by all industry groups. For the 1963–66 period the sum of the unit-cost coefficients (equation c, table 1) are 1.47, 1.83, and 1.49 for moderate, high, and low groups, respectively.

A comparison of the estimated price equations across time periods suggested that pricing behavior is affected by general economic conditions. Significance tests on the regression equations as a whole indicate that the pricing behavior of the moderate- and low-concentration industries differed across the two time

27. For the sample period 1966–69 the computed F-statistics (using the Chow test) for each basic equation across industry groups are:

Equations	F	Equations	F
1a and 2a	3.54*	2b and 3b	8.06*
1a and 3a	.52	1c and 2c	4.69*
2a and 3a	12.66*	1c and 3c	1.40
1b and 2b	2.57*	2c and 3c	17.06*
1b and 3b	.55		

*Indicates that the sets of regression coefficients are significantly different at the .05 level or higher.

28. Using analysis of covariance, the t-statistics for the dummy variates for the individual variables for each basic equation across industry groups for the period 1966–69 are:

Equations	ULC	ULC*	AHE	Prod	UMC	UKC	I/S
1a and 2a	1.83				3.92*	2.45*	.71
1a and 3a	.27				.58	.25	.45
2a and 3a	5.12*				7.28*	4.49*	.70
1b and 2b			.14	.60	3.71*	2.41*	.28
1b and 3b			.08	.17	.59	.15	.29
2b and 3b			.18	1.75	6.35*	4.31*	.13
1c and 2c		2.06*			4.45*	2.88*	1.28
1c and 3c		1.03			.43	1.06	1.27
2c and 3c		6.07*			8.78*	4.08*	.76

*Indicates regression coefficients are significantly different at the .05 level or higher using a two-tail test.

periods.[29] With respect to the significance tests on the regression coefficients of the individual variables, the regression coefficients on *UMC*, *ULC*, *ULC**, and *UKC* are significantly lower in the 1966–69 period as compared to the 1963–66 period for moderate-concentration industries.[30] In low-concentration industries, the regression coefficients on *ULC*, *ULC**, and *UKC* are significantly higher in the 1966–69 period as compared to the 1963–66 period.[31]

Cost changes were more fully passed on during the noninflationary 1963–66 period in partial oligopolies since cost changes tended to be relatively small and infrequent. However, during the 1966–69 inflationary period cost changes were large and frequent. During this period price adjustments to cost changes by partial oligopolists were relatively small since failure of rivals to respond to large price increases would result in significant decreases in market share.

In competitive industries costs were passed on more rapidly during the 1966–69 period. Competitive firms, anticipating continued large and rapid increases in costs during the inflation, passed on their costs as quickly as

29. The Chow test was used to test whether the sets of regression coefficients estimated for each basic equation within industry groups are significantly different across the sample time periods. The computed F-statistics are:

Equations	F	Equations	F
1a	1.36	2c	24.28*
1b	.99	3a	8.99*
1c	1.31	3b	5.22*
2a	20.92*	3c	5.65*
2b	11.41*		

*Indicates that the sets of regression coefficients are significantly different at the .05 level or higher.

30. Using analysis of covariance, the t-statistics for the dummy variates for the individual variables for each basic equation across the two time periods 1963–66 and 1966–69 are:

Equations	ULC	ULC*	AHE	Prod	UMC	UKC	I/S
1a	.23				.25	1.01	.40
1b			.86	1.72	.90	1.72	.13
1c		.59			.30	1.08	.69
2a	1.57				8.07*	3.09*	.94
2b			1.23	.64	6.92*	2.30*	.41
2c		2.24*			8.59*	3.13*	1.04
3a	3.96*				.80	2.77*	1.99*
3b			.62	.56	.98	2.89*	1.95*
3c		2.12*			.04	1.25	2.23*

*Indicates regression coefficients are significantly different at the .05 level or higher using a two-tail test.

31. The regression coefficients on the *I/S* variable were significantly lower in the 1966–69 period.

possible. Although cost increases in the 1963–66 period represented pressure on profits, the empirical results suggest that competitive firms' perceptions of less rapidly increasing costs allowed them some leeway in the timing of their price increases.

The explanatory power of the price equations estimated for both the high and moderate groups is substantially lower in the 1966–69 period than in the 1963–66 period. The greater variability of price responses during the 1966–69 period may reflect large uncertanties surrounding the oligopolists' long-term pricing decision during this period.[32]

In noninflationary periods estimates of future costs are likely to be highly correlated with current costs and price changes with current cost changes.[33] However, in periods of accelerating inflation current costs are no longer seen as reflecting long-term cost changes. In this situation each industry's perception of the rate of inflation and its effects on the industry's rate of return is likely to be quite different. Thus, oligopolists' price changes are likely to be less correlated with current cost changes in inflationary periods than in noninflationary periods.

The greater variability of price responses by ologopolistic industries in the 1966–69 period may also reflect breakdowns in interseller coordination mechanisms. This period was not only characterized by increasing inflation but also by a marked slowdown in the rate of growth in the economy. Due in large part to the credit crunch of 1966, a result of the monetary authority's growing concern with the increasing inflationary pressures in the economy, real output in the manufacturing sector remained almost constant between 1966 and 1967. Although real output in the manufacturing sector did increase slowly after 1967, the over-all 1966–69 period was not a period of stability and sustained growth.[34] Since these conditions generate the best environment for successful collusive behavior, many industries may have experienced significant breakdowns in their collective arrangements. The likelihood of such breakdowns would have depended on the particular demand conditions and structural characteristics of the industry.[35]

32. Oligopolistic industries avoid uncertainties with respect to productivity changes by basing prices on standard rather than actual costs. However, during rapid inflations, standard costs may be difficult to estimate.

33. This is consistent with the lower variability of industry price responses during the 1963–66 period.

34. During the 1963–66 period, real output in the manufacturing sector increased by $43.3 billion; between 1966 and 1967 real output decreased by$0.3 billion. Real output increased by $20.1 billion from 1966 to 1969 (*Economic Report of the President*, January 1972, Table B-9).

35. For example, breakdowns may have been more likely in industries where the distribution of output among the largest firms was relatively symmetrical than in those where one firm controlled a significantly larger share of the market.

The greater variability of industry price responses in oligopolistic industries during the 1966–69 period implies a greater variability in industry profit rates during this period than during the 1963–66 period. Additionally, the price equations estimated for the moderate-concentration industries imply lower profit rates in partial oligopolies during the 1966–69 period relative to the 1963–66 period. Both these phenomena may account for the general lack of opposition on the part of large corporations to the imposition of wage and price controls by the Nixon administration in August 1971.

The relatively similar explanatory power of the price equations estimated for the low-concentration industries for both time periods is consistent with the independent pricing behavior underlying the competitive pricing model. Competitive industries possess no discretionary power with respect to price. All price decisions are short-run decisions that reflect current cost-and-demand conditions.

3. CONCLUSIONS

The major conclusion of this paper is that market structure does influence industry pricing behavior. More specifically, the empirical analysis suggests that atomistic industries follow a competitive pricing model, and that tight and partial oligopolies tend to use some form of standard-cost pricing. Additionally, estimates of current standard costs explain less variability during inflationary periods than during noninflationary periods in oligopolistic industries. This may result from oligopolists viewing their current standard costs as being "less permanent" during inflations or from breakdowns in interseller coordination mechanisms during the 1966–69 period.

General economic conditions also appear to substantially affect the rate of cost pass-through in partial oligopolies. Whereas all industries passed on costs to the same degree during the 1963–66 noninflationary period, partial oligopolists passed on significantly less of their cost increases than either the tight oligopolistic or atomistic industries during the 1966–69 inflationary period. Thus, partial oligopolists contributed less to the inflationary spiral during the 1966–69 period. The impact of this behavior on the aggregate price level during the 1970–71 period is difficult to predict.[36] In those partial oligopolies where profit rates fell to critically low levels, firms may have attempted to increase prices by more than the increases in current costs. This behavior would have extended the duration of the inflation and may partially explain the phenomenon of jointly rising prices and unemployment rates during this period.

The results of this paper support the major conclusion reached by Eckstein

36. At the time of this study, data were not available to estimate industry price equations for the period 1969–71.

and Wyss (1972) that market structure does affect industry pricing behavior. However, the evidence presented in this paper suggests two conclusions different from those reached by Eckstein and Wyss.[37] First, Eckstein and Wyss conclude that all industries appear to use some form of standard-cost pricing. Our results suggest that atomistic (low-concentration) industries do not appear to use standard-cost pricing. Second, contrary to Eckstein and Wyss, our results suggest that general economic conditions do affect industry pricing behavior.

The empirical analysis presented in this paper adds to the growing body of evidence on the relationship between market structure and industry pricing behavior. However, the different conclusions with respect to the effects of general economic conditions on industry pricing behavior between this study and the Eckstein and Wyss study clearly indicate the need for further research. One specific area for further investigation is the degree to which general economic conditions affect interseller coordination mechanisms in oligopolistic industries.

37. The use of cross-section data at the four-digit SIC level does not enable tests of many of the Eckstein and Wyss findings. However, one interesting comparable point is our finding that during the non-inflationary period price increases in high- and moderate-concentration industries appeared to be keyed to wage increases. Eckstein and Wyss find similar results for their moderate-concentration industries.

Interesting also is that the demand variable in this study was significant in the low-concentration industries during the non-inflationary period. Eckstein and Wyss find demand influences most significant in the moderate-concentration group. The demand variable, I/S, is never significant in the high- and moderate-concentration groups. This particular measure of demand may be unable to pick up short-run demand changes. An alternative measure that future cross-section studies might use is deviations from the trend growth of sales. With respect to the demand variable, the Eckstein and Wyss results may be more reliable since they experimented with several demand measures. Additionally, their method may be more likely to capture the impact of demand pressures since quarterly changes measure short-run changes better than do three-year changes.

References

Beals, R. E., *Statistics for Economists: An Introduction* (Chicago: Rand McNally & Co., 1972).

Chow, G. C., "Tests of Equality between Sets of Coefficients in Two Linear Regressions," *Econometrica* 28 (June 1960).

Eckstein, O., and G. Fromm, "The Price Equation," *American Economic Review* 58 (December 1968).

Eckstein, O., and R. Brinner, *The Inflation Process in the United States,* U.S. Congress, Joint Economic Committee, Washington, D.C., 1972.

Eckstein, O., and D. Wyss, "Industry Price Equations," in *The Econometrics of Price Determination,* Board of Governors, Federal Reserve System, 1972.

Esposito, F. F. , and L. Esposito, "Excess Capacity and Market Structure," *Review of Economics and Statistics* 56 (May 1974).

Kaplan, A. D., J. B. Dirlam, and R. F. Lanzilotti, *Pricing in Big Business: A Case Approach* (Washington, D.C.: Brookings Institution, 1958).

Laden, B. E., "Perfect Competition, Average Cost Pricing, and the Price Equation," *Review of Economics and Statistics* 54 (February 1972).

Schwartzman, D., and J. Bodoff, "Concentration in Regional and Local Industries," *Southern Economic Journal* 37 (January 1971).

Shepherd, W. G., *Market Power and Economic Welfare* (New York: Random House, 1970).

Stigler, G. J., and J. K. Kindahl, *The Behavior of Industrial Prices* (New York: National Bureau of Economic Research, 1970).

Weiss, L. W., "Business Pricing Policies and Inflation Reconsidered," *Journal of Political Economy* 74 (April 1966).

——, "The Role of Concentration in Recent Inflation," *Appendix to Statement of Richard W. McLaren,* Assistant Attorney General, Antitrust Division, U.S. Department of Justice, before the Joint Economic Committee, 10 July 1970.

United States Silver Coinage:
What Remains of an Extinct Specie

David A. Belsley

0. INTRODUCTION AND SUMMARY

United States silver coinage is no more. With the recent striking of the Eisenhower dollar, the last planned U.S. silver-bearing coin has been made. This, therefore, is a particularly suitable moment to take stock of what remains of outstanding U.S. silver coinage and the potential supply of silver this stock represents.

There are two reasons why such a study is of interest. First, as noted, all the data are in, and an estimate of outstanding coinage can be made historically complete. Second, and more important, the stock of silver potentially available from outstanding U.S. silver coinage is seen to be an important source of this metal for an industrial silver market that has taken on classical problems of supply and demand—with all the implications this has for the price of silver. This latter point is best appreciated by noting that the price of silver is set

The research for this paper was carried out by the author as part of a study conducted by the Charles River Associates of Cambridge, Massachusetts, for the General Services Administration (contract #GS–00–DS–(P)–85005). An earlier version appears as Appendix C of the Charles River Report to GSA, *An Economic Analysis of the Silver Industry*. The author is indebted to the staff of Charles River Associates, in particular to Mr. Jean Paul Valette, for their assistance. The author is further indebted to his colleague, Edward J. Kane, for many helpful suggestions. This paper was written while the author was a Fellow at the Center for Advanced Study in the Behavioral Sciences at Stanford.

through supply and demand in an active world market. In the years since World War II the pressures on this price have been growing. In both the world in general and the United States in particular, industrial demand for silver has greatly exceeded new mining supplies.[1] For various reasons both industrial silver demand and silver mining supply appear quite inelastic (at least over a period of several decades), and hence the discrepancy between supply and demand has been made up from existing silver stocks, notably those of the U.S. Treasury acting to preserve the monetary value of U.S. silver coinage. Recently, however, this source has been exhausted, and alternative stockpiles, such as silver coinage, have taken on a greatly increased importance. Indeed, a quantitative estimate of the potential supply of silver from U.S. coinage is essential to understanding future price movements in the silver market. This paper, then, seeks to measure the retrievable stocks of silver represented in U.S. silver coinage.

The amount of silver potentially recoverable from coinage is great. From 1920 to 1968 the U.S. government minted approximately 2.1 billion troy ounces of silver into subsidiary coinage, and the Treasury's lifting of the ban on melting and exporting silver coins in May 1969 has made privately held stocks of U.S. coins a legal source of supply of silver to industrial users. Clearly not all silver coins minted can be recovered for their silver content. Many coins have been retired from circulation through combined losses of various kinds (including coin collection), and most of these coins should be regarded as irretrievable under any reasonable economic conditions. To estimate the potential stock of silver available from U.S. coinage, then, one must first estimate the value and composition of these irretrievably lost coins. Such an estimate proves quite difficult to obtain and forms the basic econometric task of this paper. It next seems reasonable to assume that all silver coins net of those estimated as irretrievably lost are potentially available for their silver content. But it cannot be assumed that all of these coins are held in private hoards, for, in recent years, the government itself has engaged in large withdrawals of silver coins. These withdrawals, however, have become negligible since mid-1968 and it is clear that virtually the entire stock of outstanding U.S. subsidiary coinage had been withdrawn from circulation as of, say, 31 December 1968,[2] and held either in private hoards or by the Treasury. Hence we may estimate total government

1. In 1966, for example, world industrial consumption was 356.5 million troy ounces (1 troy ounce equals 1.09715 avoirdupois ounces) and world production of new silver was only 231.0 million ounces. In the United States in that year, consumption was 150.0 million ounces, and mining output was but 42.0 million ounces. These figures are available in Handy and Harman, *The Silver Market 1966*. "World" refers here to the free world.

2. Indeed, the Federal Reserve Bank of Boston found it unprofitable to continue operations of their "separation machine" beyond February 1969.

withdrawals by their cumulative magnitude to that date and thereby reduce the stock obtained above to arrive at an estimate of silver available in private hoards.

Using this procedure, it is estimated that the private holdings of silver subsidiary U.S. coinage are in the neighborhood of 800 million troy ounces. This stock of silver is equivalent to approximately 20 years of U.S. new production of silver or over 5 years of industrial consumption at recent rates. Clearly such a stock is an important source of supply to a tight silver market. It is to be noted, however, that this stock will not be supplied inelastically. There are many liquidation costs to the coin hoarder, and the price of silver net of transactions, melting, and refining costs can be significantly less than the New York price. It is to be expected, therefore, that the flow of silver from coin hoards to industrial users will respond both to the time structure of the price of silver and to collection costs. Other things being equal, an increase in the price of silver will speed liquidation of coin stocks, but only after other, more inelastically supplied stocks (such as those held by the Treasury and other large-scale non-coinage hoarders) have been substantially reduced. Sales from these latter stocks, particularly the Treasury's,[3] have helped stabilize the price of silver in recent months, and hence, rather generally, it is to be supposed that speculation against the future price of silver is another major factor determining supply from private hoards. Further, for a given silver-price structure, supply from private coinage hoards can be expected to increase with the introduction of organized collection methods that, through economies of scale, are able to reduce transactions and purifying costs.

Part 1 of this paper constructs a simple model of coinage circulation and losses. Part 2 presents the data series employed and prepares the loss model for estimation. The estimation of losses and the calculation of the available silver stock are described in Part 3. Additional effort is required in this last section to estimate the effects of collectors—an activity for which data are wholly lacking.

1. A SIMPLE MODEL OF COINAGE CIRCULATION

Coinage Losses

For given denomination ξ (ξ = d[imes], q[uarters], h[alf-dollars]) we define:

$P_T{}^\xi$ = production of ξ in vintage-year T ,

---

3. At this writing the Treasury has just stopped selling (through the General Services Administration) silver from its stocks at the rate of 1.5 million ounces per week. Cf. Handy and Harman, *The Silver Market, 1969*, p. 7.

$S_{T,t}{}^{\xi} = $ stock of ξ of vintage T remaining in year $t (t \geqq T)$,

$S_t{}^{\xi} = \sum\limits_{T=T0}^{t} S_{T,t} = $ total stock of ξ remaining in year t^4 .   (1)

In year T, then, $P_T{}^{\xi}$ coins of denomination ξ are minted. It is assumed that all of these coins are placed into circulation at the beginning of the year.[5] Over the years some of these coins will be retired from circulation for various reasons, each having different implications for this study. We define four types of losses. (1) Direct loss of coins (thrown away, irretrievably misplaced, mutilated, buried, illegally melted, and so on). These coins, net of recovered losses, are, of course, unavailable to any potential silver supply. (2) Retirement of coins by the U.S. Treasury. The silver from these coins is presumably returned to some existing Treasury silver stock (perhaps new coins).[6] (3) Removal of coins from circulation by coin collectors for their collection value. We partition losses of this type into (3a) coin collectors' purchases of proof sets and uncirculated coins from the mint at the time that the coins are first issued, and (3b) coins retired "out-of-pocket" from circulation. In either case we assume that the collected coins would not be sold for their silver value at any realistic price of silver. (4) Hoarding of coins for speculative purposes. Such coins are held for their silver value, and presumably certain future movements in the price of silver would draw these coins into the silver market. Losses in this category seem to have assumed major proportions in recent years.

The Assumptions

A "true" model of coinage circulation that completely incorporates the four types of losses just listed would be complex indeed, and could not be estimated with the scarce data available. The actions of coin collectors, for example, are apparently varied and are very incompletely known. It is not even possible to give a reliable estimate of the number of collectors of U.S. coins, much less to determine the number of coins they remove from circulation. Similarly, the behavior of speculators is almost entirely unobserved. It is necessary, there-

4. Where T_0 is taken small enough to assure that coins of earlier vintage account for an insignificant part of the total stock currently in circulation. T_0 is taken to be 1920 in this study.

5. For the most part, dimes and quarters were issued within a year of their pressing. Half-dollars of some vintages, however, appear to have been issued over a period of several years following their pressing.

6. Government retirement of coins in this way is to be contrasted with the wholesale withdrawal of coins attempted by the Treasury since 1967. These latter stocks of coins are held by the Treasury and will be removed from our estimates of the total available silver-coinage stock to arrive at a figure for private holdings in a later section.

fore, to work with a less-than-complete model and to make simplifying assumptions that are capable of capturing the flavor of "normal" coinage losses of the various types.

First, it is assumed that the losses of types 1 and 2 during any given year t and for denomination ξ are proportional to the stock of coins of that denomination existing at the beginning of the year. Further this loss rate is assumed invariant to vintage and time. That is,

$$\Lambda^1_{t,\xi} = r^\xi_1 S^\xi_t$$
$$\Lambda^2_{t,\xi} = r^\xi_2 S^\xi_t \tag{2}$$

where $\Lambda^i_{t,\xi}$ is the loss of coins of denomination ξ over year
t due to the ith loss type, and
r^ξ_i is the rate of losses of coins of denomination ξ
due to the ith loss type.

This assumption has certain obvious weaknesses. First, one may speculate that the increased hardship placed on coins through the widespread introduction of coin-operated vending machines has increased both type 1 and type 2 losses since the 1950s. Second, retirement of excessively worn coins no doubt affects older vintages proportionately more than younger ones. Third, the fact that older coins generally contain less silver per unit due to losses through abrasion in circulation has been ignored. Thus it would be better to assume that losses in each year are more generally distributed across the existing stocks of each vintage. However, even so simple a generalization of the model adopted above cannot be estimated without having coinage samples taken in more than the one year available to this study. Fortunately, as later regression results substantiate, the assumption of strict proportionality, invariant to time and vintage, seems quite adequate for present needs.

Second, in regard to losses of type 3a, it is assumed that collectors remove a number of coins of each denomination ξ and of each vintage T from circulation immediately upon their issuance. Let this number of coins be denoted by C^ξ_T. There are no data on the total number of coins collected each year in this way. However, it is reasonably assumed that all proof sets and uncirculated coins sold by the mint[7] constitute a part of this figure. A more complete estimate of the C^ξ_T series is obtained in a manner described below.

7. In the Treasury's words: "Uncirculated coin sets, popularly known as "Mint Sets," contain pieces minted on high-speed presses for general circulation purposes. No attempt is made to impart a special finish. Although only the best uncirculated coins are used in the sets, the Mint cannot guarantee to furnish coins that are entirely free of blemish." Each set consists of 10 pieces: one each of $.50, $.25, $.10, $.05, $.01, from both the Philadelphia and Denver mints.

Proof sets are special sets of all denominations minted on slow-speed presses and finished so as to insure a blemish-free piece.

In regard to losses of the type 3b it is assumed that coins of a given denomination are removed "out-of-pocket" in each year in proportion to the existing stock. It may seem more reasonable to assume that this loss rate would be larger for coins of greater vintage. However, it is not true that older coins are necessarily more valuable to the collector;[8] more recent coins, for example, may be more valuable if significantly less of them were originally minted. Because of this and because of the lack of data required to consider more complex hypotheses, we will retain the assumption of simple proportionality, i.e.,

$$\Lambda^3_{t,\xi} = r^\xi_3 S^\xi_t \tag{3}$$

where $\Lambda^3_{t,\xi}$ = loss of coins of denomination ξ over year t due to out-of-pocket coin collection, and r^ξ_3 is the rate of such losses.

Finally we consider type 4 losses, those due to speculative hoarding. Once again an empirical investigation is at a disadvantage, for hoarding, though known to exist, is unobserved. There are no data on the activities of speculators. However, because of the timing of the collection of sample data employed in this study, we are able to overcome this shortcoming to a large extent.

The sample data on coinage circulation (described below) were collected in 1961. Although anticipation of a rise in the price of silver may have resulted in some speculation in silver coins prior to 1961,[9] conditions were not nearly as conducive to hoarding as they have been since that year. The U.S. government removed its peg on the price of silver at the end of 1961 (28 November), and from that time the anticipation of unprecedented increases in the price of silver has made some speculation profitable. It was, however, not until September 1963 that market forces caused the price of silver to reach its monetary value. The government again stepped in at this time to peg the price of silver at its monetary value ($1.29 per troy ounce), but knowledge that this situation could not last made truly large-scale hoarding profitable. Further pressure for speculative hoarding resulted from the Treasury's switch in 1964 to "sandwich" coins in place of silver coins. Silver coins rapidly disappeared from circulation as Gresham's Law seemed to operate in its classic form.

It seems reasonable, then, to consider speculative hoarding prior to, say, 1962 or 1963 to be minimal, and it will be assumed that the sample data collected in 1961 and upon which we shall base our estimates of "normal"

---

8. At least within the limits of "old" for this study, which extends back only to 1920. Truly old coins are in a different category and need not be considered here. They will never return to circulation and will never be made available for silver supply under any reasonable conditions of the silver market.

9. Speculation for silver value as distinct from investment speculation for collector value.

coinage-loss rates reflect losses only of types 1, 2 and 3. This assumption justifies the adoption of the following procedure for estimating private stocks of silver coinage in Part 3:

> First, a normal loss rate for each denomination will be estimated on the basis of sample evidence from a period prior to 1961 for which it is assumed that speculative hoarding is insignificant. This normal loss rate (modified for collectors) is then projected forward to estimate the loss of coins of the given denomination that would be expected under conditions of minimal or no hoarding up through 1967. Finally, assuming that all coins that were minted but that are not accounted for by "normal" losses are hoarded, we can easily obtain an estimate of coins potentially available for their silver content. The motivation for this last assumption is that in recent years virtually all silver coins have been removed from circulation by hoarders or withdrawn by the U.S. Treasury and replaced by sandwich coins.

The Model

In light of the foregoing, we postulate the following simple model of coinage circulation for the years prior to 1961 or 1963, the period for which we abstract from speculative hoarding.

In each vintage year T, P^{ξ}_T coins of denomination ξ are minted and circulated (we assume all to be placed in circulation at the beginning of T). C^{ξ}_T of these coins are removed immediately by collectors. Further, during any year t, the loss of coins of denomination ξ and vintage T due to loss types 1, 2, and 3b are fractions r^{ξ}_1, r^{ξ}_2, and r^{ξ}_3 respectively of the stock of that vintage coin in existence at the beginning of the year t, i.e., $S^{\xi}_{T,t}$. Hence the total loss of such coins is

$$L^{\xi}_{T,t} = r^{\xi} S^{\xi}_{T,t} \qquad T \le t \tag{4}$$

where $r^{\xi} \equiv r^{\xi}_1 + r^{\xi}_2 + r^{\xi}_3$.

Further, in each vintage year T, C^{ξ}_T of the P^{ξ}_T coins of denomination ξ that were minted in that year are removed immediately by coin collectors. Thus,

$$S^{\xi}_{T,t} = P^{\xi}_T - C^{\xi}_T. \tag{5}$$

Combining (4) and (5), we determine the stock of coins of denomination ξ and vintage T circulating in year t ($\ge T$) simply as

$$S^{\xi}_{T,t} = (1-r^{\xi})^{t-T+1}(P^{\xi}_T - C^{\xi}_T)$$

$$= (1-r^{\xi})^{t-T+1}\bar{P}^{\xi}_T \tag{6}$$

where we define $\bar{P}^{\xi}_T = P^{\xi}_T - C^{\xi}_T$.

2. DATA AND SPECIFICATION

The model equation (6) can be used in conjunction with two basic data sets to obtain estimates of the normal loss rates, r^ξ , of coins of each denomination, as well as estimates of the series of losses by collectors C_T^ξ .

The two basic data series available to this study are:

1. a time series on mint production of each denomination by vintage, i.e., the series for P^ξ_T , ξ = dimes, quarters, and half-dollars, and T = 1920, . . . , 1967,[10] and

2. a sample of 36,000 coins for each denomination taken in 1961 and listing the number of each vintage occuring in the sample.[11]

These data are listed in tables 1 and 2 respectively.

Specification

Let us denote by $\lambda^\xi_{T,t}$ the true proportion of coins of denomination ξ in year t that are of vintage T, i.e.,

$$\lambda^\xi_{T,t} \equiv \frac{S^\xi_{T,t}}{S^\xi_t} . \tag{7}$$

We may estimate $\lambda^\xi_{T,t}$ for t = 1961 and T = 1920, . . . , 1961 from the sample data as λ^ξ_T = the sample proportion of coins of denomination ξ and vintage T among the total number of coins of denomination ξ, i.e., 36,000. For t = 1961 we have from equations (6) and (7)

$$\lambda^\xi_{T,1961} = \frac{S^\xi_{T,1961}}{S^\xi_{1961}} = \frac{(1-r^\xi)^{1961-T+1}(P^\xi_T - C^\xi_T)}{S^\xi_{1961}} \tag{8}$$

$$T = 1920, . . .,1961 .$$

10. Actually the mint figures are historically complete and extend back prior to 1920. However, it is assumed that any coins antedating 1920 are (1) insignificant in number, and (2) not likely to materialize under any reasonable economic circumstances. The 1967 terminal figure allows inclusion of virtually all silver coins produced. Silver dimes and quarters were not minted beyond 1965, and only Kennedy half-dollars (both 90 fine and 40 fine) were produced beyond 1967. These pieces, however, are highly prized by collectors and are correctly assumed to be irretrievable.

11. This sample was collected at the request of the director of the Mint for the purpose of a study of coin losses performed by A. D. Little. Each of the 36 Federal Reserve Banks and branches were asked to collect a sample of 1,000 coins of each denomination and record their vintages.

TABLE 1

ANNUAL SILVER COINAGE OF THE UNITED STATES, 1920–1967
(Millions of Pieces)

Year	Half-Dollars	Quarters	Dimes	Year	Half-Dollars	Quarters	Dimes
1920	12.8	37.8	92.0	1945	51.6	103.7	241.3
1921	1.2	1.9	2.3	1946	19.8	66.7	344.2
1922	0.1	0.0	0.0	1947	8.3	43.4	203.2
1923	2.5	11.1	56.6	1948	7.1	67.9	163.3
1924	0.1	16.9	37.9	1949	13.5	19.4	70.5
1925	2.7	12.3	36.6	1950	16.4	56.3	117.4
1926	1.1	15.7	40.5	1951	40.7	87.9	191.7
1927	2.4	13.3	37.7	1952	54.2	102.4	265.6
1928	2.0	10.6	31.0	1953	28.0	88.8	229.2
1929	2.9	14.3	35.7	1954	44.0	108.8	243.5
1930	0.0	7.2	8.6	1955	2.9	21.7	45.3
1931	0.0	0.0	6.2	1956	4.7	77.1	217.3
1932	0.0	6.2	0.0	1957	26.3	125.7	274.8
1933	1.8	0.0	0.0	1958	28.9	85.4	169.4
1934	13.2	35.4	30.9	1959	20.4	87.6	251.8
1935	16.4	43.9	85.1	1960	25.9	93.9	272.2
1936	21.5	50.5	112.8	1961	31.6	123.7	305.9
1937	13.6	28.5	80.8	1962	48.4	166.9	410.6
1938	4.7	12.3	35.8	1963	92.3	212.7	548.2
1939	13.7	43.3	102.7	1964	205.8	385.9	814.9
1940	13.7	46.8	108.1	1965[a]	186.0	878.0	1,308.0
1941	43.6	111.8	263.8	1966[b]	41.7	4.6	167.9
1942	71.5	139.0	315.5	1966[c]	63.5		
1943	78.0	137.5	324.1	1966[d]	106.7		
1944	46.9	132.1	343.1	1967	295.1		

[a]1964 coins issued in 1965
[b]1964 coins issued in 1966
[c]1965 coins issued in 1966
[d]1966 coins issued in 1966

Source: U.S. Bureau of the Mint, *Annual Report of the Director of the Mint*, 1966–1968, Table C-11.

Now we assume that

$$\hat{\lambda}^{\xi}_T = \lambda^{\xi}_{T,1961} \cdot \varepsilon_T$$

where the ε_T are assumed drawn from independent and identical log-normal distributions. Thus,

$$\hat{\lambda}^{\xi}_T = \frac{(1-r^{\xi})^{1961-T+1}(P^{\xi}_T - C^{\xi}_T)}{S^{\xi}_{1961}}\varepsilon_T \qquad (10)$$

$$T = 1920, \ldots, 1961$$

TABLE 2

Age Distribution of U.S. Coins in Circulation
(Number of Pieces Found in a Sample Taken in 1961)

Year of Manufacture	Half-Dollars	Quarters	Dimes	Year of Manufacture	Half-Dollars	Quarters	Dimes
1920	134	0	84	1942	3,137	2,009	1,588
1921	16	2	1	1943	3,603	2,060	1,763
1922	1	2	0	1944	2,194	1,950	1,888
1923	20	2	102	1945	2,448	1,635	1,306
1924	3	5	58	1946	744	977	1,842
1925	0	43	37	1947	352	646	1,074
1926	0	85	77	1948	184	1,081	868
1927	26	38	73	1949	432	275	389
1928	27	29	43	1950	657	922	732
1929	36	35	70	1951	1,861	1,469	1,235
1930	1	34	11	1952	2,547	1,768	1,653
1931	2	3	1	1953	1,295	1,486	1,492
1932	2	40	0	1954	2,431	2,065	1,786
1933	25	2	0	1955	35	295	168
1934	384	425	85	1956	135	1,330	1,555
1935	512	509	310	1957	1,405	2,324	2,133
1936	750	603	398	1958	1,405	1,616	1,289
1937	449	374	281	1959	1,253	1,630	2,074
1938	149	147	104	1960	1,619	1,686	2,512
1939	462	592	446	1961	2,001	2,642	3,196
1940	543	677	572				
1941	1,821	1,531	1,292				

Source: U.S. Senate, 88th Congress, *Additional Mint Facilities,* Hearing before a Subcommittee of the Committee on Banking and Currency–S.874, 26 March 1963, p. 118.

Taking logs of (10), we obtain

$$\ln \frac{\hat{\lambda}^{\xi}_{T}}{P^{\xi}_{T} - C^{\xi}_{T}} = - \ln S^{\xi}_{1961} + (1961 - T + 1)\ln(1 - r^{\xi}) + \ln \varepsilon_{T}$$

$$\equiv \alpha_0 + \alpha_1 \tau + \theta_T \qquad (11)$$

where
$$\alpha_0 = -\ln S_{1961}$$
$$\alpha_1 = \ln(1 - r\xi)$$
$$\theta_T = \ln \varepsilon_T$$
$$\tau = 1961 - T + 1 .$$

Equation (11) is a linear equation whose parameters α_0 and α_1 are amenable to estimation by ordinary least squares. In particular we dwell upon the estimate $\hat{\alpha}_1$ of α_1 , for we may obtain from it

$$\hat{r}^{\xi} = 1 - e^{\hat{\alpha}_1} , \qquad (12)$$

the estimate of the normal loss rate, r^{ξ} .

3. ESTIMATION AND RESULTS

All the data series for carrying out a regression estimate of equation (11) are available except for the series for C^{ξ}_T . Before turning to the estimates of this series, however, we preview the steps to be employed.

An Overview of the Estimation Procedure

Our goal is to find the potential supply of silver from silver coins. This could be accomplished easily if we knew the values of P^{ξ}_T , C^{ξ}_T , and r^{ξ} for each denomination ξ and for vintages extending from $T = 1967$ back to some date T_0 (taken here as 1920)[12] sufficiently early that few coins of earlier vintage can be expected to materialize in 1967 for their silver content. Knowledge of these data would allow us to compute $\bar{P}^{\xi}_T$, and from equation (6) (with $t = 1967$) we could in turn compute the stock of each vintage of each denomination ξ existing in 1967, i.e., $S^{\xi}_{T,1967}$. In each case this would be a "normal" stock reflecting "normal" losses of types 1, 2, and 3, but abstracting from hoarding. For each denomination we then could simply add these stocks across vintages to obtain

$$S^{\xi}_{1967} = \sum_{T=1920}^{1967} S^{\xi}_{T,1967} , \xi = \text{dimes, quarters, and half-dollars} \qquad (13)$$

the total stock of denomination ξ existing in 1967. Of course, this stock of coins would not have actually circulated in 1967, for virtually all silver coins that were not lost or collected had been privately hoarded or withdrawn by the government by this time. Thus we could assume the values calculated in equation (13) give us estimates of the number of coins of each denomination hoarded and potentially available for their silver content. Since the amount of silver per coin is known, it would then be a simple matter to calculate the silver content of these stocks.

To obtain the estimates of the C^{ξ}_T and the r^{ξ} required to carry out the above procedure, a three-step sequence is employed. The essentials of these steps are summarized here before their detailed treatment in the next section.

Step 1. To estimate the normal loss rate. Our estimates of the r^{ξ} are based on the sample of coins taken in 1961 and reported in table 2. Hence, these estimated loss rates can at best reflect losses only of vintages minted prior to 1961. Further, as we shall see, vintages minted prior to the depression seem to show loss patterns that are distinctly less regular than those of coins minted after the depression. Thus it will prove useful to distinguish among three time periods: the pre-depression period (1920–30), the post-depression period

12. See note 10 above.

(1931, 1932, or 1933–61), and the current period (1962–67). The starting date for the post-depression period differs for each denomination: 1931 for dimes, 1932 for quarters, and 1933 for half-dollars. As is clear from table 1, few coins were minted during the depression years.

For each denomination the loss patterns during the post-depression period appear to be strongly regular. There are only a few anomalies and these occur in direct association with years of unusually low production (for example, 1955). In a manner to be described below these points suggest a means of estimating the effects of coin collectors during the post-depression period. Following this suggestion, the series C_T are estimated for vintages $T = T_\xi, \ldots , 1961$ (where T_ξ is 1931, 1932, or 1933, as ξ respectively represents dimes, quarters, half-dollars). Making use of the C^ξ_T series so derived, it becomes possible to estimate equation (11) over this period, and therefore to estimate r^ξ. The estimate of r^ξ determined in this way reflects a period showing strong regularity and is hence assumed to estimate the "normal" loss rate we seek.

Step 2. To estimate pre-depression collection activity. Step 1 results in estimates a_1 and a_2 of the parameters of (11), an equation of the form

$$\ln \frac{\hat{\lambda}^\xi_T}{P^\xi_T - C^\xi_T} = a_0 + a_1\tau , \qquad (14)$$

based on data from the post-depression period. This estimated equation can now be solved for C^ξ_T in terms of the known series P^ξ_T and $\hat{\lambda}^\xi_T$ and used to project values for C^ξ_T backward for $T < T_\xi$; i.e., for the pre-depression period. Steps 1 and 2 together result in estimates of the series $\overline{P}^\xi_T = P^\xi_T - C^\xi_T$ for $T = 1920$ to 1961, and the estimates of the r^ξ. It is left only to determine $\overline{P}^\xi_T$ for $T > 1961$.

Step 3. To Estimate Current-Period Collector Activity. Although the hoarding of silver coins presumably increased quite substantially in the years following 1961, we can project the "normal" behavior of collectors determined in Step 1 to arrive at a C^ξ_T series for $T > 1961$. It is assumed by this procedure that true *collector* activities remain essentially unchanged in the current period even though *hoarding* is substantially increasing. This assumption is given more discussion below.

Step 3, then, is to project the "normal" collector behavior into the current period to determine $\overline{P}^\xi_T \equiv P^\xi_T - C^\xi_T$ for $T = 1962$–67. Steps 1, 2, and 3 together determine the $\overline{P}^\xi_T$ and r^ξ for all ξ and $T = 1920, \ldots , 1967$ that are required to determine the potential silver stock. We now carry out these three steps.

Estimation of $\bar{P}_T$ and r^ξ

If we possessed series for $C^\xi{}_T$, we could make use of equation (11) to estimate r^ξ and equation (6) to estimate coinage stocks net of losses. As a first approximation to this end, we assume $C^\xi{}_T \equiv 0$. In this case, equation (11) becomes (for each ξ)

$$\ln \frac{\hat{\lambda}^\xi{}_T}{P^\xi{}_T} = \alpha_0 + \alpha_1\tau + \theta_T , \tag{15}$$

a "two-variate" equation in observed variables.

In order to assess the worth of this relationship, we plot the scattering of $\ln\hat{\lambda}^\xi{}_T/P^\xi{}_T$ and τ for each denomination. These scatters are presented in Figures 1a, b, and c for dimes, quarters, and half-dollars respectively. $\ln\hat{\lambda}^\xi{}_T/P^\xi{}_T$ is plotted along the vertical axis, and T, going from 1920 to 1962, is plotted along the horizontal axis. Examination of these scatters reveals three interesting elements common to each. First, there is a strong tendency toward linearity in the relation among the points over their respective post-depression periods. Second, this linearity is clearly violated by several years for each denomination, this being strikingly true in each case for 1955. Third, there is a marked increase in the dispersion of the pre-depression point scatters accompanied by an obvious divergence from the post-depression experience.

The Post-Depression Experience

Centering now for concreteness on figure 1c for half-dollars, the outlying points for 1955 and 1956 require an explanation. A glance at table 1 reveals these to be years of unusually low production. This is also true for the years 1933 and 1948, which show similar departures from the basic linearity. It appears, then, that a less-than-expected proportion of coins of those vintages characterized by lower-than-usual production materialized in the sample. This phenomenon can be explained in one of two ways. First, we might assume that these coins have a greater loss rate (exclusive of collectors) than other coins of the same denomination. There is certainly no reason why this should be true, for, apart from collectors' actions, coins should be treated alike. Second, it may be the case that the number of coins removed from circulation by collectors at the issuance of the coins is sufficiently large relative to the total minting in these low production years that the use of $P^h{}_T$ in equation (11) instead of $\bar{P}^h{}_T$ seriously overstates the magnitude of coins initially placed in general circulation. Given that we have ignored coin collecting in the scatters of figure 1, this latter explanation seems quite plausible, and we adopt it here. Were we therefore able to remove C^h_T from P^h_T , a plot of the resulting $\ln\hat{\lambda}^h_T/\bar{P}^h_T$ (as opposed to $\ln\hat{\lambda}^h_T/P^h_T$) against T would be expected to exhibit strong linearity even in years of low production.

It is possible, then, to estimate C^h_T for years of low production (such as $T = 1955$) by determining that number of half-dollars that would have to be removed from circulation by collectors in those years in order to bring the "corrected" data plot into line with the weight of experience in surrounding years. For example, we may estimate C^h_{1955} as that number of coins which must be removed from P^h_{1955} in order to bring the value of $\ln\hat{\lambda}^h_{1955}/P^h_{1955} - C^h_{1955}$

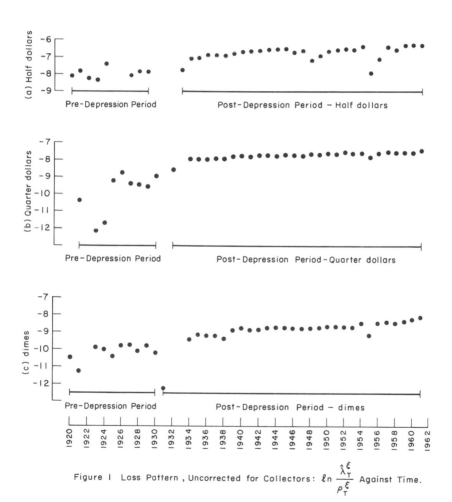

Figure I Loss Pattern, Uncorrected for Collectors: $\ell n \dfrac{\lambda^\xi_T}{\rho^\xi_T}$ Against Time.

into the region of the line defined by the majority of surrounding points. The number so determined for 1955 serves as a first approximation for C^h_{1955} . However, no further approximation will be necessary, for the magnitudes of the C^h_T that are so determined are large relative to the total production only for low-production vintages. In years of more normal production, collector activities will be a small proportion of total production and the difference between $ln\hat{\lambda}^h_T/P^h_T$ and $ln\hat{\lambda}_T/\bar{P}^h_T$ will be very small indeed.

Now we also note that 1933 is a year of low production for half-dollars and we can therefore find a similar estimate of C^h_{1933} . In order to determine the C^h_T for the other vintages we assume that C^h_T moves slowly over time between the benchmark values of C^h_{1933} and C^h_{1955} as determined above.

The series for C_T that we seek can be decomposed into the form

$$C^h_T = G^h_T + H_T \tag{16}$$

where G^h_T is the number of half-dollars initially removed from circulation by collectors and H_T is the number of proof sets plus twice the number of

TABLE 3

PROOF SETS AND UNCIRCULATED COIN SETS

Vintage	(1) Proof Sets	(2) Uncirculated Coin Sets	(3) = (1) + 2 · (2) H_T
1936	3,837	.........[b]	3,837
1937	5,542	....	5,542
1938	8,045	....	8,045
1939	8,795	....	8,795
1940	11,246	....	11,246
1941	15,287	....	15,287
1942	21,120	....	21,120
1949	.........[a]	20,739	40,478
1950	51,386	0	51,386
1951	57,500	8,654	74,808
1952	81,980	11,499	104,978
1953	120,800	15,538	159,876
1954	233,350	25,599	284,548
1955	378,200	49,656	477,512
1956	669,384	45,475	760,334
1957	1,247,952	32,324	1,312,600
1958	875,652	50,314	976,280
1959	1,149,291	187,000	1,523,291
1960	1,691,602	260,485	2,212,572
1961	3,028,244	223,704	3,475,652
1962	3,218,019	385,285	3,988,589
1963	3,075,645	606,622	4,288,889
1964	3,950,762	1,000,000[c]	5,950,762

Source: U.S. Treasury Department publications.
[a]Production of proof sets was discontinued between 1943 and 1949.
[b]None minted between 1936 and 1942.
[c]Estimated by Treasury Department.
Note: Proof sets and sets of uncirculated silver coins were discontinued after 1964.

uncirculated coin sets[13] of vintage T sold by the mint. The series for H_T is obtained from Treasury publications on proof sets and uncirculated coins. These are given in table 3.

It is necessary, then, only to estimate the $G^h{}_T$ series, coin collections net of proof sets, and uncirculated coins. It is assumed that this series moves linearly over time between its values as calculated in the benchmark years, 1955 and 1933. It is easily calculated that $C^h{}_{1955}$ must be 2.4 million half-dollar pieces, and $C^h{}_{1933}$ must be approximately 1 million coins. Of the 2.4 million coins in 1955, 0.5 million were collected in the form of proof sets and uncirculated pieces. Hence the removal from circulation must be approximately 1.9 million coins. There were no proof sets or uncirculated coins issued in 1933. The series for $G^h{}_T$, then, is estimated by the linear function in time whose value is 1.9 million in 1955 and 1 million in 1933.

The series $C^d{}_T$ and $C^q{}_T$ for dimes and quarters can be determined in a way analogous to that employed above for half-dollars. For each denomination the year 1955 was characterized by exceptionally low production and can be used to estimate $C^\xi{}_{1955}$, $\xi = d,q$. Also, for dimes, 1931 can be used for a second point to determine the line $G^d{}_T$, and for quarters 1932 can be used. The estimates of these benchmark values for G_T are summarized in table 4.

Tables 3 and 4 allow us to determine the H_T and G_T series for $\xi = d, q$, and h for the post-depression period. The C_T series for the corresponding period may now be determined by (16). These series are given in table 6.

The "Normal" Loss Rate

The C_T series derived above allow us to calculate $\bar{P}^\xi{}_T \equiv P^\xi{}_T - C^\xi{}_T$ for the post-depression period. Plots of $\ln \dfrac{\hat{\lambda}^\xi{}_T}{\bar{P}^\xi{}_T}$ against time are given in Figure 2, and these reveal the substantial linearity sought for. It is important to note that the correction applied above seems appropriate rather generally for years of low

TABLE 4

BENCHMARK VALUES FOR G_T IN SELECTED YEARS OF LOW PRODUCTION
(Millions of coins)

Dimes		Quarters		Half-dollars	
1931	1955	1932	1955	1933	1955
6.0	25.0	2.0	4.0	1.0	1.9

13. The H_T series applies equally to all denominations since the coins are sold in sets. Uncirculated coins are counted twice since each set contains two coins of each denomination. Cf. note 6 above.

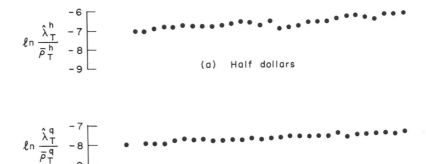

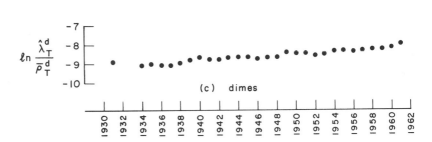

Figure 2   Post-Depression Loss Pattern, Corrected for

Collectors: $\ell n \dfrac{\hat{\lambda}^{\xi}_{T}}{\bar{\rho}^{\xi}_{T}}$ on Time.

production and not just for those chosen to define the G^{ξ}_{T} series (see, for example, $T = 1956$ for half-dollars).

We will assume the substantial regularity exhibited by the post-depression period defines "normal" collector activities and "normal" loss rates. We may therefore apply equation 11 to the respective post-depression series $\ell n \dfrac{\hat{\lambda}^{\xi}_{T}}{\bar{P}^{\xi}_{T}}$ to obtain estimates of the normal loss rates. The regression results for these periods[14] are as follows:

14. 1931–61 for half-dollars; 1932–61 for quarters; 1933–61 for dimes. The numbers in parentheses are standard errors.

Dimes: $\ln \frac{\hat{\lambda}^d{}_T}{\bar{P}^d{}_T} = -8.8087 - .0348\tau$
$$(.034) \quad (.0019) \qquad \bar{R}^2 = .917$$

Quarters: $\ln \frac{\hat{\lambda}^q{}_T}{\bar{P}^q{}_T} = -7.412 - .0171\tau$
$$(.020) \quad (.0012) \qquad \bar{R}^2 = .876$$

Half-dollars: $\ln \frac{\hat{\lambda}^h{}_T}{\bar{P}^h{}_T} = -6.225 - .0261\tau$
$$(.050) \quad (.0029) \qquad \bar{R}^2 = .730 \ .$$

Through equation (12) we obtain the estimates of r shown in table 5.[15]

TABLE 5

ESTIMATES OF THE NORMAL LOSS RATES

Dimes	.0342
Quarters	.0169
Half-dollars	.0257

The Pre-Depression Period

The method employed for estimating the series for the post-depression period does not apply well to the pre-depression period. As noted earlier, these years show greater irregularity than those of the post-depression period. For each denomination there were several years during the depression when no coins were minted at all (see table 1). Further, coin collecting, not greatly practiced in

15. A. D. Little, in a study for the director of the Mint, also estimated annual loss rates. That study made use of the same sample data but was based on a different model of coinage circulation and made use of the full data period, 1920–61. Little's results, for comparison, are:

Annual Loss Rates
(1920–1961)

Dimes	.038
Quarters	.022
Half-dollars	.028

This study is found in U.S. Senate, 88th Congress, *Additional Mint Facilities*, Hearing before a Subcommittee of the Committee on Banking and Currency, S 874, 26 March 1963, p. 117.

Another method of estimating normal loss rates has been suggested to me by E. J. Kane. This is to investigate losses of sandwich coins since their introduction in 1965. These non-silver coins are not subject to speculative hoarding, and their removal from circulation should reflect losses only of the first three types. Unfortunately, these coins have circulated too few years to fully exploit a new coinage sample at this time.

TABLE 6

ESTIMATE OF COINS RETURNED THROUGH COLLECTION AND "CORRECTED" PRODUCTION SERIES
(Millions of Coins)

VINTAGE	DIMES		QUARTERS		HALF-DOLLARS	
	C^d_t	$\bar{P}^d_t$	C^q_d	$\bar{P}^q_t$	C^h_t	$\bar{P}^h_t$
1920	57.9989	34.0221	18.9132	18.9132	11.3872	1.4099
1921	1.9188	.3912	1.8204	.0956	1.0525	.1696
1922	. . . . . .	. . . . . .	. . . . . .	. . . . . .	.0894	.0107
1923	19.3491	37.2209	10.9804	.0955	2.2369	.2152
1924	17.4983	20.4417	16.6532	.2388	.1096	.0325
1925	23.9822	12.5948	10.2265	2.0535	1.7847	.8923
1926	15.1927	25.3153	11.6739	4.0581	.7657	.3829
1927	14.4818	23.1802	11.4707	1.8137	2.1438	.2882
1928	17.8534	13.1876	9.2238	1.3838	1.6984	.3016
1929	14.9994	20.7346	12.5924	1.6696	2.4981	.4051
1930	5.4660	3.1470	5.5666	1.6214	. . . . . .	. . . . . .
1931	6.0000	.2100	. . . . . .	. . . . . .	. . . . . .	. . . . . .
1932	. . . . . .	. . . . . .	2.9000	3.3488	. . . . . .	. . . . . .
1933	. . . . . .	. . . . . .	. . . . . .	. . . . . .	1.0000	.7913
1934	8.3750	22.4770	2.9957	32.4436	1.0409	12.1836
1935	9.1667	75.9803	3.0435	40.8805	1.0818	15.3212
1936	9.9621	102.8800	3.0951	47.4107	1.1265	20.3653
1937	10.7555	69.9963	3.1446	25.3985	1.1891	12.4801
1938	11.5497	24.2760	3.1950	9.1170	1.2125	3.4633
1939	12.3421	90.3412	3.2436	40.0252	1.2542	12.4016
1940	13.1362	94.9836	3.2938	43.4630	1.2976	12.4197
1941	13.9320	249.9000	3.3457	108.5000	1.3426	42.2112
1942	14.7294	300.7400	3.3994	135.5900	1.3893	70.1316
1943	15.5000	308.5600	3.4261	134.0700	1.4091	76.5769
1944	16.2917	326.8300	3.4739	128.6400	1.4500	45.4290
1945	17.0833	224.2100	3.5217	100.2000	1.4909	50.1339
1946	17.8750	326.3200	3.5696	63.1432	1.5318	18.2623
1947	18.6667	184.5300	3.6174	39.8090	1.5727	6.7220
1948	19.4583	143.8500	3.6652	64.2576	1.6136	5.4818
1949	20.2914	50.1926	3.7544	15.6259	1.6959	11.8187
1950	21.0930	96.3314	3.8123	52.5188	1.7469	14.6143
1951	21.9082	169.1913	3.8836	84.0248	1.8113	38.8836
1952	22.7300	242.9085	3.9615	98.4036	1.8823	52.3357
1953	23.5764	205.6545	4.0641	84.7292	1.9780	25.9913
1954	24.4929	219.0044	4.2368	104.5444	2.1437	41.8628
1955	25.4776	19.8198	4.4776	17.2632	2.3776	.4988
1956	26.5521	190.7745	4.8082	72.3397	2.7013	2.0001
1957	27.8959	246.8677	5.4083	120.2977	3.2944	23.0346
1958	28.3513	141.0000	5.1198	80.2408	2.9990	25.8811
1959	29.6900	222.1630	5.7146	81.8729	3.5869	16.8961
1960	31.1709	241.0695	6.4517	87.4042	4.3171	21.6143
1961	33.2256	272.6963	7.7626	115.9563	5.6211	26.9736
1962	34.5303	376.0847	8.3234	158.6047	6.1750	42.2303
1963	35.6221	512.5834	8.6714	204.0034	6.5161	85.7928
1964	38.0758	776.8000	10.3812	375.5000	8.2190	197.5900
1965[a]	32.9167	1275.1300	4.4783	893.4700	2.3091	183.6700
1966[b]	33.7083	134.2000	4.5261	.1148	2.3500	39.3240
1966[c]	. . . . . .	. . . . . .	. . . . . .	. . . . . .	4.7100	58.8024
1966[d]	. . . . . .	. . . . . .	. . . . . .	. . . . . .	4.6116	102.1100
1967	. . . . . .	. . . . . .	. . . . . .	. . . . . .	4.2542	290.7900

[a]1964 coins issued in 1965.
[b]1964 coins issued in 1966.
[c]1965 coins issued in 1966.

[d]1966 coins issued in 1966.
Source: Tables 1, 4, and text.

the early thirties, came into its manhood in 1934 when it was observed that coin values were not greatly linked to the stock market.[16]

One can easily speculate, therefore, that the "normal" post-depression behavior of coin collectors is not representative of their behavior in the few years immediately after the depression with respect to coins minted earlier. As table 1 attests, coins were not minted as numerously before the depression, and we can assume many of these were spirited away during the depression or shortly thereafter by collectors. To approximate this removal of coins, it was decided to make use of the "normal" post-depression experience embodied in the estimated equations for dimes, quarters, and half-dollars given above, and to extend these regression lines backward to estimate what would have been normal behavior prior to the depression. A correction factor is then applied to the observed pre-depression points to bring them onto this extended regression line. The correction necessary to do this is assumed as an estimate of the number of coins of these vintages removed from circulation by collectors, i.e., as an estimate of C^ξ_T for $T < T_\xi$. While this procedure has obvious disadvantages (in particular not all of these coins were removed immediately in the vintage year), it is to be emphasized that because of the relatively small number of coins involved and because of the relatively long period of time for attrition by loss, the final estimate of potentially available silver is quite insensitive to this assumption, and the procedure used here surely gives a better estimate of this figure than one that ignores the need for such corrections altogether.[17] The estimates of C_T (and the resulting $\bar{P}_T$) obtained in this way are given in table 6.

The Current Period

It remains only to determine the C^ξ_T for the current period, i.e. $T = 1962, \ldots, 1967$. For quarters and dimes this is accomplished by extrapolating forward the "normal" collector behavior $G^\xi_T + H_T$, determined in the post-depression period. The same procedure is employed for half-dollars minted in 1963 and 1964. These extrapolated figures and the corresponding $\bar{P}^\xi_T$ are listed in table 6. The principal objection to this approach is that silver quarters and dimes issued after 1964 were given a 1964 date. Only sandwich coins were given later dates. The inclusion of these silver coins as if they were the same vintage as the year of issuance is correct in every respect except that it assumes that collectors behave similarly toward 1964-dated coins issued in

16. *Special Report: The U.S. Coin Investment Market.* Empire Investment Report, Issue #13. 3 February 1964.

17. The sensitivity of the final silver-stock estimate will be examined in the last section.

1965 as they did toward the 1964 coins issued in their mint year. This assumption is doubtful, but abandoning it for the two years in question, 1965 and 1966, will have little effect on the final estimates.

Half-dollars minted after 1964 require special treatment. These are the Kennedy half-dollars, which appear to have value as collector items or as mementos of the past that exceeds their nominal value. Coin dealers have been quoting prices as high as $2.00 for these coins since their initial issuance in 1964. It is extremely difficult, therefore, to determine what part of the silver contained in Kennedy half-dollars can be considered as potentially retrievable. Unfortunately for our purposes, these coins contain a significant fraction of the total silver coinage, and our final estimates of the available silver stock will be very sensitive to an assumption made here. We will therefore make two extreme assumptions in order to bracket the "truth." First, we assume these coins are treated just like any other half-dollars, i.e., we extend the procedure used above for dimes and quarters. This assumption will lead to an overestimate of the final silver stock. The collection series implied by this assumption is given in table 6. Second, we will assume that the Kennedy coins are so valued by collectors and souvenir holders that they will never be relinquished for their silver value. This latter assumption, while somewhat strong, is probably much closer to the truth. It would, therefore, produce a slight underestimate of the final silver stock. The collection series implied by this assumption is clearly identical to the $P^h{}_T$ series.

In passing we note that in 1966 the silver content of the Kennedy half-dollars was reduced from 90 percent (90 fine) to 40 percent (40 fine). Like dimes and quarters, 90-fine half-dollars were minted and issued in 1965 and 1966, but these coins bore the 1964 date. Kennedy half-dollars dated beyond 1964 were 40 fine.[18]

The Final Silver Stock Estimates

The $C^\xi{}_T$ and $P^\xi{}_T$ series, along with the estimates of the normal loss rates, allow us to determine via (6) the number of silver coins not collected, lost, or retired, and therefore presumed withdrawn from circulation at the end of 1967. The estimates, given in table 7, indicate that the stock of silver represented by these coins is between approximately 1 and 1.3 billion troy ounces. These bounds correspond to the two assumptions on Kennedy half-dollars made in the previous section.

At the end of 1968 the U.S. Treasury had withdrawn approximately 240 million ounces of coinage silver from circulation, and subsequent withdrawals

18. Unlike the Kennedy half-dollars, there is no question but what the entire stock of silver Eisenhower dollars struck beginning April 1971 will be hoarded by collectors. Their presence, therefore, has no effect on the final estimates given in this paper.

TABLE 7

Estimated Stocks of Hoarded Coins and Their Silver Content as of 31 December 1967

	Dimes	Quarters	Half-dollars	Total	Held Privately
Number of coins (millions)	5,333	3,010	1,098[a] 252[b]	. . . . . .	. . . . . .
Amount of silver (millions of troy ounces)	386	544	397[a] 87[b]	1,327[a] 1,017[b]	1,087[a] 777[b]

[a]Kennedy half-dollars treated as normal.
[b]Kennedy half-dollars treated as irretrievable (see text).

have been relatively very small indeed.[19] Removing these 240 million ounces from the above total stock figures results in estimates of the stock of silver held in private hoards of between 0.78 and 1.09 billion troy ounces.[20]

The accuracy of these estimates, of course, depends upon the ac. uracy of the assumptions made earlier. In particular, the pre-depression period was treated specially and somewhat arbitrarily. It is of interest, therefore, to test the sensitivity of the final silver-stock estimate to the estimate of the pre-depression stocks of coin. To this end a calculation was made of the contribution of the pre-depression vintages to the total stocks both with and without the removal of $C^\varepsilon{}_T$. These are 6 and 21 million ounces respectively. Thus, the largest possible error from the estimation of the pre-depression coin stock is 15 million ounces, or less than 2 percent of total stocks.

One additional source of error deserves discussion. Our final stock estimates do not include the silver contained in two other silver-bearing U.S. coins: silver dollars and copper-silver-manganese nickels issued in the World War II period. These coins are ignored because they are not considered as potential sources of silver. Silver dollars are kept by the public primarily for collection purposes and, to a lesser extent each year, as a medium of exchange in western casinos. As such, their value as a collector's item is always above the value of their silver content. The privately held stocks of silver dollars amount to 372.6 million ounces of silver.[21] Silver-bearing nickels containing 48.7 million ounces of silver were minted from 1942 to 1945.[22] The silver value of these nickels is equal to their nominal value when the price of silver is $0.88 to $0.89 per

19. These facts were determined through an interview between Mr. Jean Paul Valette of Charles River Associates, Cambridge, and a representative of the Treasury.

20. Additional silver has been issued in 40-fine Kennedy half-dollars over the years 1968 and 1969 in the magnitudes of 36.8 and 19.4 million troy ounces respectively.

21. *Yearbook,* American Bureau of Metal Statistics, 1967, p. 108.

22. U.S. Treasury, *Annual Report of the Director of the Mint,* 1967, p. 58.

ounce. The average annual New York price of silver reached this level in 1955 and has remained above it since. Since the ban on melting nickels was removed in 1962, it is reasonable to assume that the outstanding stocks of silver in these coins have been melted and sold as silver-bearing bullion in the 1955 to 1967 period.

Inflation, **Trade** and Taxes

Looking at Inflation in the Open Economy

Richard E. Caves

This paper arises from an international economist's curiosity about the way macroeconomic specialists view the phenomenon of inflation. There resounds a babble of demand-pull and cost-push, the quantity of money and the Phillips curve, all apparently within the shoreline of Crusoe's island. Occasionally one hears of inflation imported or exported, and domestic price-stability is victimized now and then by dearer imported raw materials. But where are the internationally traded goods, whose prices (adjusted for trade barriers) must be everywhere the same? Where is the recognition that, given the world price level, the domestic price level and the equilibrium exchange rate (price of domestic currency) must move inversely?

In the first section I set forth in simplified fashion some basic theoretical propositions about the price level in an open economy. Subsequent sections identify the channels of inflationary transfer, then take up administered (factor and product) prices in an international context and the relation of international capital movements to inflationary processes.

I. A MONETARIST MODEL

Let us start with the simplest possible account of inflation in the open economy: a "monetarist" model of a purely competitive, two-country world.[1]

1. This section owes much to suggestions by Ronald W. Jones; see Richard E. Caves and Ronald W. Jones, *World Trade and Payments* (Boston: Little, Brown, 1973), chaps. 4,16,19.

This model is descendent from David Hume's writings, but only recently has it been stated in a way that captures fully the role of internationally traded goods, whose prices must be everywhere the same.[2] A Hume-type model proves to be an effective reference point for considering complications due to administered prices, capital flows, and the like.

Assume that a disturbance increases money expenditure in the home country — either due to an increase in the quantity of money (dropped from an airplane, so that no disturbances simultaneously affect markets for goods or securities) or a decision by the public to hold smaller cash balances relative to the current level of money expenditure. If all prices are flexible and the economy is closed, prices are bid up until cash balances desired at the elevated level of money expenditure again equal the money supply. But we make the economy an open one and, indeed, small enough compared with the rest of the world that changes in its excess demand for traded goods have no effect on their world prices. The country's authority buys and sells foreign currency as needed to maintain an unchanging pegged value of home currency. The monetary disturbance creates an excess demand for goods, as in the closed economy. If all goods are traded internationally, however, their prices cannot be bid up. Excess demand for them simply spills over into an equal excess demand for foreign exchange. The monetary authority increases its domestic-currency holdings and reduces its foreign-exchange holdings by an amount equal to the excess demand. The economy absorbs a net trade deficit equal to the monetary disturbance, consisting of reduced exports and increased imports in proportions governed by its marginal propensities to spend on these classes of goods.[3] The "inflationary" disturbance causes the country to increase its consumption and reduce its net international assets (i.e., reserves) without any changes in money prices at all.

If the home country comprises a large portion of the trading world, the external prices of internationally traded goods no longer remain unaffected by its monetary disturbances. They are bid up by the public's excess demand for goods, following a monetary injection. A trade-balance deficit appears, as before, but only part of the country's monetary injection winds up in the hands of its exchange-stabilization authorities. The public abroad find themselves facing increased money prices of traded goods, and feel the need to augment

2. Arnold Collery, *International Adjustment, Open Economics and the Quantity Theory of Money,* (Princeton, N.J.: International Finance Section, Princeton University, 1971); Rudiger Dornbusch, "Currency Depreciation, Hoarding, and Relative Prices," *Journal of Political Economy* 81 (July/August, 1973): 893-915. Cf. D. Hume, "Of the Balance of Trade," reprinted in *International Finance,* ed. Richard N. Cooper (Baltimore: Penguin Books, 1969), chap. 1.

3. By invoking a model with all prices flexible, we avoid the need to consider changes in production. Transitional disturbances to relative prices hold little interest, at least in the case of the small country.

cash holdings in line with increased money expenditure. Foreigners thus temporarily reduce their real expenditure, in order to recoup the desired relation of cash balances to money expenditure. They can indeed add to their nominal balances, because the home country's exchange authority is selling foreign currency to finance its import surplus.[4] The new equilibrium for world prices and cash balances is easy to describe in this model, because the prices of traded goods must have risen by the same percentage everywhere. Therefore, nominal cash balances must have risen in the same proportion both at home and abroad, since nothing has occurred to change any country's equilibrium level of real expenditure. The home country's monetary injection winds up divided between home and foreign asset-holders, and we can infer from the equilibrium conditions that world prices must increase in the same proportion as the initial monetary disturbances increased the world's money supply. This model makes it clear why (demand-induced) inflation in a large country causes greater concern for other nations than an inflationary disturbance of equal proportion in a small nation.

Now change the locus of the monetary disturbance from the home country to the foreign land. The small trading country is strictly a price-taker. With its exchange rate fixed, its rate of inflation is simply that prevailing externally for traded goods. If its domestic money supply stays constant and its desired cash balances increase in proportion to world prices, it runs surpluses in its trade balance to the extent necessary to generate the desired cash balances. Its monetary authority, defending the fixed exchange rate, is forced to buy foreign exchange and thus provide cash balances to "validate" the increase in domestic prices. A large trading country finds itself qualitatively in the same position when inflation occurs abroad, but the change in the world price level of traded goods is no longer an exogenous variable. The larger is the country's initial money supply in the hands of the public, as a proportion of the world's publicly held cash balances, the more can it dampen world inflation by its absorption of extra cash balances. But it is still condemned, after the event, to suffer the same inflation rate as the rest of the world.

I now modify this model to allow for a nontraded-goods sector in each country. Producers of nontraded goods compete with makers of traded goods for each nation's flow of factor services; for simplicity I assume that they require no inputs of traded goods. Transport costs are assumed high enough that no price differential in the observed range between nontraded goods at home and abroad will call forth any trade: it never pays to fly to London for a haircut. A monetary injection at home, even in a small country, now causes a transitional inflation of the prices of domestic nontraded goods. A portion of the total

4. Which exchange authority undertakes this role is subject to one degree of freedom; there can be one passive country.

excess demand for goods falls upon them, and their flexible prices must be bid up unless factors of production are immediately lured from the traded- into the nontraded-goods sector. When the money expenditure circuit of the small country returns to equilibrium, however, this transitional disturbance to the relative price of nontraded goods must end. The country's real income is unchanged, and the excess demand for goods ceases once the cash-balance injection has been worked off (and deposited with the nation's exchange-stabilization authority). If the money price of nontraded goods remained in-flated, and thus their relative price above the pre-disturbance level, the quantity demanded would be less than before—a condition inconsistent with the exis-tence of a unique, stable equilibrium in the nontraded-goods market.

The role of nontraded goods is no different when the monetary injection occurs in a large country. Their prices can be inflated *relative to* those of traded goods, but only in transition. Countries—large or small—adapting to inflationary disturbances abroad would likewise experience transitional de-clines in the relative prices of nontraded goods.

Transitional disturbances can affect the relative prices of different traded goods, when inflationary disturbances occur in a large country. A monetary injection at home creates an excess demand for each traded good. As their money prices are bid up, excess supplies emerge abroad as foreigners depress their real expenditures in order to build up their nominal cash balances. In transition the *net* excess demands for the various traded goods may differ proportionally, and so their relative prices can be disturbed. Indeed, if the model is restricted to two traded goods, a criterion can be developed for the direction of change in their relative price that resembles the traditional criterion for whether a capital transfer is overeffected or undereffected by its income effects. The criterion in the case of an inflationary disturbance is more compli-cated, only because the total excess demand for goods at home and the excess supply (i.e., reduction of expenditure) abroad need not be equal at any one stage in the transition. Once the world price level for traded goods has adjusted to eliminate the initiating excess of real cash balances, however, any disturbance to the relative prices of traded goods must also be eliminated. The reasoning is essentially the same as in the case of nontraded goods.

The analysis to this point has assumed that the exchange rate remains fixed, and that the exchange-stabilization authority always holds enough reserves to defend the rate until the effects of an inflationary disturbance in one country have abated. However, should it occur, the effects of a change in the exchange rate are in fact easy to describe in this Hume-type model. From a position of initial (real and monetary) equilibrium, assume that the home country—once again, a small one— devalues its currency by x percent. The initial impact on the public is to elevate the prices of all traded goods by (approximately) x

percent, and render real cash balances (held in domestic currency) deficient relative to the going level of real income and expenditure. Expenditure is reduced, creating an excess supply of goods, and a trade-balance surplus is run until cash balances are restored to their desired relation to money expenditure. In the new equilibrium the prices of nontraded goods would be bid up to the same extent as those of traded goods, the trade balance would return to its former equilibrium, and real income would be at its original level. The same conclusions generally hold true for devaluation by a large country (otherwise, keeping the same assumption), except that the prices of traded goods now fall abroad, and rise at home by less than the percentage of the devaluation. As several economists have noted, the effects of a devaluation in a Hume-type model are thus equivalent for the devaluating country to those of increasing the money supply proportionally in the foreign country (for the foreign country, to decreasing the money supply proportionally at home).[5]

II. CHANNELS FOR INTERNATIONAL TRANSFER OF INFLATION

The role of internationally traded goods, exposed in the "monetarist" model, serves to clarify the nature of the different channels for the international transmission of inflation, and the relations prevailing among them. Country A hopes to avoid inflation that is occurring abroad and to maintain a fixed exchange rate. Along what corridors may the forces of inflation be moving? After enumerating the possibilities,[6] I shall argue that they are substitutes for one another. given a fixed exchange rate and inflation abroad, A will suffer increases in domestic prices through some mechanism, the particular one depending on the country's international economic structure.

1. Inflation might travel, first, along macroeconomic channels. Prices rise abroad, rendering foreign goods dear relative to those produced at home. Buyers both at home and abroad shift their purchases toward A's goods even if they are not perfect substitutes, improving A's balance of trade in goods and services (hereafter, trade balance).

a. The improving trade balance raises aggregate demand in the fashion

---

5. H. G. Johnson, "The Monetary Approach to Balance-of-Payments Theory," in *International Trade and Money,* ed. M. B. Connolly and A. K. Swoboda (London: George Allen & Unwin, 1973), pp. 206–24; E. A. Kuska, "The Pure Theory of Devaluation," *Economica* 39 (August 1972): 264–75. Needless to say, the assumption of initial equilibrium and flexible prices are not one's first choice for an operational approach to devaluation.

6. Cf. Leslie Dicks-Mireaux, "External Influences and Inflation in the United Kingdom," in *The Current Inflation,* ed. H. G. Johnson and A. R. Nobay (London: Macmillan, 1971), pp. 179–84.

described by the Keynesian foreign-trade multiplier. If A's money prices and factor costs rise at a rate related to capacity utilization and the employment level, inflation is transmitted through the induced increase in aggregate demand. The mechanism is self-equilibrating, in that a catch-up with foreign inflation rates eliminates the source of income disturbances—the initiating improvement in the trade balance.

b. The improving trade balance forces the exchange stabilization authority to purchase foreign currency and expand the domestic money supply. The government may sterilize this increase in high-powered money, and by keeping the exchange authority's domestic assets as deposits in the banking system, many countries try to do this automatically. If international capital flows are sufficiently interest-elastic, however, complete sterilization becomes impossible. To the extent that the public wishes to hold extra cash balances, due to increased net sales abroad, the central bank cannot deny them the option; any squeeze on cash balances tends to raise A's interest rate and attract capital from abroad. This again forces the stabilization authority to buy foreign exchange, and the government restores with one hand any of the money supply that it removes with the other. If the trade balance raises cash holdings, the effect again is to bid up domestic prices. Thus, either a monetarist or a Keynesian analysis of aggregate demand leads to the same qualitative conclusion: a favorable trade balance due to (faster) inflation abroad transmits inflation to country A.

2. Inflation might travel along microeconomic channels. Make a substantial part of A's production perfect substitutes for foreign goods. With a fixed exchange rate and rising money prices abroad, A finds itself facing rising prices without the necessary causal intervention of a trade-balance surplus. (As the monetarist model shows, however, a trade-balance surplus would be a natural concomitant even if not a causal link in inflating the domestic prices of traded goods.) In principle, these microeconomic links could also travel through two channels.

a. Links can exist in the prices of traded goods, as outlined in section one. Notice that, for a given rate of external inflation, net export or import status for particular traded goods is of no sustained consequence, so long as markets are competitive and the "law of one price" holds strictly. (I consider below the qualifications needed for dumping, oligopoly, and all that.) Inflation due to rising import prices is often recognized, but inflation due to the higher prices that exporters can command draws less attention.

b. Links can also pass through factor markets, if these are either directly international or subject to international demonstration effects. The latter possibility has gained the most attention lately, with the suggestion that trade unions might establish formal links among the European countries, or at least take purposive notice of the percentage wage increases won in other countries.[7] The exact nature of this kind of cost-push effect would then depend on what "demonstrations" get noticed. Do trade unions watch the country nearest at hand? One with similar industrial structure, or cultural ties? Do the demonstrations run from a given industry in one country to the same industry in another country?

Given inflation abroad and the maintenance of a fixed exchange rate, a country must expect to import any inflation abroad—via one channel or another. If its output is heavily weighted by internationally traded goods, inflation comes through the direct price linkages. If it trades a significant portion of its output but produces relatively unique goods (without close elasticities of substitution for foreign goods), external price disturbances intrude through the macro corridors. The two macro channels (1a and b) presumably are substitutes for one another: if aggregate expenditure is not boosted on account of increased income, it responds to increased cash balances. The same holds for the micro channels (2a and b): prices not elevated by factor-price push remain vulnerable to international-demand pull. This is not to say that, given 10 percent inflation during year t in the world at large, country A will ingest the same proportion of it by the end of $t + 1$, no matter what is the structure of its foreign trade. Rather, that structure determines how inflation will arrive and not whether A can keep a fixed exchange rate and insulate its price level.

The composition of imports can also make a difference, although none is completely safe. In countries that import large volumes of raw materials some share of general price inflation is customarily imputed to the rise in the prices of imported raw materials (weighted by their share in production costs).[8] On the other hand, if imports consist of final (consumer) goods that compete closely with domestic outputs, external inflation elevates the prices of their domestic substitutes directly. The only remaining category of imports (not inputs or producers' goods, without domestic substitutes) would be noncompeting consumer goods, such as imported foodstuffs, and they could transmit inflation if the wage-bargaining process aims to protect or increase real income. The only country that can keep its exchange rate fixed and yet be relatively safe from

7. See, for example, Michael Artis, "Some Aspects of the Present Inflation and the National Institute Model," in *The Current Inflation,* pp. 8–9.

8. For example, ibid., pp. 6–7.

imported inflation is one that bulks large in world economic activity (issues a large share of the world's money supply, in terms of the monetarist model) and has a small traded-goods sector.[9] Apparently, the United States has blessings to count.

This analysis supports the policy conclusion that nations maintaining fixed exchange rates are stuck with a common and jointly determined rate of inflation. In terms of the theory of economic policy, an attempt to maintain any other inflation rate sooner or later puts a country into a so-called "dilemma situation": either it suffers a trade-balance surplus and tendency to overfull employment, or a trade-balance deficit and a tendency to unemployment. In either case the "dilemma" is that changing aggregate demand to relieve one problem makes the other one worse, and only exchange-rate realignment (or other "expenditure-switching" policy) can extinguish the dilemma.[10]

Even a flexible exchange rate can fail to provide insulation under some conditions. Make A's rate freely fluctuating, and allow prices to increase in the rest of the world. Standard doctrine holds that an incipient tendency for A's traded goods to become cheaper on world markets leads to excess demand for A's currency, raising its price in proportion to the rate of inflation abroad and leaving the home-currency prices of A's goods unchanged. Give an extreme interpretation to the price linkages for traded goods, and suppose that their A-currency prices are marked up immediately when world prices rise, the change not depending on explicit excess demand. This instant mark-up forestalls any excess demand of foreign origin for the country's output of traded goods, and thus for A's currency. The A-currency price increases would not be sustainable, however, under monetarist assumptions about domestic expenditure. They would induce a reduction of money expenditure in A, putting traded goods *and* foreign exchange in excess supply. Therefore the price of A's currency must rise, and the A-currency prices of traded goods must fall. The trade balance cannot change the domestic money supply (an essential consequence of exchange-rate flexibility), and this process must continue until traded-goods prices are back to their original levels in A currency, and the exchange rate has done all the adjusting. Thus the theoretical insulating power of the flexible exchange rate would seem to hold for the micro as well as the macro inflation channels.

The outcome changes, however, if A's money supply is endogenous. Assume, as before, that A-currency prices of traded goods are marked up with the onset of inflation abroad. Suppose that A's central bank, responding to the

9. Even the small traded -goods sector provides only transitional insulation; it would not matter in a steady-state inflationary process.

10. See A. M. C. Waterman, "Some Footnotes to the 'Swan Diagram'—or How Dependent is a Dependent Economy?", *Economic Record* 42 (September 1966): 447–64.

increased "needs of trade," enlarges the money supply proportionally. Then no excess supply need arise in the markets for A's traded goods or foreign exchange. The domestic price level follows the world's rate of inflation and the flexible rate loses its insulating power.

III. ADMINISTERED PRICES, ASYMMETRIES, AND ALL THAT

Macroeconomic research on inflationary processes has largely lost interest in the role of administered prices per se. There seems to be general agreement with the position reached by Schultze and others that the insensitivity of product and factor prices to excess demand or supply is a question of degree, and the empirically important issue is simply the quantitative relation between the rate of change of some price measure and some measure of excess supply or underutilization.[11] If so, the significance of price rigidities and cost-push for the open economy lies in their effect on its opportunity set of policy measures. Suppose that countries are adhering to the Bretton Woods commitment to fixed exchange rates in the absence of "fundamental disequilibrium." For each (small) country a set of relations of the Phillips-curve type connects the rate of inflation in traded goods to the rate of unemployment. The external rate of inflation then determines the unemployment level for each country, along with its rates of technical progress and capital formation, the aggressiveness of its trade unions, and so on. If there is but one world price for each traded good, the individual national economy is in a sense denied an optimizing choice between inflation and unemployment by its own commitment to a fixed exchange rate. Conversely, to maintain a different rate from that prevailing in the world at large, it must indulge in a crawling devaluation or revaluation.[12]

Rather than pursue this familiar line of thought, I shall return to the old distinction between flexible and administered or cost-determined prices and wages, which still sheds some light on inflationary processes in the open economy and the international transmission of inflation.

For example, consider what we might call the Aukrust or Norwegian model of inflation in the open economy.[13] Producing sectors are divided into the

11. Charles L. Schultze, "Recent Inflation in the United States," *Materials Prepared in Connection with the Study of Employment, Growth, and Price Levels,* U.S. Congress, Joint Economic Committee, Study Paper No. 1 (Washington: Government Printing Office, 1959), esp. chap. 2.

12. See, for example, Gottfried Haberler, *Incomes Policy and Inflation: An Analysis of Basic Principles* (Washington: American Enterprise Institute, 1971).

13. Odd Aukrust, "PRIM I: A Model of the Price and Income Distribution Mechanism of an Open Economy," Norway, Statistisk Sentralbyra, Artikler Nr. 35 (Oslo, 1970), also *Review of Income and Wealth* 16 (March 1970): 51–78; Gosta Edgren, Karl-Olof Faxén, and Clas-Erik Odhner, "Wages, Growth, and the Distribution of Income," *Swedish Journal of Economics* 71 (September 1969): 133–60.

sheltered and the *exposed* or *competing,* the distinction corresponding exactly to that employed above between nontraded and traded goods. Prices in the exposed sector are determined on the world market, those in the sheltered sector by a mark-up process that maintains a constant relation between gross margins and total labor compensation.[14] Wages in the exposed sector are flexible in a special sense of being determined by the sector's ability to pay. That is, money wages in the exposed sector tend to rise at a rate equal to the sector's rate of price increase plus its rate of growth of labor productivity.[15] Wages in the sheltered sector tend to increase at the same rate as those in the exposed sector; the exposed sector contains the manufacturing and extractive industries that are the trend-setters in the wage-determination process. The model is short-run and not explicit about its macro features; presumably demand management seeks to keep unemployment within an acceptable range and the money supply is expanded endogenously to maintain stable credit conditions. Formulated this way, the Aukrust model modifies the monetarist model of traded/nontraded goods (section 1 of this paper) to incorporate noncompetitive market features and to make macroeconomic policy (to a degree) endogenous.

The model has been developed and applied in small economies with fixed exchange rates and large traded-goods sectors. The causal sequence determining the domestic inflation rate starts with the rate of increase of world prices for the country's traded goods. This and the rate of productivity growth in the exposed sector then determine the growth of money wages in that sector. The sheltered sector's wages bill increases at the same rate. Depending on the sheltered sector's rate of productivity growth, its prices are then marked up to maintain its gross margin as a share of value added. Because the sheltered sector contains the services and perhaps other industries attaining low productivity gains, its over-all productivity growth is slower than in the exposed sector. With the same rate of wage increase, it hence generates a higher rate of inflation than that transmitted to the exposed sector through world price movements.[16]

14. I will not explore the differences between this mark-up assumption and the more familiar one: that prices are set to maintain a constant percentage gross margin on labor compensation *plus* intermediate inputs. Statistical evidence of the stability of factor shares in the sheltered sectors has been advanced to support the assumption for both Norway and Sweden.

15. For evidence of the influence of traded-goods status on sectoral wage-determination practices, see Anne Romanis, "Cost Inflation and Incomes Policy in Industrial Countries," *IMF Staff Papers* 14 (March 1967): 169–206.

16. For Sweden over the years 1960–67, Edgren et al. found that prices in the exposed sector rose 1.0 to 1.5 percent annually, productivity 7.5 percent, and labor costs at 9.4 percent—approximately the sum of these two. In the sheltered sector productivity rose by 3.5 percent, wages 5.0 to 5.5 percent, and prices 2.6 to 3.0 percent. Thus the labor-cost increases for the two sectors differed, but by a smaller proportion than their rates of productivity growth.

The model has interesting adjustment properties. Consider the adaptation of the exposed sector's rate of labor-cost inflation to its "ability to pay," given by the sum of rates of price and labor-productivity increase. If wages rise less rapidly, the exposed industries enjoy windfall profits and increase their investments and outputs. The rate of wage inflation is pulled up by "wage drift," if not by the effect of high profits on negotiated wage settlements.[17] If wages overshoot, profits and investment adjust in the opposite direction, and the rate of wage is squeezed. An increase in the rate of productivity growth for the exposed sector worsens the problem of inflation for the country, because it increases labor-cost inflation in both sectors and price inflation in the sheltered sector, while having no effect on price inflation in the exposed sector. Increases in aggregate demand should not modify the price level, at least if the sheltered sector is working with excess capacity, but they will worsen the trade balance. Conversely, deflationary policies intended to curb inflation are unlikely to work unless they can break the cost-determination of prices in the sheltered sector or the link between wage increases in the exposed and sheltered industries.

The Aukrust model might conceivably apply with modifications to a relatively closed economy with a large sheltered sector containing the pace-setting industries in the wage-determination process. Keep the other assumptions as before. Now an increase in aggregate demand can raise output without increasing prices, until wages come to be bid up in the sheltered sector and higher unit labor costs are passed along in price increases.[18] If wage increases pass from the sheltered to the exposed sector, deterioration of the trade balance may be due primarily to a cost squeeze on the open sector rather than diversion of its output to domestic customers. If the exposed sector should set its prices on a cost-determined basis, of course, both its capacity utilization and the country's trade balance may become highly sensitive to the general rate of cost inflation.[19] The model in this guise may hold some interest for explaining developments in the United States, where several large industries that appear to be important wage-setters are only marginally exposed to international competition.

The Aukrust model highlights the role of cost-determined prices in the economy's sheltered sector. Without resort to formal models we can note some

17. A lag of wage costs in the exposed sector would also tend to produce a trade surplus and thus generate inflation through the macro channels outlined in section 2. Strictly speaking, the Aukrust model forestalls this by assuming away any direct dependence of prices or wages on aggregate demand or the money supply.

18. This temporal sequence is often noted empirically: see Organization for Economic Cooperation and Development, *Inflation: The Present Problem* (Paris, 1970), pp. 19–23.

19. The fact that inflation impairs the country's trade balance whether or not its traded-goods prices rise illustrates the dangers of casual judgments about the "competitiveness" of export prices or the "overvaluation" of a currency.

effects of wages being cost-determined in the open economy. The assumption is that trade unions push up wages at a rate dependent on the increase they perceive in the cost of living and insensitive to the level of unemployment. This behavior pattern has often been held a serious threat to the efficacy of devaluation as a tool for righting external imbalance. If the overspending associated with the payments deficit stems from efforts to wrest larger slices from the national-income pie, devaluation can work only if it shrinks the effective demands of some claimants. Some economists have argued that the only hope for restoring external balance then is that trade unions will suffer some money illusion and be insensitive to a loss of real income due to higher traded-goods prices following devaluation.[20] A country in which wage claims are heavily cost-determined would be particularly vulnerable to imported inflation if its absorption of traded goods (whether imports or domestically produced) is weighted heavily toward consumer goods; traded intermediate or final producer goods would inject inflation only in proportion to their cost share in the consumption bundle.

An aspect of cost-determined or administered wages much discussed lately is the possibility of international coordination of unions' wage claims, for instance, among the member countries of the European Economic Community. When colluding sellers raise the price of a product, any one of them has an incentive to cheat and shade his own price. When U.K. automobile workers raise their wages and thus the price of British-made vehicles, Continental unions may enjoy the prospect of more employment and a much enlarged wages or overtime bill if they hold off or demand less per unit of labor. The closer substitutes are to the respective outputs, the greater is the incentive to cheat. Thus, as Corden points out, the effect of integration could be to extend union solidarity across national boundaries and thereby increase the scope for wage-push, but closer product-market integration would simultaneously raise the incentive to optimize at the national level and perhaps dampen the ardor of the more aggressive unions.[21]

A familiar staple in discussions of inflation is the idea that factor or product prices may be asymmetrically flexible to upward disturbances but rigid to downward ones.[22] The notion can be applied to traded goods in the world economy as well. To make the application as sharp as possible, assume that each nation's exports are somewhat differentiated, so that French exports are

20. E. g., W. M. Corden, *Monetary Integration,* Essays in International Finance, No. 93 (Princeton, N.J.: International Finance Section, Princeton University, 1972), pp. 11–12.

21. Ibid., p. 14.

22. Schultze, "Recent Inflation in the United States," chap. 3.

never perfect substitutes for German goods. A shift occurs in world demand toward German and away from French exports. With initial exchange rates and prices unchanged, the shift tends (assuming market stability) to cause a trade-balance surplus for Germany and a deficit for France. To restore equilibrium Germany's terms of trade must improve, and France's deteriorate. If German export prices are upward-flexible, as the demand-shift model assumes, the terms-of-trade adjustment could come partly through a rise in their money price with the exchange rate constant. Revaluation, as an alternative, would substitute an increase in the foreign-currency price of the Deutschemark for an increase in the DM price of German exports. The inflationary effect for the rest of the world is the same in the two cases, but by selecting revaluation, Germany could render the adjustment approximately neutral for her own price level.[23] Symmetrically, devaluation and deflationary price adjustment would be substitute adjustment strategies for France. Aside from transitional effects, the rest of the world but not France would be indifferent to the price-level implications of the choice. If France asymmetrically chose to devalue and Germany to inflate, the ultimate effect on the rest of the world's price level would be the same as for any other response combination that effects the needed real adjustments.

The point of this example is that in the international economy exchange-rate changes provide a mechanism of adjustment to demand shifts that is not available in the national economy (or common-currency area) with downward-rigid prices. If real disturbances, such as demand shifts, have asymmetrical effects on the world price level, some combined asymmetry of market and policy responses must be involved. Consider possible French responses to the disturbance. Rather than devaluing, the French government might restrict imports or deflate domestic demand, thereby taking the (necessary) reduction of France's real income in some form that averts any decline in the world price of French goods (while potentially costing the country more in real terms). If such responses are typical of the ''losers'' in demand shifts (and if the winners' responses do not symmetrically consist in removing such restrictions or reflating aggregate demand), an asymmetry is in hand. The countries not immediately involved in the adjustment would see themselves facing demand-shift inflation.

It is interesting to relate this analysis of asymmetries to some uses (abuses?) of the concept in discussions of international monetary relations. For instance, it is asserted that surplus countries are unwilling to revalue, and thus force the

23. Germany's choice of fiscal and monetary responses to the disturbance is also relevant to the outcome. The text neglects these complications, and also assumes away any domestic production of import-competing traded goods—a feature that complicates the equating of revaluation to a terms-of-trade improvement.

countries with the counterpart deficits to devalue; this is asymmetrically inflationary for the world because surplus countries "must digest the inflationary increase in their domestic monetary circulation, caused by the accumulation of foreign-exchange reserves, and the deficit countries are forced into repeated devaluations with inflationary effects via rising import prices."[24] The trouble with this argument lies in its ambiguous treatment of the underlying source of disturbances. Suppose that all countries expand their money supplies at predetermined rates; these rates are then modified by the external imbalances they experience, the deficit countries depleting and the surplus countries augmenting cash balances in the hands of the public. Now assume, instead of the exchange-rate asymmetry specified above, that potential surplus countries revalue continuously to avert any "imported" monetary expansion. The potential deficit countries are left with greater expansions of their monetary supplies than if their deficits had been realized; they experience (on monetarist assumptions) greater inflation, but the potential surplus countries ingest less. Yet the (weighted average) effect on the world price level should be about the same. The asymmetry really lies in the implicit assumption of the argument that the deficit countries generate more demand-based inflationary pressure when they are allowed to devalue then if they were not.[25]

The same kind of asymmetry appears in a newly popular argument against flexible exchange rates.[26] A flexible exchange rate "bottles up" inflationary pressures generated within a country, whereas a fixed rate permits a trade-balance deficit to be run, injecting an extra supply of goods and venting the compressed monetary gases of inflation. However, given the rate of expansion of the country's monetary supply (or aggregate demand, if one prefers), the choice between a fixed and a flexible exchange rate simply determines whether there shall be a lot of inflationary pressure in one country or a little bit all around

24. G. N. Halm, "The Gliding Band for Variations in Exchange Rates," *New England Economic Review,* November/December 1971, p. 10.

25. Devaluation is in any case a dubious remedy to external imbalance when the deficit is created or sustained by monetary expansion, and thus is due to "overspending" rather than "overvaluation," as in the previous case of demand shifts with inflexible prices. On the theoretical importance of this distinction between the disturbances underlying external imbalance, see R. W. Jones, "Stability Conditions in International Trade: A General Equilibrium Analysis," *International Economic Review* 2 (May 1961): 199–209; also Caves and Jones, *World Trade and Payments,* chap. 19.

26. Edward M. Bernstein, "Flexible Exchange Rates and International Adjustment," in *The Economics of International Adjustment,* ed. Randall Hinshaw (Baltimore: Johns Hopkins Press, 1971), pp. 157–78; cf. comments by Gottfried Haberler in *Approaches to Greater Flexibility of Exchange Rates: The Burgenstock Papers,* ed. G. N. Halm (Princeton, N.J.: Princeton University Press, 1970), pp. 119–21.

the world. An asymmetry is involved only on a nationalistic view that "my country is better off if her inflationary pressures can be vented abroad."[27]

IV. CAPITAL TRANSFERS AND INFLATION

I have thus far largely ignored the role that international capital movements can play in the transmission or control of inflation. A useful starting point is the traditional analysis of the "transfer process" of adjustment to an autonomous change in capital flows. The transfer of purchasing power raises expenditure in the borrowing country and contracts it in the lending country. The change of expenditure, in each case, falls partly on imported goods. If the expenditure change equals the capital transfer, and the marginal propensities to import sum to unity—the razor's-edge condition appropriate to a two-country model—the trade balance changes just enough to offset the capital-account disturbance. No external balance remains to be corrected. Furthermore, the borrower's (or lender's) level of national income (employment) is left unchanged: the transfer-induced change in expenditure is just offset by the movement of the trade balance.

To isolate the relation of transfers to inflation, focus on the borrowing (recipient) country. A capital inflow could increase the excess demand for domestic goods and resource if the transfer is "undereffected," so that the current-account deterioration fails to offset the capital-account improvement; or if the transfer raises domestic expenditure by more than the amount of purchasing power received (e.g., through induced investment).[28] We would worry about capital inflows, then, as an inflationary force if these assumptions hold for a country *and* capital is attracted by domestic inflation or forces that contribute to it. This affinity of capital inflows for inflationary conditions is indeed somewhat likely. An outward shift in the marginal efficiency of investment in a potential borrowing country raises both the pressure of aggregate demand and the lure to foreign capital.

27. This is not to deny that such venting could be collectively desirable in particular cases. Suppose the rest of the world suffers from unemployment. With a fixed exchange rate the inflating country's vented excess demand increases world output; the country pays for its import surplus in a reduction of its international reserves (net foreign assets). But that cost would ordinarily fall short of the world's gain. On the general theory of the gains from policy coordination, see Richard N. Cooper, "Macroeconomic Policy Adjustment in Interdependent Economies," *Quarterly Journal of Economics* 83 (February 1969): 1–24.

28. For a more detailed account and some empirical evidence, see R. E. Caves et al., *Capital Transfers and Economic Policy: Canada, 1951–1962,* Harvard Economic Studies, No. 135 (Cambridge, Mass.: Harvard University Press, 1971), chaps. 1, 6, 7.

Furthermore, as Friedrich Lutz has argued, inflation proceeding more rapidly than abroad can induce capital inflows for other reasons. Assume that people correctly anticipate the country's inflation rate and build it into its prevailing nominal rate of interest. The fixed exchange rate is nonetheless expected—by foreign lenders, in particular—to survive inflationary pressure, at least for a time. It follows that a given nominal interest rate on a security denominated in that country's currency yields a lower expected real rate of return to a domestic lender than to a foreign lender. Capital could be attracted by a high nominal interest rate that, indeed, corresponds to a low marginal efficiency of investment.[29] Thus inflationary pressures could be augmented by capital transfers, and, furthermore, these transfers could be inconsistent with optimal allocation of real capital stocks.

These bothersome possibilities of misallocation and amplified inflationary disturbance extend symmetrically to the lending country. Take the case of international demand-shift inflation, discussed in section three. The shift of demand from French to German goods raises the marginal efficiency of investment in Germany and induces an outflow of capital from France. Let us suppose that the marginal-productivity difference is indeed real, so that France as a whole can potentially benefit from a higher real return by placing some capital in Germany. For the benefit to be realized, French real wages must fall. Because the capital transfer lowers the stock of real capital in France, it requires a change in relative factor prices. If French wages are rigid, however, unemployment increases when the capital outflow occurs, and that loss in real output can easily offset the nation's enlarged earnings on the exported capital.[30]

The international mobility of capital also affects domestic inflationary processes through its influence on the leverage of domestic policy instruments on aggregate demand. With the exchange rate fixed, for instance, high interest-sensitivity of international capital flows tends to cripple the short-run effectiveness of monetary policy while preserving that of fiscal policy for managing aggregate demand.[31] Because this theorem is well known, I stick to a few

29. F. A. Lutz, "Money Rates of Interest, Real Rates of Interest, and Capital Movements," in William Fellner et al., *Maintaining and Restoring Balance in International Payments* (Princeton, N.J.: Princeton University Press, 1966), chap. 11. Lutz recognizes the unlikelihood of prolonged exchange-rate stability in the face of differing inflation rates, but argues that disparities can prevail in the short run.

30. This case is discussed by Corden, *Monetary Integration*, pp. 26–27.

31. Some empirical evidence is now available on the size of this policy constraint. Branson finds a rather modest constraint on United States monetary policy, although the capital-flow disturbances it can create are hardly trivial for the balance of payments; see W. H. Branson, "Monetary Policy and the New View of International Capital Movements," *Brookings Papers on Economic Activity*, No. 2 (1970), pp. 235–270. More substantial short-run constraints were found for Canadian monetary policy, however; see Caves et al., *Capital Transfers and Economic Policy*, chaps. 2, 3, 8.

peripheral remarks. Whatever the impact of increasing capital mobility on the efficacy of monetary policy, it has certainly crippled the application of simple monetarist concepts such as those employed in section 1 of this paper. Sterilizing large inflows of short-term capital (whether speculative or due to interest arbitrage) is rendered difficult or impossible, and surplus countries such as Germany have watched with alarm as these flows ballooned their money supplies.

The alarm is probably misplaced, however, because a normal transactions velocity hardly applies to these balances: treasurers of multinational corporations are not likely to spend their DM assets on the products of Mercedes Benz. But the rise of capital mobility goes even farther in severing the relation traditionally assumed between money and expenditure. What matters for a large corporation (and its expenditure plans) is liquidity in any generally accepted form, and not in a particular currency. As the Euro-currency markets separate the currency of denomination from the citizenship of capital transactors, Belgium's money supply may be no more a well-defined quantity than is Vermont's. Increased capital mobility not only impairs the thermostat of monetary policy, it even makes it difficult or impossible to read the thermometer!

V. EMPIRICAL EVIDENCE: A PASSING GLANCE

These reflections on international transactions carry many implications for research on inflationary processes. I conclude with some selective comments on the studies at hand.

The distinction between traded and nontraded goods is central to any model of inflation in the open economy. How much of an economy's activity falls into the "traded goods" category? Economic sectors as defined in statistical data are always somewhat heterogeneous and seldom sort themselves neatly according to the traded/nontraded distinction. Tariffs and transport costs allow an industry's price to be insulated from external prices within a certain range, but render its output a traded good once outside this range. Imperfections in competition can reduce the substitutability between functionally similar goods produced in different countries (product differentiation) and permit nonidentical prices to persist in different markets for the same good (dumping and other forms of price discrimination). These factors suggest that we need to approach the traded/nontraded distinction by measuring the sensitivity of prices or quantities of goods produced (or sold) in one market when a change occurs in external prices of the same class of goods. Calculations of substitution elasticities are often seen, but the simple sensitivities of domestic to foreign prices have received little attention.

The empirical evidence in international price linkages broadly confirms the role of traded goods in inflationary processes, but also identifies some complications. Two studies have been made of the sensitivity of Canadian wholesale selling prices to the U.S. wholesale prices of comparable manufactured products, among other determinants. Curtis found statistically significant price linkages (with some evidence for a three-month lag) in only one-third of a sample of 50 three-digit industries; the linkages proved to be stronger, though, in industries with higher trade participation (measured by imports plus exports divided by value of domestic shipments) and large shares of Canadian production accounted for by foreign subsidiaries.[32] Thus, aside from confirming the significance of trade channels in linking the U.S. and Canadian price levels, Curtis's results add the multinational corporation as an independent link between national product prices. Taylor, Turnovsky, and Wilson analyzed the same relation at a higher level of aggregation but included more determinants of Canadian price movements, securing estimates of short-run direct price linkages about as large as Curtis's and of greater statistical significance.[33] They also carried out a more comprehensive analysis of the linkages between U.S. and Canadian prices of manufactures, including direct wage linkages between the two countries (discussed below), price-wage interactions with Canada, and indirect linkages running through the influence of imported materials prices on final prices and the impact of rising consumer prices on Canadian wage demands. With these channels allowed for, they found that a one percent increase of prices and wages in U.S. manufacturing would inflate the prices of Canadian manufactures by 0.61 to 0.70 percent. This confirms fairly strongly one's expectation that Canadian manufacturing should be counted a traded-goods sector.

The Canadian economy also appears linked to the outside world through wages, with negotiated wage rates in manufacturing subject to influence by the size of U.S. wage settlements. In the presence of international corporations and unions this link is hardly surprising. Curtis found the wage link to be of very weak significance, though of appreciable absolute size, and associated with international unions. Taylor, Turnovsky, and Wilson, concentrating on negotiated wage rates, found a link for total manufacturing and individually for several important two-digit industries.[34] At least for Canada, negotiated wage settlements must be counted another established transmission link for inflationary pressure from abroad.

32. John M. Curtis, "Direct Foreign Influences on Canadian Prices and Wages," in Caves et al., *Capital Transfers and Economic Policy,* chap. 5.

33. Lester D. Taylor, Stephen J. Turnovsky, and Thomas A. Wilson, *The Inflationary Process in North American Manufacturing* (Ottawa: Information Canada, 1974), chap. 8.

34. They also find (chap. 9) that expectations linked to international price movements affect Canadian wage demands, but not those in the United States.

Canada's experience shows an anomaly in the international transmission of inflation that may be important to the operation of a flexible exchange rate. When traded goods are produced by oligopolies and subject to administered list prices, it is not clear that the Canadian price of a traded good will respond in the short run as elastically to a change in the flexible exchange rate as to a change in the world price. Although profit conditions and arbitrage possibilities would impel symmetrical responses in the long run or for large-enough changes, oligopoly prices may be insensitive to small exchange-rate changes, especially if they are expected to be temporary. Research on Canada by Curtis and others is somewhat inconclusive, but consistent with significant insensitivity to exchange-rate changes in some sectors. Likewise, Dunn found the relation between Canadian and U.S. price changes to be independent of movements of the exchange rate for a small sample of commodities.[35] It is probably fair to conclude that the presence of seller concentration in traded-goods industries delays the ingestion of price inflation from abroad and helps to insulate domestic prices from small market-determined changes in the exchange rate. Of course, this could be economically desirable behavior in some circumstances but not others.

If international price linkages are as important for inflation as theory and selected empirical evidence suggest, they should be turning up in aggregative statistical investigations. Nonetheless, Phillips-type relations keep appearing for numerous countries—between rates of price or wage increase and measures of demand pressure or underutilization.[36] True, import prices (especially raw materials) sometimes appear among the statistical determinants of domestic price inflation. Still, if price movements show strong allegiance to their domestic determinants, the importance of international forces becomes suspect.

One rejoinder would be that the performance of "closed economy" and "open economy" models of inflation has seldom been tested competitively.

35. Robert M. Dunn, Jr., "Flexible Exchange Rates and Traded Goods Prices: The Role of Oligopoly Pricing in the Canadian Experience," in *The Economics of Common Currencies*, ed. H. G. Johnson and A. K. Swoboda (London: Allen and Unwin, 1972), chap. 16; and his "Flexible Exchange Rates and Oligopoly Pricing: A Study of Canadian Markets," *Journal of Political Economy* 78 (January/February 1970): 140–51. For another example of an asymmetrical response to a temporary disturbance to international prices, see R. E. Caves et al., *Britain's Economic Prospects* (Washington: Brookings Institution, 1968), p. 167.

36. For studies covering a broader sample of industrial countries, see OECD, *Inflation: the Present Problem*, pp. 68–76; and Erich Spitäller, "Prices and Unemployment in Selected Industrial Countries," *IMF Staff Papers* 18 (November 1971): 528–69. A recent literature survey is provided by Morris Goldstein, "The Trade-off between Inflation and Unemployment: A Survey of the Econometric Evidence for Selected Countries," *IMF Staff Papers* 19 (November 1972): 647–95.

Nordhaus, in the exception to this rule, undertook a seven-country test of several inflation models, including monetarist, Phillips, and the Aukrust model formulated to make the change of wages in manufacturing depend on import prices in the current and two past years.[37] Aukrust outperformed the closed-economy models for four of the seven countries (France, Sweden, Japan, and the United Kingdom) and did passably for West Germany. Only North America stood by Phillips. Nordhaus conjectured that the "worldwide wage explosion" of 1968–71 originated in demand pressure in the United States and traveled via international price linkages to the other industrial countries. He notes, however, that the transmission had to be suspiciously swift.

The structure of the Aukrust model indeed raises a statistical question about applying a simple Phillips-type relation to highly open economies. Suppose that the Aukrust model is correct about the prevalent source of price disturbances, namely, movements in the world prices of traded goods. Suppose also that the nation manages its macroeconomic policy with one eye on external balance. An increase in traded-goods prices raises profits and induces expansion and wage increases in this sector, and the fiscal authorities permit aggregate demand to expand and unemployment to fall because of the favorable external balance. The price increase thus leads to greater demand pressure and reduced unemployment, rather than the other way around! Faster wage increases and lower unemployment result from common ultimate causes. The curve-fitters should at least seek assurance that they have the direction of causation right.

A final empirical support for the importance of international linkages lies in the shrinking variance of national rates of inflation. The past two decades have seen important reductions in the barriers to trade among industrial countries, a sustained rise in the share of production entering into trade between nations, and a dramatic increase in the international mobility of capital (including direct investment).[38]

The tighter links between national price levels are a natural outcome of these forces, which either forge tighter links between national commodity markets or impair the ability of a country with a fixed exchange rate to repel external price changes. The OECD noted that recent years have seen more synchronization among countries in price movements without parallel behavior of demand.[39]

37. William D. Nordhaus, "The Worldwide Wage Explosion," *Brookings Papers on Economic Activity,* No. 2 (1972), pp. 431–64.

38. See Richard N. Cooper, *The Economics of Interdependence: Economic Policy in the Atlantic Community* (New York: McGraw-Hill, 1968); Winthrop G. Minot, "Tests for Integration between Major Western European Capital Markets," *Oxford Economic Papers* 26 (November 1974): 424–39.

39. OECD, *Inflation: The Present Problem,* p. 7. Let us take annual rates of increase of consumer prices for 20 OECD members (excluding peripheral, semi-industrial

VI. SUMMARY

Linkages through international trade and payments influence the process of inflation in important ways neglected in many analyses. As a "monetarist" model demonstrates, a country with a fixed exchange rate finds at least part of its price level locked to the rest of the world through the role of traded goods, and domestic inflationary disturbances may affect the trade balance instead of, or along with, domestic prices. Nontraded goods are important, but primarily in transitional adjustments.

If prices increase abroad and a country maintains a fixed exchange rate, it will ingest inflation by one channel if not another: the impact of an improving trade balance on expenditure and the money supply, or direct international price and wage links. (A flexible exchange rate provides insulation only if the money supply is strictly managed.) The presence of adminstered prices effects various qualitative changes in the working of these international linkages, as the Aukrust model conveniently demonstrates. International capital transfers can convey and contribute to inflationary disturbances, in certain conditions, and they also profoundly modify the effectiveness of policy instruments used for the control of aggregate demand.

Empirical research, although quite incomplete, documents the role of traded goods as international transmission links for inflation, and suggests that negotiated wages in some countries may strongly reflect international price movements. The apparent prevalance of "Phillips curve" relations suggests the sufficiency of a closed-economy model of inflationary processes, but international linkages could generate a spurious Phillips relation with the causality reversed.

Iceland and Turkey) in the periods 1959–64 and 1964–69. The mean inflation rate rose from 3.1 to 4.2 percent, while the standard deviation fell slightly from 1.3 to 1.2, and the coefficient of variation dropped sharply from 0.42 to 0.30. (Calculated from figures in ibid., p. 59.)

Illogic of Neo-Marxian Doctrine of Unequal Exchange

Paul A. Samuelson

The theory of comparative advantage is one of the few bits of statical logic that economists of all schools understand and agree with. A. Emmanuel in *L'échange inégal* (1969)[1] devotes more than four hundred pages to refuting that theory, replacing it with the view that the poverty of a poor nation, trading with a rich nation and importing capital from it, is importantly related to this asymmetric pattern of trade.

The thesis, if correct, is important and novel. It is seriously presented by a serious scholar. It is one of the few attempts to put Marxian analytics to work on a genuine real-world problem. Two distinguished savants, Professors Charles Bettleheim and Henri Denis, have thought it valuable enough to have given the author the benefit of their criticisms. The argument deserves a fair-minded examination. Since, at the request of students in an MIT graduate seminar, I invested some hours in studying its arithmetical tables and syllogisms in order to form a judgment of the merits in the doctrine of unequal exchange, my provisional negative findings may be of some usefulness to others.[2]

I am grateful to the National Science Foundation for financial aid.

1. Translated as *Unequal Exchange: A Study of the Imperialism of Trade* (New York and London: Monthly Review Press, 1972).

2. My 1972 paper "Deadweight Loss in International Trade from the Profit Motive," in C. Fred Bergsten and William G. Tyler, eds., *Leading Issues in International*

I. RICARDO'S RED HERRING

Begin, as Emmanuel does, with Ricardo's traditional Portugal-England wine-cloth arithmetic. In backward England it takes 100 labor to produce [her needed 1 of] cloth; and 120 labor to produce [1 of] wine. In rich Portugal it takes only 80 labor for [that 1 of] wine; and only 90 labor for [that 1 of] cloth. Ricardo, and everybody (including Emmanuel), will agree that with labor immobile between countries and competitive balanced trade freely possible between countries, England will end up specializing in cloth, exporting it to Portugal in return for wine imports from Portugal, which specializes in wine production and imports cloth.

Moreover, the final post-trade ratio of cloth's price to wine's price, it is agreed, must end up somewhere between 100/120 and 90/80. We know that J. S. Mill first told Ricardo's readers where, on that closed interval, the equilibrium terms of trade would fall. Ricardo, presumably only by way of giving a hypothetical example, says, "Thus England would give the produce of the labour of 100 men, for the produce of the labour of 80" (*Principles*, ed. Sraffa, p. 135). This suggests

$$\frac{100}{120} \le (P_c/P_w)^* = 1 \le \frac{90}{80}$$

For this gratuitous case (or for any other arbitrarily selected terms-of-trade point in the open interval), the real wage in both countries rises: English workers get one of their needed subsistence goods for less work than before (the imported one); and so do Portuguese workers. Emmanuel does not disagree with this. He does not claim that poor country's labor is impoverished by the example's trade. He does not even go into the ill-posed question, "Which nation has the *higher* percentage improvement in real wage, the rich nation or the poor?" Those who know modern economic theory know that no one answer could possibly be given; before (and *after!*) trade, all we can validly know is this:

$$\frac{80}{120} = Min \left[\frac{80}{120}, \frac{90}{100} \right] \le \frac{U.K.\ real\ wage}{Portugal\ real\ wage}$$

$$\le Max \left[\frac{80}{120}, \frac{90}{100} \right] = \frac{90}{100}$$

Economic Policy: Essays in Honor of George N. Halm (Lexington, Mass.: Lexington Books, 1973), discusses some paradoxes of apparent (but illusory) steady-state inefficiencies under competition.

It is easy to supply examples in which trade brings either country to either pole of these limits, with the other country garnering *all* the gains from trade.

And even in Ricardo's gratuitous case, where we are made to end up at $P_c/P_w = 1$, it is not possible to say which of the countries has had real wages improved by the bigger percentage. The U.K. real wage always stays the same as before in cloth; only in wine does trade ever benefit it. The Portugal real wage rises only in imported cloth.[3] Equality-of-percentage rise in the respective imported-goods' real wages can take place only if the equilibrium price ratio P_c/P_w, ends up at the geometric mean of the two limits:$[(100/120)(90/80)]^{1/2} = \sqrt{15/16}$. But it would be wrong to think that Ricardo's choice of $1 = 16/16$ for the post-trade terms of trade of the United Kingdom implies, necessarily, that poor English labor gets the larger percentage gain in real wage, for imported wine might loom small in their total consumption budget. Even in the cases of uniform homothetic tastes, an exact index number of trade-induced relative real wages movements could take on any value. (By the way, Ricardo's example gratuitously suggests that England wants the *same* wine and cloth after trade as before trade—as if the benefits from trade are spent on leisure. Perhaps this is merely a figure of speech. By his own Malthusian theory of labor supply, Ricardo would presumably suppose that trade benefits are frittered away in mere creation of more human lives. As usual, Ricardo operates simultaneously at many levels of abstraction: although his arithmetic involves only labor costs, his explanation is that of any broker talking about shifts of "capital" between various projects, and so on.)

Emmanuel's unequal exchange, he is careful to warn us (p. 92, for example), is not at all concerned with the question: Granted that both countries gain from trade in real wages, does one get more than what might be considered the point

---

3. For convenient reference in connection with later appraising of Emmanuel's tables, let me pin down with admissible numbers Ricardo's pre-trade and post-trade equilibrium. Suppose before trade that each country consumes 1 (or 1 million) of wine (quarts) and cloth (yards). Portugal has the higher per capita income because 170 man-hours (= 80 + 90) of labor produce there what it takes 220 man-hours (= 120 + 100) to produce in England. Suppose that after trade, all of England's fixed labor goes to produce 2.2 m. cloth; and all of Portugal's goes to produce $2^1/_3$ wine. Humoring Ricardo with his 1-to-1 post-trade terms of trade, suppose millian reciprocal demand causes $1^1/_9$ m. wine to be exported by Portugal for $1^1/_9$ m. English cloth. Profit not having reared its ugly head, *all can agree that trade benefits both countries.* Poor England (but not so poor as before trade) now ends up consuming $1^1/_9$ m. wine and $1^1/_{72}$ m. cloth; rich Portugal ends up consuming $1^4/_{45}$ wine and $1^1/_9$ cloth. So runs the harmonious classical story. Will Emmanuel's Marxian version of the true situation, inclusive of profits equalized by international capital movements, successfully refute comparative cost? The last section will give a definite negative answer to the question.

of fair division[4] of trade blessings? For, as he says, from that viewpoint "unequal exchange does not represent a real loss but merely a failure to gain." Emmanuel's unequal exchange is designed to bare the *harm* from the trade, not its *benefit*.

II. HARM TO WORKERS WHEN POOR COUNTRY IMPORTS PROFIT-EQUALIZING CAPITAL?

To deduce trade's evil, we must abandon Ricardo's labor-only arithmetic. Now let there be profits as well as wages, surpluses, surplus values, indirect labor (in the form of Marxian constant capital) as well as direct labor (variable capital in Marxian terminology).

Now we still keep labor immobile as between countries. But let us suppose with Emmanuel that, in the absence of trade, the profit rate is lower in the nation with high real wages. We have at least two choices. We could merely introduce balanced merchandise trade in wine and cloth, not permitting any borrowing or lending. Always, current merchandise balance of payments must then balance.

However, it seems more realistic to recognize that capital is mobile between countries. Thus, Emmanuel says (p. 54), "Let us now suppose that free circulation of capital is introduced between countries, and, as a result, equalization of profit takes place."

Before looking at his Tableaux, we may ask ourselves: "What would the conventional international textbook models give as an answer to the positive-profit unbalanced-trade case?"

III. CONVENTIONAL TEXTBOOK PROOF OF TRADE-INDUCED RISE IN REAL WAGES OF CAPITAL-IMPORTING COUNTRY

In the oversimplified world of the texts, Heckscher-Ohlin two-factor production functions are made to replace labor-only Ricardian functions. Before trade, poor England has less homogeneous capital ("leets"), K, relative to its labor supply, L. Her profit rate, equalized between wine and cloth industries, is presumably higher than in rich Portugal, with its plentiful capital. Apparently, wine must be capital-intensive relative to cloth if we are to use Heckscher-Ohlin explanations for Portugal's comparative advantage in wine.

What are the effects of trade in the textbook models?

4. Emmanuel here takes Graham's simple case where A produces in 10 hrs. 40 wheat or 40 watches, while B's 10 hrs. produces 40 wheat and 30 watches. Naïvely, some writers have thought 40 and 35 (= 1/2 of 30 + 40) represents fair division—not Ricardo's gratuitous case, but one equally gratuitous.

1. Mere balanced trade in wine and cloth, with no IOUs or movement of physical capital goods allowed, will raise real wages of the abundant factor in the poor country England, as free trade in goods serves as a partial substitute for factor mobility. The high real wage of Portugal drops as relatively specializing there in non-labor-intensive wine economizes on its initially scarce labor. In England the high interest or profit rate drops as it relatively specializes on labor-intensive cloth.

2. If we supplement free trade in goods by free movement of physical capital, the differentials in real wages between rich Portugal and backward England are further reduced. Indeed, if the only reason for England's inferiority is scarcity of capital goods, real wages must be equalized by capital flows. (Indeed, we know from the classical factor-price equalization theorem that, even before enough capital has moved to equalize capital/labor endowments, real wages will already have become equal.)

To sum up: conventional 2-factor models lead to the opposite of the "unequal-exchange" thesis. Labor in the capital-poor countries gains the most from trade and from foreign investment and absentee-ownership.[5]

IV. NEOCLASSICISM REPLACED BY NEO-NEOCLASSICISM

Although the international-trade texts have not caught up with the frontier of debates about reswitching and complexities of heterogeneous-capital vectors, we must see how Joan Robinson or Sraffa or an MIT student handling dated-input models would evaluate the probabilities of immiserating unequal exchange.

Let us begin with a Leontief-Sraffa model where primary-factor labor produces all goods at constant returns to scale but with the help of produced goods themselves as inputs needed to work with primary labor.

Make the bizarre assumption of Ricardo that England is poor and Portugal rich. If we measure poverty by lowness of the real wage alone and assume the same Leontief-Sraffa technologies everywhere in the world, then Emmanuel is

5. Imagine a 3-factor world with production functions like $Q = F(L,K,T)$, where T is immobile land. Obviously, if K had some singular pattern of rivalry with L, rather than complementarity, as shown by negative $\partial^2 Q/\partial L \partial K$, free geographical movement of K could *hurt* real wages in the land-poor country. But, contrary to the unequal-exchange thesis, the combined income of the poor country, its return from the combined dose of immobile labor-cum-land, would have to go up rather than down. (None of this denies that import of *new* technology from a rich country might sometimes lower real wages in a poor country. Thus, the green revolution of hybrid wheat and rice strains could lower rural real wages while raising proprietors' property incomes.)

right in supposing that the poor country must have the higher profit rate, for a lower real wage can occur only with a higher profit rate, as students of the factor-price frontier know.

However, we need not assume the same technological options in terms of labor and non-primary inputs. In that case, it is possible but not mandatory for the high-profit region also to be what Emmanuel wishes it to be, the low-wage region.

Now we can ask the question: "Suppose by free movement of capital, trade in goods takes place between countries that have come to a common rate of profit. Will the real wage rise in the capital-importing country whose profit rate has been brought down in contradiction to Emmanuel's alleged fall in real wage?"

The only proper Sraffa answer is clear. "Yes. Mobile-goods trade and capital flows, which permanently lower the backward country's profit rate, must permanently *raise* (not lower) its real wage.

"Moreover, the real wage will presumably be induced to rise even more than the same drop in the profits rate would induce in a no-trade autarky. This is because, in addition to the rise in real wage obtainable without trade, the possibility that one can permanently exchange goods at price ratios different from those of autarky, will (if anything) lower some equilibrium prices relative to domestic wage rates at the postulated lower profit rate and give an extra boost to real wages in terms of imported goods."

So once again, the immiseration conclusions of unequal exchange are not validated—but rather their reverse.[6]

6. Here is a paradox discussed in my cited Hahm Festschrift paper. Suppose Ricardo's data (100, 120; 90, 80) hold for *total* labor requirements. If profit rates are both zero, Portugal exports wine and England exports cloth. But suppose (in this note only) that Portugal's wine requires its labor in two periods, half to produce grape juice and half to turn grape juice into wine; suppose U.K. wine is producible in one period. Cloth everywhere is produced in one period. Then, we discover that a high-enough profit rate, equal in both countries, will give England a cheaper cost ratio of wine to cloth. England will export wine in the steady state, and Portugal will specialize in cloth production! The world *seems* to be no longer efficiently on its global production-possibility frontier.

I have italicized the word *seems* because there is no true paradox. All this is quite as it should be. The world never has a choice of going at once from one steady state to another: to do that, it would have to build up stocks of heterogeneous capital goods in some places and reduce them in others. And there is nothing "inefficient" about the reversed geographical pattern. Actually, that pattern would be efficiently reached asymptotically if the two countries (1) permitted free balanced trade in goods, (2) permitted no interregional borrowings or absentee ownership, and (3) had Ramsey planners who engineered optimal growth patterns for their stationary populations with the same high time-preference rates in the two countries.

V. SOME MARX-LIKE TABLEAUX

We are now armed to examine Emmanuel's arguments. He envisages countries A and B, with unequal profit rates in autarky, e.g., 20% and 33^1/$_3$%. After trade with mobile capital, they emerge with a common intermediate profit rate, e.g., 25%. (Each country has three industries, e.g., I wine, II cloth, . . .). Relevant tables from his chapter 2 are presented in table 1 below.

System A gives [Portugal's] low-profit before-trade situation. System B gives [England's] pre-trade high-profit situation. Systems A and B together give the alleged after-trade situation at a common intermediate profit rate.

A word of explanation may be helpful. The usual assumptions of Marxism Tableaux are made here. Thus the second column, Variable Capital, represents expenditures on direct labor, and the first column, Constant Capital, represents the cost of raw materials (or other capital goods) used. The column Surplus Value is based upon an assumed constancy of the rate of surplus value in all industries: in these first tables, more or less a happenstance, Emmanuel assumes that the rate of surplus value is the same in both countries before trade, mainly, 100%. Much less admissibly, he assumes that, although each country's

TABLE 1

SOME MARXIAN TABLEAUX

Branches	c Constant Capital	v Variable Capital	m Surplus Value (1.0)v	V Value $c + v + m$	T Rate of Profit $\frac{\Sigma m}{\Sigma c + \Sigma v}$	p Profit $T(c + v)$	L Price of Production $c + v + p$
			System A				
I	80	20	20	120		20	120
II	90	10	10	110	20%	20	120
III	70	30	30	130		20	120
	240	60	60	360		60	360
			System B				
I	40	20	20	80		20	80
II	50	10	10	70	33^1/$_3$%	20	80
III	30	30	30	90		20	80
	120	60	60	240		60	240
			Systems A and B Together				
{ IA	80	20	20	120		25	125
{ IIA	90	10	10	110		25	125
{ IIIA	70	30	30	130		25	125
{ IB	40	20	20	80	25%	15	75
{ IIB	50	10	10	70		15	75
{ IIIB	30	30	30	90		15	75
	360	120	120	600		120	600
A	240	60	60	360		75	375
B	120	60	60	240	25%	45	225
	360	120	120	600		120	600

Source: Adapted from Emmanuel, *L'échange inégal*, pp. 53–55.

rate of profit is equalized after trade, nevertheless each country continues to have the same rate of surplus value as it had before trade. Those who have had experience with Marxian categories will realize that there cannot in general be such extreme independence between the rates or profit and of surplus value. (E.g., when the organic compositions of capital are the same in different industries, or very nearly so, a large change in the profit rate must generate a sizable change in the rate of surplus value.)

In the final section of the table I have added two final rows that respectively consolidate the totals for the two countries. Emmanuel regards these totals as crucial because of his belief—wrong, as we shall see—that it is essentially the totals that are needed to describe the effects of international exchange.

How does the author use these tableaux?

Emmanuel seems to think that, if mobility of capital were not permitted to equalize profit rates, the goods would exchange between A and B at the price ratios from the final columns of A and B: 80 of B for 120 of A. Since capital mobility brings down the profit component of B's prices and raises that of A's prices, Emmanuel thinks that B's terms of trade are necessarily hurt by the process and that she must now trade 75 of B for 125 of A.

But this act is at its heart a nonsense calculation. Before trade, there was autarky: not 80 of B for 120 of A but 0 of B and 0 of A, with the terms of trade a meaningless and indeterminate form, $0/0$ = gibberish. And even if I change the comparison, and construct two post-trade situations—one where capital is immobile and the domestic profit rates are not equalized and the other where profit rates are equalized—still Emmanuel's comparison is a nonsense one. By his way of reckoning, an invention in the advanced country that lowered all costs of production there would impoverish it. Yet every college sophomore knows that a reduction in the terms of trade that is offset by productivity improvement may be highly beneficial to *both* countries.

By Emmanuel's kind of fallacious reasoning, one's heart would bleed for the capitalists in underdeveloped countries. Whenever capital imports bring down their profit rates, their whole nation suffers. Emmanuel even claims that hundreds of billions of dollars of extra real income—perhaps 30 or 40%!—could be secured for workers in the less-developed countries if his kind of unequal exchange were somehow ruled out.

The illogic of the whole procedure is much greater than has yet been indicated. GNPs (inclusive of double, triple, and multiple countings of gross raw materials at the different stages of production), of course, don't exchange against each other in international trade. Therefore, when Emmanuel uses such totals, as in 375 of A against 225 of B, we must reasonably infer that he regards these as differing only in scale (by a factor of 3 in a 3-branch model) from actual commodity prices, which is fair enough.

But it is profoundly wrong to leave after-trade industry totals what they were before trade. The whole effect of trade is to cause specialization and production shifts: Portugal contracts (even to zero) production in its cloth branch and expands it in its wine branch; in England the opposite takes place.

In Emmanuel's tables, both before trade and "after," there is no possibility of any wine-cloth trade. In every case his domestic price ratios, P_2/P_1 and P_3/P_1 are *identical* between countries both before and after trade! If Ricardo had postulated wine-cloth cost ratios as $80/100 = .8$ in Portugal and $96/20 = .8$ in England, he would have ended up with zero trade in everything.

Let us, however, extricate Emmanuel from his unfortunate choice of initial numerical examples. Let us give his argument all the rope it can use, to see fair-mindedly whether there is anything insightful—even imperfectly so—in his whole approach.

VI.   THE ACID TEST: RICARDO'S EXAMPLE

What could provide a better test case of the root merit of the theory of unequal exchange than Ricardo's own simple case of comparative advantage? After all, Professor Bettelheim, in his sponsorship of the Emmanuel work, has important doubts about Emmanuel's analysis. The principal merit of Emmanuel's work in Bettelheim's eyes is that it refutes Ricardian comparative advantage. Thus, Bettelheim claims:

> Emmanuel's critique constitutes an extremely important contribution to the over-turning of what might be called the "dogma of the theory of comparative costs and of the benefits of the capitalist international division of labor. . . .
> . . . One of the essentially interesting aspects of Emmanuel's book is, I think, that it brings out the profound inadequacy and illusory character of the classical and "neoclassical" theory of international trade.

Does the theory of unequal exchange succeed in any sense in undermining the theory of comparative advantage? Or in limiting its realism and relevance? Or in amplifying and improving it in any way?

I believe any analytically trained fair-minded reader who goes to the trouble of examining unequal exchange seriously will conclude as I have that the answers are No, No, and No. The following analysis, by the correct Marxian technique, of Ricardo's classical case should close the books on the matter.

Three tables are presented in table 2 dealing with the Ricardo example along proper Marxian lines: System A, System B, and System A and B, in the Emmanuel style. To be fair to his thesis, my example assumes differences in real wage rates in poor England and rich Portugal prior to trade. Also, to correspond with his emphasis upon equalization of profit rates by trade, I have amplified Ricardo's wine-cloth example to allow for profit. So that every Marxian can agree with the analysis, I have worked with an example in which there are no differences in organic composition of capital to put a wedge between analysis of Marx's Volume I "values" and Volume III "prices." Indeed, in the present simple Ricardo example, all constant capital is zero—permitting no one to explain away or to minimize the higher real wages of one country as the result of labor there working with more and better machinery. There is no room here for the apologetics of thrift.

To parallel Emmanuel's arbitrary profit rates, I use his pre-trade rates of 20% and 33⅓%. Like him, I use post-trade equalized rates of profit of 25%. But I do not follow Emmanuel's incorrect supposition that we can pool *after* trade his *unchanged* pre-trade surpluses. Of course, the specialization forced by trade will alter all such magnitudes, and the changed profit rates will affect the surpluses. Emmanuel fell in the same small trap here that Marxians (Sweezy, Dobb, et al.) and non-Marxians (Bortkiewicz, Seton, Samuelson,[7] et al.) agree Marx fell into when he gave his Volume III form of the transformation algorithm for going from "values" to "prices." In any case, Emmanuel is free to change my 25% to any other intermediate equalized profit rate he likes: my refutation will not thereby be affected at all. And he can use other than these admissible terms-of-trade outcomes, which I have made in table 2 to agree with an earlier footnote's version of the Ricardo case.

Let me give a word of explanation. I assume (see system B of table 2) that England consumes 1 (million or) m. qts. of wine before trade and 1 m. yds of cloth. She has a labor supply of 220 m. hrs., both before and after trade.

I assume (see system A) that rich Portugal consumes about an eighth more per head; the same 1 m. qts. of wine and 1 m. yds. cloth for her 170 m. hrs. labor, as against England's 220 m. hrs. labor.

Both before and after trade, labor is fixed in each country: at 170 m. hrs. for Portugal and 220 m. hrs. for England. I humor Ricardo in his choice of 1-cloth-to-1-wine post-trade terms of trade: to fix the numbers, I pick levels consistent with convex preference contours in each country—1⅑ m. yds. of English cloth exports to balance 1⅑ m. qts. of Portuguese wine exports. Finally, with Emmanuel, I assume free capital mobility creates equality of profit rates at 25%, bringing down the poor country's 33⅓% and bringing up the rich country's 20%. (It is not possible to humor Emmanuel and keep post-trade rates of surplus value at pre-trade levels because the case has such balanced organic composition. So I resist doing the impossible.)

The postulates of the example are now complete. It is just a question of working out all the numerical entries of the three tableaux, adhering to standard

7. I have reviewed this in the 1971 *Journal of Economic Literature*.

Marxian c + v + . . . calculations. Table 2 presents the corrected analysis, whose results are quite contrary to the unequal-exchange claims. To move beyond the fetishistic level of prices and aggregates, I have appended two columns to show actual physical commodity outputs—in quarts of wine and yards of cloth. Subtracting exports, or adding in starred imports, the final column shows national consumptions. With the profit rates known, the physical per capita consumptions or workers can be easily calculated by the reader.

VII.   UNEQUAL EXCHANGE REFUTED

Emmanuel and Bettelheim will, I am sure, now agree with me that this careful and valid exercise, in which Ricardo's comparative-cost case has profit rates appended to it—and which do get equalized by trade—does benefit both countries in exactly the same manner that Ricardo claimed! See the last two columns of table 2, and note its identity with Ricardo's results (e.g., as spelled out carefully in an earlier footnote). Moreover, even if we improve on Ricardo's gratuitous way of selecting one of the possible range of final equilibria, we see that no single valid point has been scored by this Marxian model of unequal exchange against classical or neoclassical trade theory. Q.E.D.

Of course, wine is traded against cloth in the model. Anyone who wants to

TABLE 2

CORRECTED ANALYSIS OF RICARDIAN CASE

Branches	c Constant Capital	v Variable Capital	m Surplus Value	T Rate of Profit	p Profit $T(c + v)$	L&V Price and Value $c + v + p$	Q Physical Production	Consumption (Q-exports) or (Imports*)
System A: Rich Portugal before Trade (170 m. hrs. total labor)								
I Wine	0	80 m.	16	20%	16	96 m.	1 m. qts.	1 m. qts.
II Cloth	0	90 m.	18		18	108 m.	1 m. yds.	1 m. yds.
	0	170 m.	34		34	204 m.		
System B: Poor England before Trade (220 m. hrs. total labor)								
I Wine	0	120 m.	40	33⅓%	40	160 m.	1 m. qts.	1 m. qts.
II Cloth	0	100 m.	33⅓		33⅓	133⅓ m.	1 m. yds.	1 m. yds.
	0	220 m.	73⅓		73⅓	293⅓ m.		
Systems A and B: After Trade and Profit Equalization (Unchanged Total Labor Hours)								
IA Wine	0	170 m.	42½	25%	42½	212½ m.	2⅛ m. qts.	1¹/₇₂ m. qts.
IIA Cloth	0	0	0		0	0	0	1¹/₉ m. yds.*
	0	170 m.	42½		42½	212½ m.		
IB Wine	0	0	0	25%	0	0	0	1¹/₉ m. qts.*
IIB Cloth	0	220 m.	55		55	275 m.	2¹/₅ m. qts.	1⁴/₄₅ m. yds.
	0	220 m.	55		55	275 m.		

say that a certain number of high-wage hours of A has been traded against a certain larger number of hours of low-wage B is free to do so. (David Ricardo did.) But that tautology does not mean that there is a meaningful par for such a ratio and that a deviation on one side from it represents "unequal" exchange. Unequal exchange in this sense is not the result of wage differentials; nor is it the cause of wage differentials; rather, it is tautologically a restatement of the fact of assumed wage differentials!

It is a cruel hoax on the laborers in poor countries to pretend that there is some way of increasing their real incomes[8] by 100% or 200% or even 2% by choking off trade, or by some other proposed way of eliminating unequal exchange. Indeed, romantic dilettantism has always been the enemy of social progress for the masses. Whether wrapped in Marxism symbolism or otherwise, logical nonsense is logical nonsense.

VIII.   CONCLUSION

I have spared the reader further details of a thorough post-mortem on the Emmanuel model of unequal exchange, including a careful auditing of his dialogue with Professor Bettelheim. Because it is less mainstream economists than Marxians who are interested in the model, I have checked my negative autopsy report by *redoing his analysis completely in terms of Volume I "values," eschewing all prices.* The same negative finding emerges.

No new light has been thrown on the reason why poor countries are poor and rich countries are rich. What is a quite different and less important matter, no flaw in the theory of comparative advantage has been uncovered, and no improvement on that theory is provided by the doctrine of unequal exchange.

Let me also report that there is much else in *Unequal Exchange* to disagree with and to agree with. The analysis has the merit of being clear, if incorrect, a compliment that not all critiques and defenses of modern economics can warrant.

8. Actually, the trade-induced reduction in the poor country's profit rate adds an additional increase to the real wage there; i.e., along with the higher real wage in terms of the cheaper imported good, there is an increase in real wage in terms of its home product too. The trade-induced rise in the rich country's profit rate must depress its workers' real wage in terms of the exported good, and this same factor *could* even wipe out the higher real wage in terms of the imported good, leaving the rich-country employers with all the gains from trade.

Devaluation and Absorption: An Alternative Analysis

Randall Hinshaw

The purpose of this essay is to explore the macroeconomics of currency devaluation (or of exchange depreciation) in those cases where excessive "absorption" is due to domestic inflation—or, more precisely, to a more rapid rate of inflation at home than abroad. My excuse for undertaking what some might regard as a superfluous exercise is that the ensuing analysis departs from the current standard presentation as stated in terms of aggregate price elasticities, income elasticities, and export multipliers. Although the standard analysis has provided numerous valuable insights, it is riddled with serious pitfalls—pitfalls that have not been entirely avoided in the alternative language of absorption.

For better or worse, the analytical framework presented here is at least partly original.[1] It is the result of many painful efforts to find a simpler and more direct way of looking at situations of international disequilibrium—in particular, a way that would provide more reliable signals for the makers of policy. Attention will be concentrated on the relation between a country's level of absorp-

---

1. Elements of this analysis are prominent in the writings of Frank D. Graham, J. E. Meade, Michael Michaely, I. F. Pearce, and others. I also owe much to discussions with graduate students grappling with the same problems—in particular, John Chambers and Paul W. Gaebelein, Jr. But none of these individuals can be blamed for the ensuing synthesis, for which I accept full responsibility.

tion, in money terms, and what will here be called its "absorption price level." A devaluation will typically induce both a rise in absorption *in money terms* and a rise in the absorption price level, but it will here be argued that, with appropriate monetary and fiscal policies, the absorption price level will rise by a greater proportion than absorption in money terms, in which case real absorption *must* fall.

BASIC CONCEPTS

But first a word about concepts, beginning with absorption (in money terms). Absorption, that highly useful concept developed by Sidney Alexander, can be defined as the total amount spent by a country, per period, on goods and services (avoiding, of course, all double counting), including imports of goods and services, but excluding exports, since exports are "absorbed" by the rest of the world. Thus absorption can be regarded as national aggregate demand—at a given absorption price level—and output (national product) can be regarded as national aggregate supply. A country's absorption (aggregate demand) will exceed its output (aggregate supply) when its imports of goods and services exceed its exports.

In this terminology devaluation can be regarded as an attempt to reduce excessive absorption (or as a substitute for other methods, such as direct controls on payments, of holding absorption down). Excessive absorption is not, of course, synonymous with an excess of imports over exports of goods and services, since the deficit on current account may be balanced by a net inflow of long-term capital or unilateral transfers. In these circumstances the balance of payments is in over-all equilibrium and, so long as the situation continues, no adjustment is called for. By the same token, absorption may be excessive even if there is a current-account surplus, since the surplus may be more than offset by a net outflow of long-term capital or unilateral transfers. Thus the United States, which throughout the twentieth century until the 1970s had an export surplus (including services) in every single year, has been chronically in over-all deficit since 1949. For the purposes of this essay, excessive absorption will be defined as absorption resulting in an over-all payments deficit.

As indicated earlier, attention will be focused in this analysis on the relation between a country's level of absorption, in money terms, and its absorption price level. The absorption price level may be thought of as a properly weighted price index embracing all goods and services absorbed, including purely domestic output (output that is currently neither exported nor imported), plus international goods and services — a broad category consisting of three subdivisions: imports, import-competing domestic output (output that is supplemented by imports of the same goods and services), and domestic consumption of those goods and services—so-called "exportables"—that are absorbed by both the domestic and the foreign market.[2] The absorption price level is equivalent conceptually to the price index required to correct absorption for price-level changes. Except for the usually slight difference in weighting, it is also equivalent to the price deflator used to correct national product for changes in the price level.[3]

In reflecting on a country's absorption price level, it should be noted that part of it—the price level of purely domestic goods and services—is exclusively determined by domestic demand and domestic supply, whereas the other part of it—the price level of international goods and services—is mainly (and for small countries, almost exclusively) determined by the rest of the world. A small country such as Luxembourg, for example, accounts for only a tiny fraction of world demand and world supply, and thus, at a given exchange rate, has little influence on its international price level as expressed in domestic currency. It can inflate—or deflate—until it is blue in the face without perceptibly affecting either its import price level or the price level of the goods it exports, a fraction of which will typically be absorbed at home. For countries that account for a substantial fraction of world demand and world supply, the picture is somewhat different; but even here, inflationary policies have a much greater effect on the price level of domestic goods and services than on the international price level. Even a country as large as the United States accounts for only a modest fraction of the global demand for, and supply of, international goods; but it accounts for the entire demand for, and supply of, domestic goods and services.[4]

These observations lead to a very clear way of looking at excessive absorption. Excessive absorption means two things: first, that a country's absorption

2. It should be noted that the essential distinction between purely domestic output and international output derives from the existence of transportation costs and trade barriers. If transportation costs were zero and if trade barriers were entirely suppressed, all *commodities* would be international goods, and would appear either in a country's import schedule (frequently supplementing domestic production) or in its export schedule. The only exception to the latter generalization would be those rare cases where the national demand for a given commodity was exactly equal to national supply.

3. The two price indexes are identical when absorption equals output (when exports of goods and services equal imports).

4. In the case of most commodities, the United States accounts for less than one-fourth of world consumption and production. In 1971, for example, the United States accounted for 14% of world sugar consumption, 14% of world cotton consumption, and 22% of world consumption of steel; in the same year, it accounted for 11% of world production of iron ore, 17% of world cattle production, and 19% of world cotton production. Only in rare cases does the fraction exceed one-third for either consumption or production.

price level is too low in relation to its level of absorption in money terms; and second, that its international price level is too low in relation to its price level for domestic goods and services. The first proposition means that the existing level of disposable money income (including, of course, government transfer payments) has excessive purchasing power, leading to excessive domestic purchases of imports and exportables; and the second proposition means that relative prices (international prices in relation to domestic prices) also encourage excessive purchases of international goods and services.

INFLATION, ABSORPTION, AND THE ABSORPTION PRICE LEVEL

How can such a situation arise? Very easily. It can arise in several ways, of which perhaps the most common—the case examined in this essay—is through inflation. The matter can be illustrated by starting with a situation of internal and external equilibrium, and then introducing an inflationary policy which disturbs the equilibrium.

Consider first the case of a rather small country, such as Norway, and assume a situation of full employment and external equilibrium, with price stability both at home and abroad. To simplify matters at this stage, assume also that both the number employed and output per man-hour in Norway are stationary. This means, of course, that Norwegian real output cannot increase. To make matters still simpler, assume that Norway is in balance on current account, with exports of goods and services equal to imports. One can than look at this situation as a circular flow in which Norwegian absorption per period is exactly equal to Norwegian output. Norwegians divide their absorption between Norwegian output and foreign output, and any domestic output not absorbed by Norwegians is absorbed by the rest of the world, so that exports equal imports. In this situation Norway's absorption price level is in the appropriate relation to its level of absorption in money terms, assuring an equilibrium level of real absorption; and its international price level is in appropriate relation to its price level of domestic goods and services, assuring an equilibrium distribution of Norwegian purchases of domestic goods, imports, importables, and exportables.

Assume now that a new government gains power on a platform of sharply increased social security benefits, with no increase in taxes. Assume that the increased benefits are entirely financed by an increase, *per period*, in the money supply. What will happen? Part of the increase in disposable income will be spent on imports, part will be spent on output that would otherwise have been exported, and part will be spent on purely domestic goods and services. The first two developments—the increase in imports and the decline in exports—will produce a deficit in the balance of payments. But the increase in

Norwegian purchases of international goods—imports and exportables—will not appreciably raise the price level of such goods, since Norway accounts for only a small fraction of world demand. Only in the case of domestic goods and services will prices be free to rise significantly. This means that the effect of the inflationary policy will be twofold: to create a payments deficit and to induce a rise in the Norwegian absorption price level almost exclusively limited to the price level of domestic goods and services. In this situation Norwegian real output remains unchanged per period, but absorption, both in money and real terms, increases, the increase taking the form of a payments deficit. The increase in real absorption means, of course, that the absorption price level has risen by a smaller fraction than absorption in money terms.

In the case of a large country, the only qualification is that an inflationary policy might have an appreciable upward effect on the country's international price level. Under a regime of fixed exchange rates strong inflationary pressures in the United States, for example, could significantly raise prices throughout the world. This is the real meaning of "exporting" inflation. But the rise in the U.S. international price level would be less than the rise in the price level of domestic goods and services, since the United States accounts for only a fraction of the demand for international goods, whereas it accounts for the entire demand for purely domestic output.

Whether the country is small or large, there is one variable that under present assumptions cannot rise—namely, real output. For it has been assumed that the inflating country is characterized by full employment, a stationary labor force, and no growth in output per man-hour. But several other key economic variables can and do rise. Absorption rises in both money and real terms. In money terms absorption rises because of increased government transfer payments financed by an increasing money supply. In real terms absorption rises because the constant real output per period is augmented by rising net imports of goods and services. To put the matter another way, absorption in money terms rises by a greater proportion than the absorption price level, yielding an increase in real absorption.

MONETARY IMPLICATIONS

Does an inflationary policy of the type here considered produce, per period, a stationary payments deficit and a once-for-all rise in absorption and in the absorption price level, or does it produce a continuously rising deficit and a continuously rising price level? To answer this question, it is necessary to examine the monetary implications.

The inflationary policy here assumed is an increase in disposable money income brought about, not by an increase in real output, but by an increase in government transfer payments financed by an increase, per period, in the money supply. Against this gross increase in the money supply must be offset, however, the monetary leakage induced by the payments deficit. Assuming that the deficit is financed by an outflow of international monetary reserves involving an equivalent subtraction, per period, from the domestic money supply, this monetary leakage will at first be less than the new money created, since only a part of the increase in disposable income will be spent on imports. Thus, for a time, there will be a net increase per period in the domestic money supply, resulting in a rising absorption price level—the rise of course being concentrated on the price level of domestic goods and services.

But this rise in the absorption price level will not continue indefinitely. With the price level of domestic goods rising in relation to the price level of international goods, an increasing fraction of disposable income will be spent on imports and on exportables. Thus the payments deficit will gradually expand to the point where the monetary leakage per period is no longer less than the monetary creation per period. At this point the domestic money supply on a net basis ceases to grow, and the price level no longer rises.[5]

Thus, under present assumptions, there sooner or later emerges a stationary net money supply, a stationary price level, and a stationary payments deficit per period. But this situation can continue only so long as the deficit can be financed. The one element which does not remain stationary is the supply of international monetary reserves, which is continuously declining. The loss of reserves is a reflection of excessive real absorption, and, long before reserves are exhausted, officials in the inflating country may see the handwriting on the wall and take remedial action.

DEFLATION AS A CURE FOR EXCESSIVE ABSORPTION

All successful methods of reducing excessive absorption that do not rely on direct interference with the price system achieve their aim by altering the relation between a country's level of absorption in money terms and its absorption price level. This is clearly true, for example, of deflation. Deflation is generally thought of as a painful policy, which it may be—and certainly will be in a situation of *global* deflation. Indeed, in a situation of competitive deflation, as in the Great Depression, the problem may be insoluble. But in a situation where income and price levels abroad are stable—or, *a fortiori*, are rising—the story is clearly different.

5. Of course, by augmenting the money supply of the rest of the world, the country's payments deficit can continue to exert upward pressure on world prices. But it has already been assumed that price levels abroad are stable, which implies that foreign countries are taking appropriate monetary measures to offset any external addition to their money supplies.

In any case, it is instructive to examine exactly how deflation reduces excessive absorption. Under present assumptions it should be noted that deflation will *automatically* take place in the country that has arrested the inflation if the country's monetary policy henceforward is passive and if the payments deficit cannot be financed by borrowing from abroad. In these circumstances the deficit must be financed with reserve assets, and, as these decline, the country's money supply will decline by at least the same amount per period.[6] The decline in average cash balances will induce a decline in absorption in money terms—a decline, that is to say, in domestic expenditure on domestic goods and services, imports, importables, and exportables. The fall in absorption will have a depressing effect on the country's absorption price level, but this effect, for reasons already stated, will be much greater on the price level of domestic goods and services than on the country's international price level, which in the case of small countries will hardly drop at all. Since the decline in absorption (in money terms) will be greater than the decline in the absorption price level, there will also be a decline in real absorption.

But deflation may be painful—even under present assumptions—for the underlying disequilibrium is one in which factor prices—notably money-wage rates—are too high. Where wage rates are rigid downward, the deflationary process, as Keynes long ago emphasized, may induce substantial unemployment, and thus may be needlessly painful if it can be shown that excessive absorption can be eliminated by methods that do not induce unemployment.[7]

In practice, of course, central banks—precisely to avoid unemployment—have long interfered with any form of automatic adjustment mechanism involving deflation. If a central bank chooses to replace, per period, any monetary leakage resulting from a payments deficit, excessive absorption can continue for as long as the deficit can be financed. This may be a very long time, as the chronic U.S payments deficit illustrates. In any case, the setting in which alternatives to deflation should be evaluated is one in which excessive absorption is persisting precisely because the central bank is actively preventing any decline in the money supply that might otherwise occur. In the ensuing analysis, then, it will be assumed that the country under consideration, because of inflationary policies in the past, is in a position of excessive absorption that is persisting, not because the country is *currently* increasing its money supply at

6. Under a fractional-reserve banking system, the monetary contraction may, of course, be much greater than the decline in reserves.

7. Of course, if, because of unemployment, real output falls as rapidly as real absorption, the outlook is hopeless. But this eventuality is unlikely under the present assumption of price and income stability abroad, since the decline in the deflating country's expenditure on exportables will be accompanied by a corresponding expansion of exports.

an unwarranted rate,[8] but because the central bank is taking measures to prevent the monetary contraction that would automatically occur if monetary policy were passive.

A NEW LOOK AT DEVALUATION

As a means of reducing excessive absorption, devaluation (or exchange depreciation) has long been preferred to deflation, because it does not entail unemployment. The question, of course, is whether devaluation is effective, and the answer is: it all depends. Some postwar devaluations have been spectacularly effective in reducing excessive absorption; others have not. The failures have often been explained in terms of low import and export price elasticities, but, if the ensuing analysis is correct, the explanation lies elsewhere—and can be expressed much more simply.[9]

In the broadest macroeconomic terms, devaluation, if effective, reduces excessive absorption by altering the relation between the level of absorption expenditure and the absorption price level. In this sense, devaluation is like deflation. But deflation operates by lowering the level of absorption (in money terms) by a greater degree than it lowers the absorption price level, whereas devaluation, if effective, operates by raising the absorption price level by a greater degree than it raises absorption expenditure. Since real absorption is nothing more than absorption expenditure corrected for changes in the absorption price level, it *must* fall if the absorption price level rises by a greater fraction than absorption in money terms. And if real absorption declines sufficiently, the payments deficit will disappear, since devaluation—unlike deflation—has no tendency to reduce real output via unemployment.

It will be helpful to go over these matters point by point, taking first the rise in the absorption price level, which, as already indicated, is a blend of the import price level, the price level of exportables, and the price level of domestic goods and services. Devaluation of course raises the import price level in domestic currency, the degree of rise depending, inversely, on the devaluing country's importance in world demand. For a very small country—a country accounting for only a negligible fraction of world demand—the import price level will rise by almost the same proportion as the rise in the price of foreign currencies.

But so will the price level of exportables, for a small country will account not

8. At a rate in excess of any growth in real output.

9. This is not to deny that low average price elasticities exist, particularly on the import side. But to discuss all the misapplications of low price elasticities to problems of international disequilibrium would require a separate essay. My own views on this matter are spelled out in "Elasticity Pessimism, Absorption, and Flexible Exchange Rates" in *Essays in Honour of Jan Tinbergen,* ed. Willy Sellekaerts (London: Macmillan, 1973).

only for a small fraction of world demand but also for a small fraction of world supply. The products it sells abroad will also be produced by other countries, and any momentary price discrepancies occasioned by devaluation will be removed by middlemen—immediately in the case of primary products and more gradually in the case of other goods. The *momentary* effect of a devaluation is to reduce the devaluing country's export prices, as expressed in foreign currencies, by the full extent of the devaluation. But export prices cannot remain at that level unless the country can supply the entire world demand at those prices. This is manifestly impossible—certainly for a small country. Thus the price level of exportables, in the devaluing country's currency, will tend to rise by almost as much as the price of foreign currencies, since the increase in the country's contribution to the supply of goods absorbed in the rest of the world is negligible in relation to the rest of the world's total supply.

For a large country the import and export price levels will rise by a smaller proportion than the price of foreign currencies, the degree of rise depending, inversely, on the importance of the country in world demand and world supply. In the absence of information to the contrary there is no reason to assume that the rise in the import price level will be any greater—or any less— than the rise in the export price level. Thus there is no presumption that devaluation will affect the country's terms of trade. In some cases, of course, such an effect may occur, but it can be in either direction.[10] And in the case of really small countries, the terms of trade cannot be appreciably affected in either direction by devaluation, since both the import price level and the export price level must rise by approximately the same proportion as the rise in the price of foreign currencies.

In any case, devaluation raises the absorption price level, since two of the components—the import price level and the price level of exportables—clearly rise, while the third component—the price level of domestic goods and services—at least does not fall. But for devaluation to achieve a reduction in real absorption, the absorption price level not only must rise, but must rise by a greater fraction than the level of absorption in money terms.

10. This is not merely theory. As of December 1972, the U.S. import price level was 10.6% higher than in the third quarter of 1971—the quarter immediately prior to the December 1971 devaluation. But the U.S. export price level, despite government price restraints, rose during the same period by almost the same amount—by 10.1%. And in the U. S. devaluation of 1933–34 (undertaken expressly to raise the U.S. agricultural price level), the U.S. export price level actually rose somewhat more than the U.S. import price level. In the final quarter of 1934, the export price level was 35% higher, and the import price level was 31% higher, than in the first quarter of 1933; during the same period, the dollar price of foreign currencies, on a trade-weighted basis, increased by about 40%.

To see whether this condition can be satisfied, it is necessary to reflect only briefly on the inflationary disturbance examined in this essay. It will be recalled that, in that instance, the payments deficit was the direct result of an increase in (money and real) absorption induced by an increase in government transfer payments financed, not by an increase in taxes, but by an increase in the money supply per period. In the situation now under scrutiny, it is assumed that the monetary authorities, while not permitting the deflation that would automatically result from a passive monetary policy, are no longer augmenting the money supply. With real output per period constant, devaluation can work only if real absorption declines—which means, of course, that devaluation must raise the absorption price level by a greater proportion than it raises the level of absorption in money terms.

But this is an entirely reasonable conclusion under present assumptions. Some rise in absorption in money terms is to be expected, since there will be a rise in money income—notably in the sector of international goods (exportables and importables), where devaluation will induce a price rise. Money income in other sectors, however, will rise at a lower rate or not at all. Much, of course, will depend on the reaction of organized labor, but many forms of income (e.g., the salaries of college professors) will either not rise at all or will rise only slowly and after a considerable lag. In particular, that part of disposable income reflecting government transfer payments will not rise unless the government chooses to raise it; and it should be unnecessary to add that it would be foolish for government to boost transfer payments—at least by inflationary methods—since, in the case here considered, that is how all the trouble began.

In any case, it is clear that devaluation *can* raise the absorption price level more than it raises the level of absorption in money terms. Moreover   and this is very important—even in those sectors where money incomes have gone up by as high a proportion as the absorption price level, real absorption may fall, since, with a fixed money supply and a higher price level, real cash balances—certainly on the average—will have fallen. In old-fashioned terminology, if one assumes, as is surely reasonable, that domestic "absorbers" of all kinds make an effort to equate the marginal utility of real expenditure with the marginal utility of real cash balances, then a decline in real cash balances will induce a decline in real absorption.

CONCLUDING OBSERVATIONS

The assumptions thus far have been rather restrictive, and have stacked the cards against devaluation as an effective measure. In the real world inflation at home is often accompanied by inflation abroad, which of course makes external balance easier to achieve. Indeed, in an environment of global inflation, a country with a fixed exchange rate will find itself under pressure to inflate in some degree if it is to avoid a persistent—and expanding—payments surplus.

Also restrictive, of course, is the assumption of constant real output per period. Where devaluation has been preceded by unemployment, real output can increase rapidly, and thus may obviate any need for a lasting cut in real absorption. Even under full employment, real output will ordinarily rise gradually in response to rising output per man-hour, so that if the excessive absorption preceding devaluation is small in relation to total output, as it usually is, any reduction in real absorption immediately following devaluation can often be entirely reversed during the course of a year or two.

This does not mean that devaluation is always the appropriate response to a payments deficit. Devaluation can be a painful affair, as Americans are now learning. It avoids the pain of unemployment—and in this respect is preferable to deflation—but, in the absence of direct controls, it always confronts the consumer with a higher cost of living. Thus devaluation should not be undertaken lightly; in the American case, I am strongly persuaded, it should have been avoided both in 1971 and in 1973.

But the question here examined is whether devaluation is an effective method of reducing excessive absorption, and the answer here given is that, when coupled with appropriate policies in other sectors, it is. Where devaluation is a failure, as it often is, the explanation is almost always to be found in far more mundane matters than low or perverse price elasticities.

Basic Considerations on International Monetary Reform

Robert Triffin

I hope my readers believe firmly in the old Latin proverb *Bis repetita placent.* For indeed, my former writings—and those of others—have left me very little to say that is new about basic considerations on international monetary reform.

Events have fully confirmed the warnings that I have been repeating for more than a decade about the inherent instability and ultimate unviability of the gold-exchange standard of yesteryear. The system died in fact many years ago and was officially buried by President Nixon on 15 August 1971. Unfortunately, the paper-dollar standard put provisionally in its place by the Smithsonian agreement is even more absurd and fragile than its predecessor.

As to the basic features of the new system that countries are now trying to negotiate, they too bear a striking resemblance to those that I have been advocating, ever since 1959, and even 1957.[1] In brief, both the adjustment of world reserves to world needs and the preservation of adjustment disciplines on individual countries' balances of payments urgently require the adoption of a reserve system based on truly international reserve deposits with the Interna-

1. R. Triffin, *Europe and the Money Muddle* (Yale University Press, 1957), pp. 296–301; R. Triffin, *Gold and the Dollar Crisis* (Yale University Press, 1960), pp. 3–14; Statement of 28 October 1959 to the Joint Economic Committee of Congress; R. Triffin, *Our International Monetary System: Yesterday, Today and Tomorrow* (Random House, 1968).

tional Monetary Fund, rather than on the vagaries of the private gold market and of the balance of payments of the so-called reserve-currency countries.

FUNDAMENTAL SHORTCOMINGS OF THE SYSTEM AND
GUIDELINES FOR REFORM

The marathon debate on international monetary reform launched by the International Monetary Fund and the Group of Ten more than twelve years ago has elicited a virtually unanimous consensus on at least three broad principles that Monsieur de La Palisse himself might have ventured to advance if his counsel had been asked:

1. The expansion of international monetary reserves should adjust to the reserve requirements of the noninflationary potential of world economic growth, rather than be abandoned to the vagaries of the private gold market, of the balance of payments of one or two reserve-center countries (the United Kingdom in former years and the United States today), and of the—inevitably waning—ability of these latter countries to preserve confidence in their currency issues precariously absorbed as *international* reserves by other countries.

2. These needed increases in international monetary reserves should be earmarked for the support of *internationally agreed policies* rather than for the unlimited financing of the deficits inevitably foisted—under the present system—upon the reserve-currency countries.

3. The international settlements and reserve system should put pressure on persistent surplus countries as well as on persistent deficit countries to correct fundamental disequilibria in their balances of payments.

All three of these common-sense principles are totally flouted by the two reserve systems that have succeeded one another in the postwar years: the gold-dollar standard and the paper-dollar standard.

Under both systems central banks used *in fact* primarily the dollar—rather than gold—as means of market intervention to stabilize their rates of exchange. They sold dollars to the market to prevent an excessive depreciation of their national currency and bought dollars to prevent an excessive appreciation. This practice had not been anticipated in the IMF Articles of Agreement, which did not single out any currency for that purpose. After European countries restored convertibility in 1958, the Executive Board of the Fund felt obliged to specify that the Fund would not object to exchange margins double those (1%) authorized by Article IV, section 3(a) of the Fund Agreement, as long as these resulted from the maintenance of margins of no more than 1 percent from parity "for a convertible . . . currency."[2] Most countries indicated that they used the dollar as the reference currency in question, thus allowing their exchange rates vis-à-vis other currencies to move by twice as much as the margin legally maintained vis-à-vis the dollar. With the main exceptions of sterling area and French franc area currencies, the U.S. dollar was thus legally confirmed in its role of "international intervention currency."

Until 15 August 1971, however, the central banks that bought dollars to stabilize their exchange rate could *legally* present them at any time to the U.S. Treasury for conversion into gold metal. Under the Smithsonian paper-dollar standard, in operation since 18 December 1971, this option has vanished. Foreign central banks are now expected to redeem from the market, and retain as reserves, any overflows of dollars that would otherwise depress their price on the exchange markets beyond the new, and enlarged, margins authorized in the Smithsonian Agreement. They can escape that obligation only by reducing the dollar overflow either through an increase in their own prices and costs levels, or through an upward readjustment of their own exchange rate—toward all other currencies as well as toward the dollar—or by exchange restrictions against foreign currency inflows and/or against their own exports.

The main difference between the two systems is that under the gold-dollar standard, actual conversions of dollars into gold by foreign central banks could put some pressure on the United States to readjust its own domestic policies, exchange rates, or exchange controls, whereas under the paper-dollar standard no such pressure can be put by them on the United States. In fact, however, actual conversions—though legally permissible—had gradually fallen into disuse long before the dollar was declared legally inconvertible on 15 August 1971. Gold-convertible obligations to foreign central banks had begun to exceed the total U.S. gold stock as early as 1964 and had risen by July 1971 to more than five times the declining gold holdings available to the U.S. Treasury to honor demands for gold conversion. The facade of the system could only be salvaged by more and more reluctant voluntary restraints by foreign countries in the actual exercise of their gold conversion rights. Such restraints were impelled upon them both by the fear of bringing the open collapse of the system and by the various forms of financial, economic, and political pressures that the United States could bring to bear upon the countries that attempted to cash their claims for gold metal at the Treasury.

2. Decision No. 904, of 24 July 1959. The General Council of the Fund considered that this enlargement of margins constituted technically a multiple-currency practice but could be authorized as such under Article VIII, section 3 of the Agreement.

TABLE 1

SOURCES OF WORLD GROSS RESERVES, 1937–71
(In billions of U.S. dollars)

	As of the End of			Changes over Period		
	1937	1949	1971	Total 1950–71	20 Years 1950–69	2 Years 1970–71
I. Gold	25.3	35.0	44.8	9.8[a]	6.0	3.8[a]
II. Credit Reserves	2.4	10.6	87.4	76.9	26.7	50.2
1. Reserve Currencies	2.4	10.4	70.7	69.3	22.0	47.3
a) Dollars	0.4	3.4	51.1	47.7	12.7	35.1
b) Euro-Currencies, etc.[b]	0.2	0.1	20.7	20.6	7.4	13.3
c) Sterling	1.7	6.9	7.8	0.9	2.0	− 1.1
2. Credit from Int'l Monetary Organizations[c]	....	0.2	0.8	0.7	4.7	− 4.0
3. SDR Allocations	x	x	6.9	6.9	x	6.9
Total	27.7	45.5	132.1	86.6	32.7	53.9

Source: *International Financial Statistics* and Supplements. See also table 4 below.
[a]Of which $3.5 billion due to gold revaluation from $35 to $38 per ounce.
[b]Of which a large component of Euro-dollar liabilities (see line 1 b) and footnote 2 of table 2.
[c]IMF, Bank for International Settlements and European Fund.

A few figures cast a crude light upon the actual functioning of the system and its utter contradiction of the three principles enunciated above.

1. First, we examine the current system's impact upon the *over-all growth of the world reserve pool* (see tables 1 and 2).

Increases in global reserves averaged a modest 3% per year over the 20 years 1950–69, but actually declined in 1949 and 1959, for instance, while rising to 7% in 1950, and exploding to 18% in 1970 and 43% in 1971. Reserve increases over these last *two years alone* reached $53.9 billion, i.e., more than the $51.6 billion increase of the previous 32 *years* (1938–69).

Gold played a minor, and declining, role in these increases: only 4% of total reserve growth in the 1960s and less than half of 1% in 1970–71. The inflationary explosion of world reserves was essentially due to the disproportionate and growing impact of *national* currency issues—primarily dollars—accumulated as *international* reserves by other countries. Dollar, Euro-currency, and—to a minor extent—sterling balances added more than $69 billion to world reserves in the postwar years 1950–71, accounting for more than 90% of their total growth (see line II, 1, of column 4, table 1).

2. The second common-sense principle gradually rallying agreement is that needed increases in international monetary reserves should be earmarked for the financing of *policies internationally agreed* among the reserve holders. In fact, four-fifths of the $92.4 billion of net reserves accumulated by foreign countries over the 22 years 1950–71, served to finance large and persistent net reserves losses of the United States, totaling over these years $73 billion. Foreign countries' net reserves rose from a paltry $12.4 billion at the end of 1949 to a record $104.8 billion at the end of 1971, while U.S. net reserves fell from *plus* $22.7 billion to *minus* $50.3 billion (see table 3).

TABLE 2

NET AND GROSS MONETARY RESERVES
(In billions of U.S. dollars)

End of	1937	1949	1959	1969	1970	1971	June 1972
I. Net Reserves = Monetary Gold	25.3	35.0	40.2	41.0	41.3	44.7[a]	44.9[a]
A. United States	12.4	22.7	10.9	− 0.1	− 10.7	− 39.8	− 43.8
1. Assets	12.8	26.0	21.5	17.0	14.5	13.2	13.3
2. Liabilities	− 0.4	− 3.4	− 10.6	− 17.0	− 25.2	− 52.9	− 57.1
a. to Nat'l Mon. Auth.	− 0.4	− 3.4	− 10.1	− 16.0	− 23.8	− 50.7	− 54.6
b. to IMF	x	....	− 0.5	− 1.0	− 0.6	− 0.6	....
c. SDR Allocations	x	x	x	x	− 0.9	− 1.7	− 2.5
B. Other Countries	13.2	12.4	28.4	47.0	65.4	104.8	113.8
1. Assets	14.9	19.5	35.9	61.2	78.1	118.9	133.1
2. Liabilities (−)	− 1.7	− 7.1	− 7.5	− 13.4	− 12.7	− 14.1	− 19.3
a. to Nat'l Mon. Auth. (f bal)	− 1.7	− 6.9	− 7.0	− 8.0	− 6.6	− 7.8	− 11.0
b. to IMF	x	− 0.2	− 0.4	− 4.1	− 3.3	− 1.5	− 1.1
c. to BIS & European Fund	....	0.1	− 0.1	− 0.4	− 0.2	0.4	0.4
d. SDR Allocations	x	x	x	x	− 2.5	− 5.2	− 7.6
C. Undetermined	− 0.2	− 0.1	0.9	− 6.8	− 13.4	− 20.3	− 25.1
1. Euro-Currencies, etc.[b]	− 0.2	− 0.1	0.8	− 7.5	− 14.1	− 21.2	− 25.9
2. IMF Profits	x	....	0.1	0.7	0.8	0.8	0.8
II. Credit Reserves	2.4	10.5	17.2	37.2	51.3	87.4	101.5
A. Reserve Currencies = − (IA2a + IB2a + IC1)	2.4	10.4	16.2	32.4	44.5	70.7	91.5
B. IMF Credits = − (IA2b + IB2b)	x	0.2	0.8	4.4	3.1	1.2	0.3
1. Reserve Positions in IMF	x	1.7	3.3	6.7	7.7	6.9	7.0
2. Minus Gold & SDR holdings	x	− 1.5	− 2.4	− 2.3	− 4.6	− 5.7	− 6.7
C. BIS and EF Credits = − (IB2c)	....	− 0.1	0.1	0.4	0.2	− 0.4	− 0.4
D. SDR Allocations = − (IA2c + IB2d)	x	x	x	x	3.4	6.0	10.1
III. Gross Reserves = (I + II)	27.7	45.5	57.4	78.2	92.5	132.1	146.1
A. United States = (IAI)	12.8	26.0	21.5	17.0	14.5	13.2	13.3
B. Other Countries = (IB1)	14.9	19.5	35.0	61.2	78.1	118.9	133.1

Sources: *International Financial Statistics* (October 1972) and varia for earlier estimates

[a]Of which $3.5 billion from dollar devaluation.
[b]Of which estimated U.S. liabilities of $2.9 billion in 1969, $8.8 billion in 1970 and $9.3 billion in 1971 (see IMF 1972 *Annual Report*, p, 27, estimates in billions of SDR's).

TABLE 3

SOURCES OF NET RESERVE INCREASES
FOR COUNTRIES OTHER THAN THE UNITED STATES, 1937–71
(In billions of U.S. dollars)

	AS OF THE END OF			CHANGE OVER PERIOD		
	1937	1949	1971	Total 1950–71	20 Years 1950–69	2 Years 1970–71
I. U.S. Reserve Losses[a]	−12.4	−22.7	50.3	73.0	25.6	47.3
A. Reported	−12.4	−22.7	40.2	62.9	22.7	40.1
B. Unreported[b]	....	....	10.1	10.1	2.9	7.9
II. World Monetary Gold	25.3	35.0	44.8	9.8	6.0	3.8
A. At $35 an ounce	25.3	35.0	41.3	6.2	6.0	0.2
B. Impact of 1971 dollar devaluation	x	x	3.5	3.5	x	3.5
III. Other[c]	0.2	0.1	9.8	9.7	3.8	5.9
Total	13.2	12.4	104.8	92.4	35.5	57.0

Source: *International Financial Statistics* and Supplements.
[a]Minus sign in first two columns indicates cumulative reserve gains of the U.S.
[b]Euro-dollar liabilities of the U.S. to monetary authorities, as estimated in Table 7, p. 27 of the 1972 *Annual Report* of the IMF (recalculated from SDR's into dollars).
[c]Difference between foreign-exchange assets and liabilities, other than described in footnote 2, minus undistributed IMF profits.

The U.S. policies thus financed by foreign central banks probably commanded widespread support in the first part of this period. U.S. deficits could be ascribed largely to U.S. expenditures for common defense against actual or widely feared communist aggression and to U.S. foreign assistance for reconstruction of countries ravaged by World War II and the financing of the less-developed areas of the world. In the latter part of the period, however, more and more questions could legitimately be raised by the lenders about the role of the escalation of the Vietnam War and of American penetration or take-over of European business firms in the U.S. deficits they were financing.

3. Last, but not least, the system flagrantly contradicted the third objective of a well-functioning monetary order, i.e., the preservation of an international discipline putting pressure on persistent surplus as well as on persistent deficit countries to correct fundamental disequilibria in their balances of payments.

Persistent surplus countries could elude such readjustment by intervening in the exchange market, in the defense of undervalued (overcompetitive) exchange rates and by absorbing (through indefinitely growing monetary reserves) the dollars overflowing from the deficit countries. The United States, on the other hand, could avoid readjustment of either its internal policies or its exchange rate by palming off more and more dollar IOUs on foreign central banks. The figures quoted in paragraph 2 above indicate the extent to which this occurred in fact.

INTELLECTUAL CONSENSUS ON THE
OUTLINE OF A REFORMED SYSTEM

These glaring shortcomings of the postwar international dollar standard have finally elicited a broad intellectual consensus, in official as well as in academic circles, on the need for total reform and on the basic characteristics that should be guided by the three common-sense principles summarized above.

1. First and foremost, future reserve increases should consist essentially in *reserve accounts* with the IMF, similar to the SDR's, and whose creation should be systematically adjusted to the reserve requirements of the potential for noninflationary growth of world trade and production. They should no longer be abandoned, as in the past, to the irrelevant vagaries of the gold and dollar markets. The role of gold and dollars—or any other so-called reserve currencies—in the future settlement and reserve system should be sharply circumscribed to implement this objective.

a. As far as *gold* is concerned, short-term and long-term goals are both reasonably clear. In the short run, the only essential commitment to be required from member countries is the observation of article IV, section 2, of the Fund Agreement: "No member should buy gold at a price above par value plus the prescribed margin, or sell gold at a price below par value minus the prescribed margin."[3] Since the market price of gold is nearly certain to fluctuate in the future well above its par value, the first part of this rule is all that matters: members might therefore be allowed to sell, *but not to buy,* gold at a price above par value plus the prescribed margin. Such sales were barred in effect by the March 1968 agreement among Gold Pool members, but there are various indications that officials might be ready to scrap this prohibition—as strongly suggested by the chairman of the U.S. Joint Economic Subcommittee on International Exchange and Payments—and to revert to the Articles of Agreement authorizing such sales. This would unblock the present gold holdings of members, blocked in effect by the two-tier system now in operation.

It would be highly desirable—even if not strictly indispensable—to channel such sales through the IMF, in order to assure orderly marketing of the gold that members might wish to sell. Members might sell gold to the Fund on consignment and be credited, in their reserve account, at a price corresponding to that obtained by the Fund when selling to the market.

Fund sales at market prices to the monetary authorities—as distinct from the private market—might also be contemplated, but this would require fundamen-

3. This margin was set by rule F-4 (adopted 10 June 1947, amended 15 October 1954, and extended 5 November 1954) at either one-quarter of one percent plus various charges, or one percent inclusive of such charges, at the option of each Fund member.

tal changes in the Articles of Agreement, so as to divorce exchange rates from gold, in terms of which they are now defined. Gold would have to be replaced as *numéraire* by the IMF unit of account, i.e., exchange rates as well as reserve accounts with the Fund would have to be defined in terms of this unit of account, rather than in gold. Gold would become merchandise, like any other, and would ultimately be phased out of the monetary system, thus following the same fate as silver. This demonetization process, however, would be a slow and gradual one, as central banks would not wish to hurry it and to depress unduly the price of a commodity of which they still hold nearly $40 billion in global reserves.

All that matters in the near future is that current gold production and private holdings should not be monetized by central banks' purchases from the market, except in the highly unlikely event of a drop of the market price to, or below, parity.

The only logical alternative to the proposal above would be a steep increase in the official gold price to about twice its previous level, or more. This, however, would be absurd on two counts:

(1) It would flood world reserves overnight with about $40 billion or more of additional reserve assets and add more fuel to already bloated reserve levels and other disturbing inflationary pressures on monetary policies.

(2) It would once more enthrone the vagaries of private gold production and absorption as a main determinant of world reserve creation—or destruction—thus contradicting the first basic objective of the international monetary reform now under negotiation. Nobody could predict the impact of the new gold price on the future evolution of the world reserve pool, but it would certainly not adjust it to the reserve requirements of the noninflationary growth potential of the world economy.

b. The second problem raised by the concentration of reserves in "reserve accounts with the Fund" is that of the *national* currencies—overwhelmingly the U.S. dollar—now used as *international* reserves. Such currencies will inevitably continue to be used as "intervention currencies" by the monetary authorities to keep market rates of exchange within agreed margins,[4] as long as reserve accounts with the Fund are reserved to the monetary authorities and cannot be held by private banks, firms, and individuals.

In order not to frustrate the basic objective of the reform, however, such holdings should be held down in the future to the modest amount of "working

4. Note, however, that the reduction of such margins between EEC and associated currencies will result in a bypassing of the dollar in many of these operations.

balances'' needed for daily interventions in the market. Any balances acquired from the market and exceeding an agreed ceiling—which might be set up realistically at about 5% of annual imports, or 15% of global reserves—would be converted immediately into reserve accounts with the IMF. Conversely, central banks would draw on their reserve account to procure, at any time, the currency, or currencies, needed to replenish their working balances, whenever depleted to excess by their sales of foreign exchange to the market.

All such operations should, of course, be credited to, and debited from, the IMF reserve account of the two countries involved in each transaction. An exception would have to be made, however, at the initiation of the system for the enormous excess balances in reserve currencies—overwhelmingly U.S. dollars—inherited from more than half a century of functioning of the previous international monetary system. This outstanding "overhang" could not be deducted overnight from the debtor countries' reserve accounts. It should preferably be retained by the Fund as *consols*—or *rentes perpétuelles*—carrying appropriate interest rates and exchange-rate guarantees, but to be amortized only when the debtor countries' reserves increase beyond "normal levels" (as discussed later in this paper, in connection with the adjustment mechanism).

This semi-consolidation of the "overhang" is indeed essential to permit the restoration of the convertibility of the dollar.

The first and most obvious reason for this is that outstanding U.S. liabilities to foreign monetary authorities now approximate $60 billion, i.e., more than 4½ times the total reserve assets—gold, SDRs, reserve positions in the Fund, and foreign exchange—into which they could possibly be converted. These assets ($13.2 billion as of the end of September 1972) are only about 23% of the current annual rate of U.S. imports, and might be deemed inadequate to sustain convertibility, even if not overmortgaged by the overhang of past debts. Consideration should certainly be given to strengthening them through stabilization loans floated on the international market and/or subscribed by central banks of the largest reserve holders.

The second reason requiring consolidation of the overhang is that it would be indispensable to enable the U.S. to earn reserves when in surplus and to lose reserves only when in deficit. Without consolidation

(1) the settlement of surpluses might often take the form of debt reduction, while

(2) reserve losses could occur, even when the United States is in equilibrium or in surplus, whenever any foreign country settles with previously accumulated dollars deficits with countries that do not wish to add such

dollars to their existing holdings and present them, therefore, to the United States for conversion.

2. The second common-sense principle on which agreement is slowly emerging is that reserve increases should be used for internationally agreed-upon objectives. The implementation of the first principle, just discussed, would already ensure that they are not automatically used—as in the past—to finance the private gold market and the deficits of the United States. Reserve increases would center on the accumulation of SDR types of reserve accounts with the Fund.

SDR allocations, however, are now distributed among all Fund members *pro rata* of their Fund quotas, irrespective of the national policies that they may help finance. Richer countries receive the major share of that pie. Widespread support is gathering now for an old proposal of mine that would allot a portion of SDR allocations to financing of the underdeveloped countries by the IDA, the IBRD, and so on, without, however, changing the monetary criteria governing the total size of SDR creations.[5]

Other internationally agreed objectives that would qualify for support would include the traditional objectives of IMF operations, and particularly the recycling of reversible capital movements in accordance with the criteria now observed by the IMF General Arrangements to Borrow.

One could even envisage, in the longer run, when responsible officials and public opinion have become sufficiently familiar with the problem, the use of reserve creation for the financing of other objectives commanding high priority in the international community, such as the fight against war, pollution, contagious diseases, illiteracy, and so on.

3. Third and last, but not least, is the wide consensus that has been reached regarding the need to accelerate the adjustment process and enforce it symmetrically on surplus countries as well as on deficit countries.

The implementation of the first principle above would, by itself, remove one of the main shortcomings of the present system. Reserve currency countries would no longer enjoy the unique and extravagant privilege of escaping reserve pressures for readjustment by being able to settle their deficits with their own IOUs rather than with their limited reserve assets. Persistent deficits would deplete such reserves and make it impossible for them—as has always been the case for all other deficit countries—to postpone indefinitely the readjustment of their exchange-rate and/or domestic policies.

5. This recommendation has been unanimously endorsed by the Subcommittee on International Exchange and Payments of the Joint Economic Committee of the United States Congress.

Yet, the process might still be slow for countries in deficit, and would not put any corresponding pressures on surplus countries, since these are always able to resist adjustment by selling their own currency—rather than foreign exchange—to the market.

A large consensus has now emerged on the need to accelerate the readjustment of inappropriate exchange rates that force persistent surpluses on some countries and persistent deficits on others. The most radical proposal, espoused by a number of academic professors, would be to bar all exchange interventions and let exchange rates float freely on the markets. Such a view has found little favor so far in official circles, and for excellent reasons. Exchange-rate changes have a destabilizing impact on domestic prices and wages, and this impact is practically irreversible, under modern conditions, for price and wage *increases* prompted by a devaluation. Revaluations, as well as devaluations, may also be totally inappropriate—and indeed destabilizing—to correct temporary balance-of-payments disequilibria unrelated to competetive distortions in prices and costs, but arising, for instance, from capital movements prompted by exchange-rate speculation, interest-rate differentials, and so on. Countries should be able to choose, in such cases, other and more appropriate methods to correct their deficits or surpluses.

I have long suggested that the IMF be empowered to force persistent surplus or deficit countries to consult with the Fund on the internal or external policy readjustments most adequate and acceptable to restore equilibrium. Such consultations might be requested by members, or triggered automatically by any given increase or decrease (e.g., 25%) of global reserves above or below "normal" levels. In the absence of agreement, the country might be enjoined from engaging in further market interventions in defense of a clearly overvalued or undervalued exchange rate. Other sanctions might also be considered, along the lines suggested by the U.S. secretary of the treasury at the 1972 IMF meeting.

4. All three of these basic suggestions received considerable support from many governors at the 1972 IMF meeting. Other points of agreement—which space bars me from discussing here—relate to the need to discourage or offset huge and destabilizing capital movements. Some, however, place the main emphasis here on the broadening of exchange margins—increasing the risks for speculators—and others would advocate more effective consultations on interest rates and/or cooperative definition and implementation of measures aiming at restricting undesirable types of capital movements and encouraging others.

5. Prospects for ultimate agreement on worldwide monetary reform certainly brightened at the 1972 IMF meeting, especially after the very substantive and

conciliatory speeches of the U.S. secretary of the treasury and the French minister of finance. A broad, preliminary, outline agreement may emerge at a subsequent IMF meeting, but the finalization and ratification of proposed amendments to the IMF Articles of Agreement will still take considerable time.

Ad hoc cooperation between the major powers will be badly needed in the meantime to surmount the dollar crises that are bound to be triggered, not only by the huge—even though hopefully tapering-off—deficits of the United States, but also by the deficits of any other country, under the present system of universal paper-dollar settlements. Progress toward regional monetary union in the European Community—and in other parts of the world—would be helpful in this respect if it enables member countries, as Mr. Shultz said at the 1972 IMF meeting, "to speak with one voice and to be treated as a unit for purposes of applying the basic rules of the international monetary and trading system."

This brings me to a third topic, of basic significance for international monetary reform, but on which I shall be exceedingly brief: the role of the emerging monetary union of the European Community in the worldwide monetary system.

THE EMERGING EUROPEAN MONETARY UNION

The Paris Summit Conference of 19–21 October 1972 solemnly reaffirmed the determination of the member states of the enlarged European Communities irreversibly to complete their economic and monetary union before the end of the present decade, and spelled out the broad objectives that they will have to implement *jointly* both as to their internal relations and as to the growing world responsibilities incumbent upon Western Europe in its relations with other industrial countries, the less-developed countries, and the socialist countries of Eastern Europe.

The first steps toward monetary union have been taken already, but the crucial decision reached at the Paris meeting was to set up before 1 April 1973 a European Monetary Cooperation Fund, and to request a report, before the end of 1973, on the conditions for the progressive pooling of the member countries' international monetary reserves.

If this program is adhered to, it will have an enormous impact on the negotiation and implementation of the worldwide monetary reforms discussed above.

1. First of all, it would make the *system of intra-European settlements* less exclusively dependent on the U.S. dollar than it was until March 1971. Stabilization interventions by central banks in the exchange market could be carried out directly in member currencies, reducing the margins of fluctuations among them at least by half of the margins that would be entailed by dollar

settlements, and making it possible to reduce such margins further and even to eliminate them entirely, as envisaged in the final stages of the program for full monetary union.

This is, of course, the exact opposite of the provisions for enlarged margins adopted in the Smithsonian agreement and likely to be retained—or even expanded further—in the worldwide reform of IMF rules. Full use of the widened IMF margins would, of course, be the very antithesis of monetary union, and might even spell the doom of the Common Market itself, since it would allow exchange rates among member currencies to fluctuate in a way tantamount to the adoption of export subsidies and import tariffs among member countries. No customs union has ever operated, historically, or could ever be expected to survive in the future, under such conditions of exchange-rate instability.

Secretary Schultz himself agreed, at the 1972 meeting of the IMF, that countries in the process of forming a monetary union—with the higher degree of political and economic integration that that implies—may want to maintain narrower bands among themselves, and should be allowed to do so.

The Summit Meeting communiqué provides that the European Monetary Cooperation Fund will, in the initial phase of its operation, make intra-Community settlements multilateral, use for this purpose a European unit of account, and regroup under a renovated mechanism the interim financing and short-term monetary support operations already agreed to. These financing provisions will be reviewed, and presumably enlarged considerably in time.

Far more important is the progressive pooling of reserves. The claims and debts arising from interim finance and short-term monetary support operations are now "settled" very largely in inconvertible dollars. This so-called settlement, however, does *not* extinguish the creditor country's claim. It merely substitutes a nonmember debtor (the United States) for the European debtor country, and without any guarantee whatsoever against any later depreciation of the U.S. dollar in terms of gold, SDRs, or any national currency.

As noted by the Belgian minister of finance, Mr. Vlérick, in some recent speeches, it is paradoxical to limit parsimoniously in amount ($1.4 billion today) and in time (normally six months) the settlement credits available to members, while granting credits unlimited in amounts (more than $30 billion, as last reported) and duration to a nonmember country, without any previous agreement or guarantees whatsoever.

A better settlements system, more acceptable to creditors and debtors alike, should be devised and implemented by the European fund. Net credits and debts—after multilateral compensation—should be denominated in SDRs or in a European unit of account, and could be consolidated in the form of medium-term, or even long-term, obligations denominated in the same unit, transferable, as dollar balances are today, among central banks, and negotiable in the market whenever it is desirable to mop up inflationary levels of liquidity. Such obligations could be used as an instrument for the open-market operations indispensable to the effective management of the European monetary union. They could be redeemed, at any time, by the debtor country through transfers of gold, SDRs, or any currencies acceptable to the creditors.

2. *Settlements with nonmember countries* will inevitably continue to be carried out primarily in dollars until agreement is reached on the worldwide reforms discussed above.

The restoration of dollar convertibility, however, and the limitation of dollar reserves to agreed working balances could be accelerated by the European fund through the conversion of excess dollar balances into special reserve certificates essentially similar to SDRs, and exchangeable for them or any so-called substitution account, if and when IMF amendments making this possible are enacted as envisaged in the report of the IMF executive directors on the *Reform of the International Monetary System* (see particularly p. 32). As noted in the same report (p. 3), this and other aspects of the reforms now under negotiation could, if this were considered useful, be put into practice as soon as they were agreed—and before any amendments that might be required had become effective.

Close cooperation among the major financial powers (the United States, the expanded European Community, and Japan) will indeed remain crucial both

a. to palliate, in the interim period, the shortcomings of a still-unreformed international monetary system, and particularly to overcome the crises likely to be triggered by huge and persistent—even if, hopefully, tapering off—dollar overflows;

b. to promote, even in the longer run, the minimum of policy harmonization indispensable to the smooth functioning of the reformed system.

3. This brings me to a third, and final, observation on the role that an incipient European monetary union could play in the strengthening of the *adjustment mechanism* with nonmember countries, and particularly the dollar area.

The countries of the enlarged Community have been accumulating in recent years, and are still accumulating today, enormous external surpluses, financed by inflationary reserve increases totalling $9.5 billion in 1970, $17.5 billion in 1971, and—at an annual rate—well over $8 billion in the first nine months of 1972. Over the two years 1970 and 1971, these external surpluses alone—if not offset in part by domestic credit contraction—would have resulted in increases

TABLE 4

IMPACT OF 1970–71 NET RESERVE INCREASES
UPON RESERVE MONEY AND MONEY SUPPLY

	IN MILLIONS OF DOLLARS			PERCENTAGE OF 1970–71 Surpluses	
	1970–71 Surpluses	End 1969 Reserve Money	End 1969 Money Supply	To Reserve Money	To Money Supply
I. Common Market	19,617	51,830	113,010	38	17
German Federal Republic	10,702	15,200	24,600	70	44
France....................	5,221	15,000	37,100	36	14
Italy	1,920	15,200	37,100	26	5
Netherlands	1,149	2,740	6,480	42	18
Belgium-Luxembourg	625	3,690	7,730	17	8
II. Other Industrial Europe......	13,315	21,270	40,790	63	33
United Kingdom	9,445	10,130	20,530	93	46
Switzerland	2,293	4,700	9,120	19	25
Austria	600	1,860	2,550	32	24
Norway..................	359	1,120	1,980	32	18
Sweden..................	359	2,340	2,810	15	13
Denmark..................	257	1,120	3,800	23	6
III. Other Industrial Countries excluding U.S............	13,933	19,400	60,600	72	23
Japan	11,466	14,800	47,000	78	24
Canada	2,467	4,600	13,600	54	18
Total....................	46,865	92,500	214,400	51	22

Source: *International Financial Statistics.*
Column 1: item 76.
Column 2: item 14 converted into dollars at December 1969 par value.
Column 3: item 34 converted into dollars at December 1969 par value (seasonally adjusted).

of central banks' internal monetary liabilities ranging from 17% in Belgium to 70% in Germany and 93% in the United Kingdom (see table 4). It is obviously of vital interest to the Community to reduce such excessive and inflationary surpluses.

The European Fund for Monetary Cooperation should develop the means to deal with this problem more realistically and efficiently than is possible for national monetary authorities acting independently from one another.

Pressure should, of course, continue to be applied on the major deficit countries to reduce their deficits through monetary and fiscal policies. Full-employment objectives must be accepted as a must, but should be pursued primarily through fiscal and budgetary policies, and interest-rate policies should be primarily earmarked for balance-of-payments equilibrium. Close consultations between the European Community and other major financial centers, particularly the United States, should be given a high priority in this respect.

A realistic appraisal of the political forces at work, however, strongly suggests that feasible harmonization of internal policies will remain insufficient to ensure reasonable balance-of-payments equilibrium between independent and sovereign countries, in the future as well as in the past. The European

Community must accept this disabused conclusion as a fact of life, and choose, therefore, between the two alternative courses of action realistically open to it, or a combination of them.

The first, and most appropriate, would be to revalue its currencies upward to the extent necessary to reduce to acceptable limits its stabilization interventions on the exchange market. Such a course of action has been chosen only sparingly in the past because of the opposition of export industries and import-competing industries to the implied worsening of their competitive position in world markets, resulting in lower profits for the shareholders and loss of employment by their workers.

This obstacle would be vastly reduced if such currency revaluations were, in the future, decided and implemented *jointly* by the countries of the Community and those most likely to join them in a European monetary area. Mutual trade among such countries currently encompasses ⅔ to ¾ of their total exports, as compared with about 8% only for their exports to the United States. Exchange-rate readjustments with nonmember countries would raise far less resistance, when needed to restore competitive conditions with these countries, if stability could be preserved among the currencies of the European area itself.

The progressive pooling of reserves, envisaged at the Summit meeting in 1974, would be the logical instrument for such joint decisions and their joint implementation by members. The limits of stabilization interventions in the exchange market could be decided directly—letting the exchange rate itself be determined as a consequence by the market—or, alternatively, the buying rates of foreign currencies could be moved *parallelly* upward, reducing as a consequence the size of needed market interventions. A combination of these two alternative policies, limiting either the size of interventions or the pace of exchange-rate fluctuations could possibly prove to be the most acceptable solution to the problem.

Another way of limiting excessive and inflationary reserve increases by the surplus countries of the Community has been widely resorted to recently. This is to limit, through various forms of exchange controls, excessive capital inflows into the exchange market. These measures, however, have been taken primarily so far on a purely national scale, thus interfering unnecessarily with the freedom of capital movements within the Community itself. One of the first objectives of the European Fund should be to resume the movement toward a unified European capital market by limiting the applications of such controls to undesirable capital inflows from outside the Community.

Once the machinery for such joint controls has been established, close consultations with other major financial centers—particularly the United States and Japan—would make it possible to seek a joint definition and implementation of measures designed,

a. not only to restrain the types of capital movements deemed most disequilibrating and undesirable by all concerned,

b. but also to stimulate capital movements deemed readjusting and desirable both by the capital-exporting and the capital-importing countries.

In brief, no single panacea has ever proved feasible to solve the major disequilibria that have confronted monetary authorities in the past, and will inevitably confront them again in the future, even under a reformed international monetary system. Each type of policy is subject to a margin of tolerance dictated by political as well as by economic factors. The countries of the Community will have to concert together, and to the extent possible with their major partners, the combination of policies that will prove most desirable, or least damaging, to all in dealing with such problems:

a. harmonization of internal fiscal and monetary policies, particularly with regard to a reequilibrating pattern of interest rates;

b. other measures designed to stimulate reequilibrating capital movements and to restrain or discourage disequilibrating ones;

c. temporary financing of residual disequilibria through fluctuations in monetary reserves;

d. appropriate realignment, or flexibility, of exchange rates between independent countries and countries grouped in regional monetary and economic unions.

The International Monetary Fund will remain the main forum for such concertation of policies between countries and among groups of countries, but will be able to perform this task far more smoothly and efficiently than in the past, if countries closely interdependent on one another—such as those of the European Community—are able to develop the institutional framework indispensable to devise joint, compatible policy decisions and to implement them effectively in practice.

Summary and Conclusions

The intellectual consensus that emerged both at the September 1972 IMF meeting in Washington and at the October 1972 summit meeting in Paris is impressive and opens the path toward a long overdue reform of the international monetary system and the completion of economic and monetary union by the countries of the enlarged European Community.

Two major political obstacles have been lifted by the acceptance of Britain into the European Community and by the reiteration at the Paris meeting of Europe's determination "to affirm its personality while remaining faithful to its traditional friendships and alliances."

European progress toward full economic and monetary union will greatly enhance the chances of a successful negotiation and effective implementation of worldwide monetary reform. The two objectives must be viewed as complementary rather than alternative to one another. They both have been solemnly reaffirmed, in Washington and in Paris. The laymen that we are can only hope and pray that our political leaders will, at long last, be able to translate into concrete action the objectives on which they have, at long last, reached such an impressive agreement.

United States Direct Investment in Europe and Canada, 1955–1970: A Regression Study

Sarah Montgomery

For more than a decade the growing direct investment flow from the United States to Europe and Canada has caused concern both in the United States and in the countries receiving this capital. In the United States worry has been about the potential of these flows for increasing the deficits in the balance of payments; abroad, fears have been of growing American control of major economic sectors. Table 1 presents data on U.S. direct investment in all of Western Europe, the United Kingdom, the European Economic Community (EEC),[1] and Canada, for the years 1955 through 1970. Direct investment is measured here as the sum of the flow of direct investment in the capital account of the U.S. balance of payments and American owners' share of the reinvested earnings of the foreign companies. The percentage increases from 1955 to 1970 in the last line of the table indicate the very different time trends for the several

The computations for this study were done at the University of London Computer Centre (ULCC) with financial support of a Faculty grant from Mount Holyoke College. I am grateful to both institutions. My special gratitude goes to Professor J. D. Sargan and Mr. P. Wakeford of the London School of Economics and Political Science and to Mr. P. Alpiar of ULCC for their gracious and essential help in obtaining access to the facilities of ULCC. Also, I am indebted to Judith Voris Reppy and to the editors David A. Belsley and Edward J. Kane for very helpful comments on earlier drafts of this paper. Finally, I must thank John L. Bridge for answering numbers of questions.
    1. The EEC data in this study cover only the original six members of the Community.

areas. The most rapid growth is in investment in continental Europe, the slowest, in Canada. The table also shows the book values of U.S. direct investment in each area at the end of 1954 and the end of 1970 and their percentage growth over the period. These also grew most in continental Europe and least in Canada.

Much has been written analyzing the possible cause of this direct investment.[2] Few attempts, however, have been made to subject these data and some of the more worrisome conclusions of previous studies to statistical

TABLE 1

U.S. DIRECT INVESTMENT IN CANADA AND WESTERN EUROPE, 1955–1970[a]

(In Millions of U.S. Dollars)

Year	Total Western Europe		Western Europe Excluding U.K.	U.K.		EEC	Canada
1955	349		190	159		148	695
1956	740		338	402		254	1,042
1957	581		249	332		212	1,035
1958	428		256	172		219	700
1959	750		420	330		283	810
1960	1,325	(958)[b]	576	749	(382)[b]	436	840
1961	1,056		738	318		406	568
1962	1,160		899	261		565	685
1963	1,442		1,099	343		733	898
1964	1,796		1,415	381		902	798
1965	1,876		1,308	559		854	1,502
1966	2,269		1,671	598		1,246	1,700
1967	1,727		1,315	412		893	1,052
1968	1,457		883	574		546	1,397
1969	2,102		1,635	467		1,163	1,608
1970	2,902		2,045	857		1,499	1,695
Percentage of change, 1955–70	+732		+977	+439		+913	+144
Year-end	Book Value of U.S. Investments, 1954 and 1970						
1954	2,643		1,380	1,263		1,016	6,043
1970	24,516		16,520	7,996		11,774	22,790
Percentage of change,[c] 1954–70	+828		+1097	+533		+1059	+277

Sources: [20]; [23], various issues; data provided by Bureau of Economic Analysis, U.S. Dept. of Commerce.

a Annual flows as recorded in the U.S. balance of payments plus U.S. owners' share of reinvested earnings of foreign companies. See text footnote 9 for a more detailed description.

b The number in parentheses is that used in this study. It excludes a single $367 million transaction by which an American manufacturing firm acquired the remaining foreign equity in its U.K. affiliate. This one adjustment in the data was made because of the size of this transaction relative to all the other direct investment flows to the United Kingdom during this period, and because the transaction would not be expected to have any direct connection with plant and equipment expenditures by the affiliate. (If U.S. direct investment in U.K. manufacturing, 1957–70, is regressed against plant and equipment expenditures of U.S. manufacturing affiliates in the United Kingdom, the RSQC is only .05 when this transaction is included, but is .49 when it is excluded.)

c The dollar change in the book value equals the sum of the annual direct investments plus certain valuation adjustments. See text footnote 3.

2. See [15] for a summary of both the theoretical and the empirical literature.

analysis. Two published studies include changes in the size of the foreign market as a potential factor explaining U.S. investments in Europe: V. N. Bandera and J.T. White [1] and A. E. Scarperlanda and L. J. Mauer [13].[3] Although a strong theoretical case can be made for including change in foreign GNP as an explanatory variable, both studies find that it had little effect on investment flows from the United States.[4] Both assign most of the explanatory power to the *level* of foreign GNP,[5] a variable for which it is difficult to find theoretical justification.

Bandera and White say that demand-oriented investment will go into "high—and growing— income areas" as businessmen attempt "to capture a share of a market" [1, p. 118]. However, the absolute size of the market (as distinguished from its absolute annual growth) should affect the desired amount of annual investment only if businessmen aim each year to increase their share of the market by a fixed percentage.

Scaperlanda and Mauer distinguish between the hypothesis that relates investment to changes in demand and the size-of-market hypothesis which "is that foreign investment will take place as soon as the market is large enough to permit the capturing of economies of scale" [13, p. 560]. This latter hypothesis is the basis for their including GNP as an independent variable. There appears to be little reason, however, to assume that the investment stimulated by increasing opportunities to exploit economies of scale would be proportional to the size of the market. A more promising hypothesis appears to be that the new investment opportunities and their induced levels of investment would vary directly with the growth in the size of the market.[6]

3. In [1] change in each country's total GNP is an independent variable in an analysis of U.S. direct investment, 1954–1962, in each of seven Western European countries. Investment in manufacturing, in petroleum and in trade are considered separately. In [13] change in the EEC's GNP is included in a study of U.S. total direct investment, 1952–66, in the Common Market countries, combined. In both studies direct investment flow is measured as the difference from year-end to year-end in the value of U.S. direct investment abroad. These data differ somewhat from the annual series in Table I because they include certain adjustment in valuations made in the books of the foreign companies. These changes are often associated with liquidation of assets.

4. Bandera and White find a close association between the level of GNP and the book value of direct investments, but "only a modest evidence" [1, p. 127] that annual changes in these two series are related.

5. Both pairs of authors test several other independent variables but do not find them significant.

6. The effects of lagged adjustments of the actual to the optimal capital stock have so far been ignored. If there were a large and sudden increase in the size of a market, the lag might be long, and for a substantial period the level of investment might be quite independent of any further increases in the size of the market.

I. DESIGN OF THE PRESENT STUDY

The purpose of this paper is to explore further the effect of changes in market size on U.S. foreign direct investment in developed countries, while simultaneously considering the possible influence of other factors. It is thought that the study is strengthened by the use of more annual observations than were available to earlier investigators[7] and by the inclusion of both Canadian (*C*) and Western European (*WE*) data. To this end a model explaining direct investment flows (*DI*) is developed and subjected to regression analysis. Included as independent variables are (1) change in economic activity abroad (dO_f), (2) change in U.S. economic activity (dO_{us}), (3) residual cash available to U.S. corporations (*L*), (4) a dummy to capture structural changes caused by the formation of the EEC (*M*), and (5) a dummy to reflect the program, beginning in 1965, to limit *DI* (*P*).

In linear form, the basic equation tested is:

$$DI = a + b_1 dO_f + b_2 dO_{us} + b_3 L + b_4 M + b_5 P + u \qquad (1)$$

For all areas dO_f and *P* prove significant,[8] while *M* is rejected as insignificant. *L* is significant in the European but not in the Canadian equations. dO_{us} proves significant for DI_c but is dropped from the equations for Europe because of intercorrelation with *L*. Before examining the evidence in detail, the theoretical basis for the choice of variables is developed.

This study is based on a well-known theory developed by James S. Duesenberry [7] in which the equilibrium level of real investment is that at which the marginal cost of funds used to purchase additional capital stock equals the marginal efficiency of capital. The marginal cost of funds to the firm is normally lowest for internal funds. External funds cost more and become increasingly expensive as firms expand their borrowing.

If, under these circumstances, a firm has an internal cash flow that is less than its investment needs, an increase in internal funds will lower the marginal cost of funds at the old equilibrium level of investment and, thereby, increase the desired level of investment.

In addition, the equilibrium level of investment will rise with an increase in the marginal efficiency of capital at each level of investment. This will occur if

7. A major reason for the paucity of regression studies in this field has been the very short period appropriate for investigating a number of questions about foreign investments in Europe. Lawrence B. Krause, for example, rejects the possibility of using "multivariate techniques" in analyzing direct investment in the EEC, because only eight observations (1958–65) are available [12, p. 131].

8. The equation for *DI* to the United Kingdom is an exception. In it the only significant variable is dO_f.

the desired capital stock increases relative to the actual capital stock. With given technology and factor costs and thus an unchanged optimal capital-output ratio, such increases in the desired stock will be directly related to increases in expected sales. If past sales serve as a guide to future sales, investment will be a function of changes in these.

Several extensions and adaptations of this familiar model are necessary for its application here. First, this investment theory does not indicate where new capital stock should be located. Firms investing in new facilities in response to growth in a foreign market could locate them at home or in a third area and plan to expand exports as an alternative to investment in the country where they anticipate growing sales. If they aim to maximize profits, they should locate where costs, including tariffs and transportation costs, are lowest. Assuming cost differentials are unchanging and are such that American firms choose to produce in each foreign area some part of what they sell there, investment to serve overseas markets implies some investment abroad by U.S. firms.

Secondly, the analysis in this study assumes that the collection of short-term and long-term loans and equity-capital flows that comprise U.S. direct investment[9] are closely associated with purchases of capital stock. Statistical evidence suggests that this is a defensible assumption. Equations (2) and (3) show the results of regressing DI_{we} and DI_c for 1957–70 against the plant and equipment expenditures by foreign affiliates of U.S. corporations (PE) in equations that also include P.[10]

$$DI_{we} - 141 + .62PE_{we} - 593P \tag{2}$$
$$(.96) \quad (8.77) \quad (2.28)$$
$$RSQC = .89; \ D.W. = 1.87$$

$$DI_c = -42 + .66PE_c + 7P \tag{3}$$
$$(.21) \quad (5.12) \quad (.04)$$
$$RSQC = .79; \ D.W. = 2.61$$

The corrected R^2's ($RSQC$) are .89 and .79, while the coefficients of PE are

9. The part of direct investment that is included in the capital account of the U.S. balance of payments "measures capital transactions by U.S. residents with foreign enterprises in which the U.S. residents by themselves or in affiliation with other U.S. residents own 10% or more of the voting securities or of other ownership interests" [6, p. 55]. Excluded are "any loans to foreign affiliates by U.S. banks and agencies of the U.S. Government, and commercial claims of unaffiliated U.S. persons" [26, pp. 9–10]. The dependent variable examined in this study is this total plus "United States equity in earnings on common stock after deducting applicable dividends" [20, p. 201].

10. As in all the equations, the numbers in parentheses are *t*- values.

similar for the two areas and suggest that each dollar of PE generates almost two-thirds that amount of DI.

To recapitulate, it is hypothesized that DI is closely associated with PE and that the determinants of PE will include the internal funds available to U.S. corporations (L) and changes in the size of overseas markets (dO_f). In allocating both internal and external funds, however, American firms have the alternative of expanding production facilities at home to meet the demands of the domestic market. DI should be larger as alternative domestic market opportunities are less. Change in the size of the U.S. market (dO_{us}) should, therefore, be included separately as an independent variable. This proves possible in the equation for DI_c where dO is measured by changes in industrial production (dIP). In the European equations, however, dO is measured by $dGNP$. $dGNP_{us}$ is highly correlated with L. dO_{us}, therefore, is omitted with L serving to reflect both the expected positive influence on DI of corporate liquidity and the expected negative influence of changes in the U.S. market.

Two dummy variates are also included. One reflecting the formation of the EEC (M) attempts to depict two structural changes. First, the EEC lowered trade barriers within the Community relative to the common external tariff, thereby changing the relative cost of local production for sales within the Community. Second, it is argued that the emergence of the EEC increased awareness of profitable investment opportunities in that area which had previously existed but had not been exploited [12, pp. 122–23].

The final independent variable is that designed to reflect the impact of the mandatory Foreign Direct Investment Program (FDIP) of 1968–70 and the voluntary program that preceded it. Both programs sought to lessen the balance-of-payments impact of foreign investment activity of American firms. The restraints were aimed especially at investment activity in continental Europe. Investment flow to the United Kingdom was discouraged less and that to Canada was, fundamentally, exempt.[11]

II. STATISTICAL DATA

As explained earlier, DI is measured as the sum of direct-investment flows in the U.S. balance of payments and the U.S. owners' share of reinvested earnings of overseas companies.[12] The latter data are available only in annual series,

11. Partway through the voluntary program, there was a rather muted request to restrain investment in Canada, and Canada was briefly included in the mandatory program. Soon after FDIP began, however, DI_c was exempted. The provisions of the program and its possible effects on DI are considered in more detail in section III D below.

12. See footnote 9 above for a description of what these series measure.

thus forcing this study into the many difficulties and limitations from the use of annual data. Separate equations are estimated for the flows to (1) Canada (*C*), (2) the United Kingdom (*UK*), (3) the EEC, (4) Western Europe (*WE*), and (5) Western Europe excluding the United Kingdom (*RWE*).

In early stages of the study dO_f and dO_{us} were measured by two alternative series: year-to-year changes in industrial production (*dIP*) and annual changes in *GNP* at current prices (*dGNP*). The *GNP* series has the advantage that, like *DI*, it is measured in current prices. However, because the coverage of *GNP* and *IP* is so different, and because the pattern of prices of goods bought with *DI* may differ greatly from that of the *GNP* deflator, it appears good practice to try both series in the equations.

Another question arises in this context: whether to measure *dGNP* in dollars at a fixed exchange rate (or in domestic currency units, which is a parallel series) or in dollars at current exchange rates. The greatest discrepancies between these two series occur in those years in which exchange rates were altered. Current-dollar exchange rates show much larger positive or smaller negative changes in *GNP* in those years for countries appreciating their currency and much smaller positive or larger negative changes for countries depreciating their currency.[13] The potential distortion arising from this source appears large relative to any difficulties arising from the use of fixed exchange rates. Therefore, the choice was made[14] to use Canadian *GNP* in Canadian dollars and European *GNP* in U.S. dollars at 1963 exchange rates.[15]

L is measured by corporate capital-consumption allowances plus profits after taxes and dividends. Dividends (*D*) are excluded because of the empirical and theoretical case made by studies that portray these payments as fundamentally fixed obligations.[16] It is impossible to test here for the significance of *D* because the simple *R* between *D* and *L*, 1955–70, is .9874.

13. In appreciating countries, negative changes in *GNP* measured at fixed exchange rates may become positive changes at current exchange rates, and in depreciating countries positive changes in *GNP* may become negative.

14. The best criterion for resolving the question of whether to use fixed or current exchange rates, of course, would be which *dGNP* series best reflects the factors influencing the U.S. investor. To answer that, however, would require a great deal of knowledge of the relationship between national rates of inflation and exchange rate adjustments and of the effect of exchange rate changes on the expectations of investors. No simple assumptions seemed defensible.

15. Early in the investigation, however, a number of regressions were run using *dGNP* for European areas at current dollar exchange rates. The equations for the United Kingdom were seriously affected by the 1967 devaluation. The regressions for the rest of Europe were not greatly changed.

16. For a brief discussion and references, see [4, pp. 149, 166].

M is set at zero through 1958, the last year before the EEC's internal tariffs began to fall, and at unity for subsequent years.

Two series are used to measure P: P_{we}, which is employed in all equations except that for the United Kingdom, and P_{uk}. They are derived from a dummy variable developed by R. Herring and T. D. Willett for their study of the impact of FDIP [11]. When measuring the relative annual severity of the restraints, they set all years before 1966 at zero and assign the following values to 1966 through 1969: .1; .2; 1.0; and .8. These figures are used for P_{we} with the addition of a 1970 figure of .65. The latter was chosen quite arbitrarily to reflect the further easing of controls between 1969 and 1970, which, however, entailed no radical changes in the regulations.[17] The expected sign of the coefficient of P_{we} in the European equations is negative. In the equations for DIC, P_{we}, if significant, is expected to have a positive coefficient as DI is diverted from Europe to Canada.

The voluntary program treated foreign investment in the United Kingdom like that in the rest of Europe. Under the mandatory program, however, investment in the United Kingdom was less severely limited. To reflect this difference in the treatment of the United Kingdom, P_{uk} is the same as P_{we} through 1967, but is only 54% as large for 1968–70.[18]

Herring and Willett say that their series "must be regarded as a very impressionistic approximation of the stringency of the various control programs" [11, p. 68]. The adaptations of it used here are even cruder, but they do have the virtue of having been developed independently of this study and of not having been subject to tampering or experimentation designed to improve the statistical results.

17. A number of sources, for example, [9, p. 28], refer to this further easing of the regulations. In addition, there may have been some lessening of the influence of the regulations because firms were both increasingly unwilling to postpone expenditures abroad and increasingly able to find ways of making expenditures under given regulations.

18. The United Kingdom was on Schedule B while all of the continental European countries (except Greece and Finland) were on Schedule C. Investment in Schedule C countries was limited to 35% of that in 1965–66 while investment in Schedule B countries was to be no more than 65% of 1965–66 level. On this basis the restraints on DI_{uk} were 54% as severe as those on DI_{we}.

The restrictions applied to the investment in all countries on a schedule, combined, not to that in each country individually. This may cause difficulty with the equation for the United Kingdom, only one of a diverse group of nations on Schedule B, but would be expected to cause less trouble in the equations for aggregates of continental European countries, since they predominate in Schedule C.

For information on the voluntary and mandatory programs, see [11] [21, 1 March 1965, pp. 11–24; 23 December 1965, pp. 2–4; 8 January 1968, pp. 2–7]; and [27, 1971, p. 145].

Both theoretical analysis and empirical evidence strongly indicate that models of real capital formation should include lagged relationships among the variables and that the effects of changes in the independent variables should be spread over extended periods. Since *DI* is assumed to be closely linked with *PE*, such time patterns also should be part of this model. The use of annual data and the limited number of observations, however, preclude sophisticated formulation of the lags. Instead, several alternatives were tried using simple annual lags and two-year moving averages. The averages ultimately were selected because the more gradual influence that they portray appears more defensible economically and because statistically the equations with the series averaged were about as satisfactory as those with simple annual lags.

III. REGRESSION RESULTS

Table 2 presents the final estimates for the Western European areas. dO_f is measured by $[(GNP_t - GNP_{t-1}) + (GNP_{t-1} - GNP_{t-2})]/2$. As already indicated, dO_{us} measured in the same way is highly correlated with L.[19] One of the two variables has to be excluded, and the other has to serve as a proxy for the combined effects of both. Whichever variable is chosen, its coefficient is positive. Since that would be the expected sign for L if both variables could be included in the equation, while dO_{us} would be expected to be negatively related to *DI*, the influence of L appears to dominate. The interpretation of the results is, therefore, more straightforward if L serves to represent both effects. It is an average of t and $t - 1$ values.

Equations (4) through (7) include *M,* but it does not prove significant and, in the case of the EEC itself, has a negative coefficient. The equations reestimated without *M* are (8) through (11).

The final estimates for Canada are in table 3. Here dO_c is measured by *dIP*. Although it is anticipated that a series that measures *dO* in current prices would better "explain" direct investment than a volume series, in the Canadian equations *dIP* outperforms *dGNP*. It may be that, in the Canadian case, the relative composition of *GNP* makes it a poor measure of the market served by affiliates of U.S. parent companies, whereas the composition of the industrial production index is more appropriate. Since dO_c is measured by dIP_c, it appears preferable to measure dO_{us}, which may compete for *DI* dollars, by dIP_{us}. Not surprisingly, however, given the close interrelations of the two nations, dIP_c

19. For the sample period the simple $R = .9723$. Two reasons for the collinearity between L and dO_{us} probably are (1) that both are strongly influenced by the upward trend in the economy and (2) that most components of national income change gradually and, therefore, when income rises particularly rapidly (slowly), profits, the residual component, will be at high (low) levels.

TABLE 2

Equations for U.S. Direct
Investment in Europe, Anually, 1955–70

DI_{we}	$= \quad -832$	$+ \quad 23.7L$	$+ \quad 30.3dO_{we}$	$+ \quad 128.9M$	$- \quad 792P_{we}$ (4)
	(5.79)	(4.72)	(8.25)	(1.36)	(5.31)
					RSQC $= .97$; D.W. $= 3.10$
DI_{uk}	$= \quad 33$	$- \quad 1.6L$	$+ \quad 79.5dO_{uk}$	$+ \quad 30.8M$	$+ \quad 23.0P_{uk}$ (5)
	(.29)	(.34)	(3.37)	(.44)	(.11)
					RSQC $= .75$; D.W. $= 2.42$
DI_{rwe}	$= \quad -856$	$+ \quad 21.5L$	$+ \quad 26.5dO_{rwe}$	$+ \quad 129.0M$	$- \quad 780P_{we}$ (6)
	(6.96)	(5.11)	(7.54)	(1.59)	(6.10)
					RSQC $= .97$; D.W. $= 2.87$
DI_{eec}	$= \quad 712$	$+ \quad 19.8L$	$+ \quad 23.8dO_{eec}$	$- \quad 18.1M$	$- \quad 616P_{we}$ (7)
	(6.73)	(5.91)	(6.64)	(.25)	(5.46)
					RSQC $= .95$; D.W. $= 3.18$
DI_{we}	$= \quad -885$	$+ \quad 26.8L$	$+ \quad 30.7dO_{we}$	$- \quad 855P_{we}$	(8)
	(6.19)	(5.76)	(8.09)	(5.82)	
				RSQC $= .97$; D.W. $= 3.10$	
DI_{uk}	$= \quad 15$	$- \quad .5L$	$+ \quad 77.6dO_{uk}$	$- \quad 11P_{uk}$	(9)
	(.15)	(.12)	(3.46)	(.05)	
				RSQC $= .77$; D.W. $= 2.50$	
DI_{rwe}	$= \quad -908$	$+ \quad 24.4L$	$+ \quad 27.0dO_{rwe}$	$- \quad 844P_{we}$	(10)
	(7.22)	(6.11)	(7.29)	(6.54)	
				RSQC $= .96$; D.W. $= 2.52$	
DI_{eec}	$= \quad -704$	$+ \quad 19.4L$	$+ \quad 23.7dO_{eec}$	$- \quad 607P_{we}$	(11)
	(7.22)	(6.91)	(6.94)	(5.91)	
				RSQC $= .96$; D.W. $= 3.15$	

Symbols:

DI = U.S. direct investment in millions of U.S. dollars (data in table 1).

L = U.S. corporate undistributed profits after taxes plus capital consumption allowances, in billions of current dollars, moving averages of t and $t - 1$. (Original data in appendix.)

dO = Moving average of annual changes $[(t - 1) - (t - 2)]$ and $[t - (t - 1)]$ in GNP at market prices, billions of U.S. dollars at 1963 exchange rates. (Original data in appendix.)

M = Dummy for formation of EEC: 1955–58 $= 0$; 1959–70 $= 1$.

P_{we} = Dummy for programs limiting foreign direct investment to continental Europe: 1955–65 $= 0$; subsequent years: .1; .2; 1.0; .8; .64.

P_{uk} = Dummy for programs limiting foreign direct investment to the United Kingdom: 1955–65 $= 0$; subsequent years: .1; .2; .54; .43; .35.

and dIP_{us} are highly correlated. The equation, therefore, does not include dO_{us} but the difference between dO_c and $dO_{us}(dO_{us-c})$.[20] dO_c and dO_{us} and L are averages with a year-longer lag than those specified in the European equations.[21]

20. For the sample period the simple R between dO_c and dO_{us} is .9297, whereas that between dO_c and dO_{us-c} is only .2264.

TABLE 3

EQUATIONS FOR U.S. DIRECT
INVESTMENT IN CANADA, ANNUALLY, 1955–70

$$DI_c = 341 + 1.9L + 81.6dO_c - 126.0dO_{us-c} - 22.2M + 634P \quad (12)$$
$$(.88) \quad (.11) \quad (1.59) \quad (2.85) \quad (.10) \quad (1.28)$$
$$\text{RSQC} = .74; \text{D.W.} = 1.84$$

$$DI_c = 367 + .4L + 85.4dO_c - 126.1dO_{us-c} + 671P_{wc} \quad (13)$$
$$(1.35) \quad (.04) \quad (2.47) \quad (2.99) \quad (2.06)$$
$$\text{RSQC} = .77; \text{D.W.} = 1.82$$

$$DI_c = 377 + 86.5dO_c - 126.2dO_{us-c} + 682P_{wc} \quad (14)$$
$$(3.26) \quad (4.79) \quad (3.12) \quad (4.44)$$
$$\text{RSQC} = .79; \text{D.W.} = 1.82$$

$$DI_c = -91 + 23.8L + 26.7dO_c - 119.3dO_{us-c} - 223.5M \quad (15)$$
$$(.47) \quad (3.64) \quad (.92) \quad (2.64) \quad (1.46)$$
$$\text{RSQC} = .73; \text{D.W.} = 2.13$$

$$DI_c = -59 + 18.1L + 38.2dO_c - 114.4dO_{us-c} \quad (16)$$
$$(.29) \quad (3.29) \quad (1.30) \quad (2.43)$$
$$\text{RSQC} = .70; \text{D.W.} = 1.59$$

Symbols:
L = U.S. corporate undistributed profits after taxes plus capital consumption allowances, in billions of current U.S. dollars, moving average of $t - 1$ and $t - 2$. (Original data in appendix.)
dO = Moving average of annual change $[(t - 1) - (t - 2)]$ and $[(t - 2) - (t - 3)]$ in industrial production index, 1963 = 100. (Original data in appendix.)
For other symbols see notes at end of table 2.

When all the variables are included in the Canadian equation, only dO_{us-c} is significant. If M, which is rejected in the European equation, is dropped, dO_c and P become significant while L remains insignificant. When in (14) the equation is reestimated without either M or L, the t-values for the coefficients of dO_c and P rise very substantially. Before settling on (14), however, a very different alternative must be considered.

Although Canada was exempt from the restrictions of P, the program did not aim at encouraging investment in Canada. Its major intent was to improve the U.S. balance of payments. To the extent that DI was redirected to other foreign areas from Europe, the goal was to encourage investment in less developed countries [11, p. 68]. If these explicit goals were the only results of the program, P_{we} should be insignificant in the equation for DI_c. This is the case in (12), and so in (15) P is dropped with the resulting equation radically different from (12). The coefficient of L rises from 1.9 to 23.8 and becomes significant, while the coefficient of dO_c falls from 81.6 to 26.7 and is insignificant. If M,

21. With both simple lags and moving averages, longer lags for dO give substantially better statistical results for Canada, whereas shorter lags yield the better results with the European data.

still insignificant, is dropped, the equation, (16), is not changed substantially from (15).

The instability of the coefficients between (12) and (16) suggests there is multicollinearity. The following correlation coefficients

Variables	R
P, L	.7954
P, dO_c	.3097
L, dO_c	.7312

point to the relationships between L and P and L and dO_c as the crucial ones. The choice of P and dO_c rather than L as the significant variables and, therefore, of (14) as the final equation is made on two grounds. First, the equation including P has a higher RSQC. Second, even stronger evidence is found by examining (17), estimated for 1955–65, the period before there were any restraints on DI.

$$DI_c = 512 \quad - 2.9L \quad + 77.1dO_c \quad - 120.1dO_{us-c} \tag{17}$$
$$\quad\ (1.35) \quad\ (.22) \quad\ (1.86) \quad\quad (1.73)$$
$$\text{RSQC} = .34; \text{D.W.} = 2.01$$

The coefficient of dO_c conforms to that in (14) and not to that in (16). Moreover, the t-values of the coefficients of both dO_c and dO_{us-c} though not

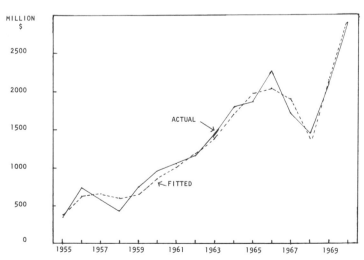

CHART I. – ACTUAL AND FITTED VALUES FOR DI_{we}

CHART II. - ACTUAL AND FITTED VALUES FOR DI$_{uk}$

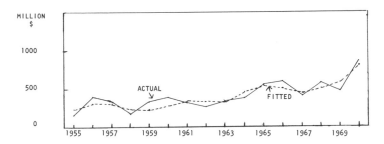

very high are significant at 10%, while the coefficient of L is negative and insignificant. This certainly suggests that in (16) L is significant only because it serves as a proxy for P.

Charts I–V show the actual values for DI and the values fitted from equations (8) through (11) and (14). In every case the actual series is more volatile than the fitted. The Canadian equation generates fitted values that track most closely the cycles in the actual data. The actual series for WE, RWE, and EEC show few turns, and the fitted series miss the short cycle with a peak in 1964 and a trough in 1965. The U.K. data are more cyclical. The fitted series with some timing differences, as well as with substantial smoothing, picks up all of the cycles except that with a peak in 1968 and a trough in 1969.

A. *Plant and Equipment Expenditures*

As further confirmation of the results of the regressions for DI and as an aid in their interpretation, equations are estimated for PE_{we} and PE_c with the same

CHART III. - ACTUAL AND FITTED VALUES FOR DI$_{rwe}$

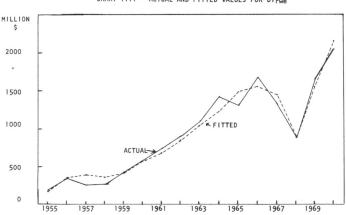

CHART IV. - ACTUAL AND FITTED VALUES FOR DI$_{eec}$

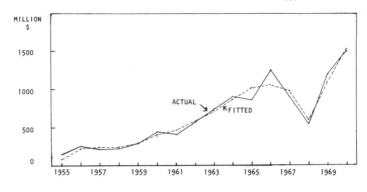

CHART V. - ACTUAL AND FITTED VALUES FOR DI$_{c}$

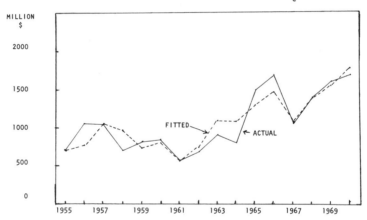

independent variables as in (8) and (14). They cover 1957–70, the period for which data for *PE* are available.

$$PE_{we} = -1732 \quad + \quad 54.8L \; + \; 35.2dO_{we} \quad - \quad 291P \tag{18}$$
$$(5.63) \quad\quad (6.07) \quad\quad (4.98) \quad\quad (1.04)$$
$$\text{RSQC} = .97; \text{ D.W.} = 1.76$$

$$PE_{c} = \quad 666 \quad +137.7dO_{c} - 85.8dO_{us-c} + 935P \tag{19}$$
$$(4.80) \quad\quad (6.71) \quad\quad (2.00) \quad\quad (5.71)$$
$$\text{RSQC} = .88; \text{ D.W.} = 1.86$$

If we substitute (18) and (19) into (2) and (3), the equations for *DI* as a function of *PE*, give

$$DI_{we} = -933 + 34.0L + 21.8dO_{we} - 773P \tag{20}$$

$$DI_c = 398 + 90.9dO_c - 56.6dO_{us-c} + 624P \tag{21}$$

These can be compared with equations for DI, 1957–70, estimated directly.[22]

$$DI_{we} = -910 + 27.1L + 30.7dO_{we} - 860P \tag{22}$$
$$(5.22) \quad (5.30) \quad (7.67) \quad (5.42)$$
$$\text{RSQC} = .96; \text{ D.W.} = 2.91$$

$$DI_c = 305 + 93.7dO_c - 132.0dO_{us-c} + 710P \tag{23}$$
$$(2.43) \quad (5.05) \quad (3.40) \quad (4.79)$$
$$\text{RSQC} = .82; \text{ D.W.} = 1.83$$

The coefficients in (20) are quite similar to those in (22), and those in (21) come close to those in (23) with the exception of that for dO_{us-c}. Its coefficient is much larger in the directly estimated equation for DI_c. These results further support the hypothesis that the forces determining DI are to a large extent those that determine PE. They also suggest, however, that there are additional reasons why DI_c is inversely related to dO_{us-c}. To investigate further this last relationship, the equation for DI_c as a function of PE_c is reestimated with dO_{us-c} included as an independent variable.

$$DI_c = -76 + .63PE_c - 75.6dO_{us-c} + 132P \tag{24}$$
$$(.43) \quad (5.53) \quad (2.09) \quad (.70)$$
$$\text{RSQC} = .84; \text{ D.W.} = 2.34$$

dO_{us-c} is significant in (24), and when (19) is substituted into (24) the result

$$DI_c = 344 + 86.8dO_c - 129.7dO_{us-c} + 721P \tag{25}$$

is similar to (23).

According to (24), DI decreases relative to PE when the United States grows more rapidly relative to Canada. Part of the explanation may be that during these periods affiliates of U.S. corporations find Canadian funds cheaper and more abundant compared with U.S. funds and so use relatively more of them and less DI in financing PE.[23]

22. It should be noted that (22) and (23) covering 1957–1970 are not markedly different from (8) and (14) estimated for 1955–1970.

23. In his study of Canadian firms in 1956, 1959, and 1962 John F. Helliwell concludes, however, that foreign controlled firms are less affected than domestic companies by changing credit conditions because of their greater reliance on parental financing and on internal funds [10, pp. 150–51, 156].

The equations for PE and the relation of these equations to those for DI are of special interest in analyzing the influence of P. The coefficients of P are discussed below after briefer consideration of the coefficients of the liquidity and output variables in the equations for DI.

B. Change in Foreign Economic Activity

dO_f is of particular interest because, as explained in the introduction, two studies of DI in Europe rejected it as insignificant. The evidence here in equations (8) through (11) and (14) is quite the contrary. For each of the several areas of Europe, dO_f is significant and, specified somewhat differently, it is also significant in the Canadian equation.[24]

To gain some perspective on the size of the coefficients of dO_f and to aid in their interpretation, the implied elasticities of the book value of U.S. direct investments (BV) to O_f are given below.[25]

Area	Elasticity
WE	1.05
RWE	1.18
EEC	1.09
UK	1.39
C	.55

Econometric studies of real investment in U.S. manufacturing suggest that

24. Because other investigators using data for earlier parts of the period have such different findings about DI in Europe, it appeared advisable to test the stability of the relationships found here. The sample period was divided into 1955–62 and 1963–70 and the Chow test applied. The resulting F-values are: WE, .24; RWE, .44; EEC, .10; UK, .07; C, .52, well below the one percent critical value of F of 3.84. The null hypothesis, therefore, cannot be rejected.

25. The elasticities are measured at mean values. In the published series BV is not revalued to reflect changes in prices after foreign investments are made. Therefore, when prices are rising, a comparison of DI with BV will overstate the percentage growth of BV at either fixed or constant prices. This in turn will give an upward bias to the elasticities. To roughly and partially correct for this, the published BV series are adjusted upward for use here. Beginning with the figures for year-end 1954 given in table 1 the series in each subsequent year are increased by the actual dBV for the year and by an estimate of the increase in the current value of BV_{t-1} because of the past year's inflation. The rate of inflation is measured by the annual change in the GNP deflator. The mean value of the inflated BV series are used to find the percentage of change in BV associated with a one percent change in O_f. The resulting measures of elasticity are, however, probably still somewhat overstated because (due to data limitations) no adjustments of BV are made for any inflation occurring prior to 1954.

the long-run elasticity of the capital stock to output is approximately unity.[26] If the long-run elasticity of the capital stock of foreign affiliates to foreign output is also unity and if DI is proportional to PE, the elasticities of BV to European output appear reasonable. It may be noted that according to these estimates, BV_{uk} is more responsive to changes in the size of the British market than is BV_{rwe} to changes in continental European GNP. Over the sample period, however, O_{uk} rose at an average rate of 6.6% while O_{rwe} grew by 9.4% annually. It was only because of this that market growth caused more expansion in U.S. investments on the continent than in the United Kingdom.

The implied elasticity for Canada is quite low compared with the estimates for Europe and to the results of the studies for U.S. manufacturing.[27] This may be partly because 14% of DI_c went to mining, whereas investment in mining was inconsequential in Europe.[28] The data available [3, p. 20] [25, pp. 71–72] [26, pp. 71, 73] indicate that other U.S. affiliates produce primarily for the local market, but mining affiliates produce mainly for export, with the result that a smaller proportion of sales of U.S. affilitates in Canada than in Europe are for the local market and thus a smaller part of BV_c is responsive to changes in home demand. This would tend to lower the measured elasticity.

C. U.S. Cash and Changes in U.S. Economic Activity

The Canadian, U.K., and continental European equations differ greatly in the roles assigned to dO_{us} and to L. In equation (14) for DI_c, dO_{us-c} is significant.[29] Faster growth in the American economy works to discourage investment in Canada. However, combining the coefficient of dO_{us-c} (-126.2) with that for dO_c ($+86.5$), the U.S. economy would have to grow 1.69 times as fast as Canada before the depressing effect on DI_c of U.S. expansion would completely neutralize the positive influence of dO_c.

26. Michael K. Evans computes the elasticities implied in four studies and finds they range from .6 to 1.0. He concludes that "although further results would be helpful, it is reasonable for the long-run capital-output elasticity to equal unity" [8, pp. 136, 148].

27. The measure for Canada appears low in comparison to the estimates for U.S. domestic investment especially since it is thought that not all of the upward bias has been removed from the estimate for Canada.

28. The figures for the industrial composition of DI given here and in section III.C, below, are based on data from the same sources used for table I.

29. It must be noted, however, that the coefficient of dO_{us-c} (unlike the other coefficients in the equation for DI_c) is very sensitive to the lags that are specified for dO_c and dO_{us-c}. Whereas it is -126.2 ($t = 3.12$) in (14) with $(dO_{t-1} + dO_{t-2})/2$, it is only -39.7 ($t = 1.77$) if dO_{t-1} is specified and -10.9 ($t = .29$) in an equation with $(dO_t + dO_{t-1})/2$.

While dO_{us-c} is significant in the Canadian equation, L is not. In contrast, in all the European equations except that for DI_{uk}, the coefficient of L is positive and significant; and given the high correlation between L and dO_{us}, this is interpreted to mean that any inverse relation between dO_{us} and DI is weaker than the positive influence of corporate cash on DI. Finally, L is insignificant in the U.K. equation, which suggests that any positive effect of rising U.S. cash is counterbalanced by the negative influence of dO_{us}.

Some of the difference in the importance of L for DI in the several areas may result from variations in the industrial composition of the investment. DI in manufacturing was 55% of the total in Western Europe but only 42% of that in Canada. Since the evidence from studies of the U.S. economy is that corporate liquidity affects the rate of capital formation in manufacturing but not in the other sectors [8, p. 138], this may help account for the insignificance of L in the Canadian equation.[30] Also, the proportion of BV that is in long-established affiliates is probably considerably larger in Canada than in Europe, and these are the affiliates that account for most of the overseas earnings of American corporations.[31] These earnings are not included in L but are an alternative source of cash. If the timing of the earnings is not completely synchronized with that of L, they may serve as substitutes for it, weakening any statistical relation between L and DI.

The insignificance of L in the equations for DI_{uk} may also be partly explained by the relatively older age of affiliates there. It may also be connected with the relative importance of DI in petroleum in Britain. From 1955 through 1970, 27% of DI_{uk} was in petroleum, while 23% of DI_c and 20% of DI_{rwe} went to that industry. Before the investment control program began, international petroleum firms had started to use substantially more foreign funds in their financing. It has been suggested that their reasons may have included the greater availability of these funds and the desire to protect themselves against exchange rate fluctuations by having liabilities and claims in the same currencies. [25, pp. 28–29]. A policy of switching toward foreign funds would be expected to lessen the impact of L on DI.

Not only is L significant in the equations for continental Europe and for total Western Europe, but its coefficients appear high. According to equations (8),

30. Caves and Reuber, however, find Canadian corporate cash a significant variable in their equations for total Canadian plant and equipment expenditure based on quarterly data for 1950 to 1962 [4, pp. 164–169].

31. That BV_c is in longer-established affiliates than BV_{rwe} seems most likely given the larger BV in Canada at year-end 1954 and its slower growth over the sample period (see table 1). The evidence that most earnings are made by older affiliates comes from the 1966 benchmark study of U.S. overseas investment [5, p. 15] [24, p. 85].

(9), (10), and (11) for every billion dollars of L there is DI_{we} of \$24 to \$27 million, about three-quarters of which goes to the EEC. The implied elasticities of DI relative to L are:

Area	Elasticity
WE	.96
RWE	1.24
EEC	1.44

These appear high when they are compared with the findings of econometric studies of real capital formation in the United States. Reviewing a number of studies, Evans concludes that in manufacturing the elasticity of investment to corporate cash over a two year period is .25 to .50, but that there is no evidence that changes in cash have an effect on investment in the non-manufacturing sectors [8, p. 138].

What economic explanation might there be of the high elasticities of DI in Europe to L? A number of observers have suggested that American firms have become increasingly well-informed about investment opportunities in Europe. It was suggested above that this might have been associated with the formation of the EEC and resulted in a structural change that could be captured by the dummy M. M, however, proved insignificant, suggesting that if there was such a learning process, it probably was more gradual. Since in most years dL was positive, perhaps a major part of the dynamics of American firms' reactions to this new information was the way they allocated their incremental cash. When their cash grew, they may have chosen to devote an increasing proportion of it to investment in continental Europe. This is suggested as a tentative hypothesis. It is recognized, however, that the large coefficients for L may have a very different sort of explanation. They may have arisen because L is serving as a proxy not only for dO_{us} but also for some unidentified variable positively associated with DI.[32]

32. L and foreign GNP are highly correlated. The simple R's are:

L, O_{we}	.9698
L, O_{rwe}	.9690
L, O_{eec}	.9660

Moreover, foreign GNP was the variable found in [1] and [13] to be the principal determinant of U.S. direct investment in Europe. However, since, as argued above, it is so hard to justify theoretically why O_f should be an ultimate determinant of DI, it does not appear a promising candidate for a variable for which L may be serving as proxy. Indeed, it is instead hypothesized that in [1] and [13] foreign GNP acted as a proxy for L (and also perhaps for some other unidentified variable).

D. Direct Investment Control Program

Before examining the coefficients for P, it is necessary to elaborate more fully on the provisions of the control program and to consider its possible effects on corporate behavior. The aim of the program was to decrease the net impact of U.S. direct investment on the balance of payments. The regulated flow, therefore, is not DI but that net of long-term borrowing by U.S. parent firms. Parents of European affiliates could comply with the program by borrowing abroad with no effect on DI_{we}. Foreign borrowing, however, instead may be undertaken by the foreign subsidiaries themselves. If that is the case, or if subsidiaries acquire foreign equity funds, DI will decline because the expenditure of funds acquired abroad by a subsidiary is not included in DI[2, p. 51].

If the amount borrowed by the parent or acquired by the subsidiary abroad is equal to what would otherwise have been spent out of U.S. funds, there will be no effect on PE_{we}. Herring and Willett argue that such would be the case if firms operated in a perfect capital market where the imputed cost of funds is the same no matter what their source. Regulations affecting the use of funds from one source would not affect the marginal capital costs and so would not change the desired level of real investment [11, pp. 60–61]. But, Herring and Willett conclude, firms are in a different kind of world where there are "transactions costs, taxes, default risks and less than perfectly elastic arbitrage schedules" and where, therefore, costs rise when the use of one source is restricted. Therefore, Western European affiliates would be expected to have lower levels of PE because of P [11, p. 61].[33]

No matter what happens to DI_{we} and PE_{we}, as long as firms use fewer U.S. funds to finance expenditures in Europe there will be U.S. financial resources released for spending elsewhere, including in Canada. If as a result DI_c increases, the higher flow may substitute for Canadian funds with no effect on PE_c or it may increase PE_c because it lowers marginal capital costs. In the latter case, there simultaneously may be some substitution of U.S. for Canadian financing and therefore some change in the relationship between DI_c and PE_c.[34]

Table 4 shows the estimated impact of the program on DI in millions of dollars. To indicate the relative magnitude of these effects, the calculated

33. There are, however, problems in analyzing the data. "Contemporaneously with and, partially, because of the imposition of the control program there was a growing awareness in the U.S. of opportunities for financing abroad as well as an actual increase in such opportunities and a decrease in the cost of foreign relative to domestic sources" [11, p. 61]. There may, therefore, have been no increase in financing costs due to P or there may have been no increase that can be isolated statistically.

34. The possibility that there is such substitution is suggested above in the discussion of the coefficient of dO_{us-c} in (24).

TABLE 4

ESTIMATED EFFECT OF CONTROL PROGRAM ON
U.S. DIRECT INVESTMENT IN EUROPE AND CANADA, 1966–70*

(In millions of U.S. dollars)

Year	DI_{we}	DI_{rwe}	DI_{eec}	DI_{uk}	DI_c
1966	−86	−84	−61	−1	+68
1967	−171	−169	−121	−2	+136
1968	−855	−844	−607	−6	+682
1969	−684	−675	−486	−5	+546
1970	−556	−549	−395	−4	+443
Total	−2,352	−2,321	−1,670	−18	+1,875
Estimated effect as percentage of:					
Actual *DI*, 1966–70	22	31	31	1	25
BV, 1970	10	14	14	0.2	8

*Calculated from coefficients of P_{we} and P_{uk} in equations (8) through (11) and (14).

impact for 1966–70 is shown as a percentage of actual *DI* for those five years combined and of *BV* for year-end 1970.

Except for the impact on DI_{uk},[35] the restraining effects on investment are large especially after the program becomes mandatory in 1968. Approximately 70% of the estimated decline is in DI_{eec} and 30% in *DI* to the other countries of continental Europe. This is also the approximate division between the two areas of actual *DI*, 1966–70, and of *BV* at the end of 1970.

For all of Europe the estimated decrease is $2,352 million or 22% of actual *DI*, while the estimated increase for Canada of $1,875 is 80% of the decline in DI_{we} and 25% of actual DI_c. Finally, according to these estimates, BV_{we} and BV_{eec} would have been 10 and 14% higher at the end of 1970, and BV_c, 8% lower without the program.[36]

Although the effects of *P* on DI_{we} and DI_c are of roughly similar size but with opposite signs, the same is not true of its effects on *PE*. Table 5 summarizes the

35. Although the coefficient of P_{uk} is not significant, the implicit effect on DI_{uk} when added to the estimated effect of P_{we} on DI_{rwe} falls only slightly short of the estimated effect of P_{we} on DI_{we}.

36. Since the proportion of Canadian assets owned by Americans is already large, an 8% decline in BV_c would have a substantial effect on the amount of U.S. ownership of the Canadian economy, about which many Canadians are concerned. A rough measure of the importance of American ownership is the percentage *BV* is of foreign *GNP*. For Canada this rose from 25.8% in 1954 to 28.8% in 1970. Had BV_c been 8% less in 1970, this ratio would have equaled only 26.4%. In Europe the percentage of *BV* to *GNP* rose from 1.3% in 1954 to 3.0% in 1970. Without *P* the increase would have been larger. Since, however, the ownership ratio is so much lower than in Canada, the estimated effect is much less in percentage points. A 10% larger *BV* in 1970 would have raised the ratio only from 3.0 to 3.3%.

TABLE 5

COEFFICIENTS OF P_{we} IN
EUROPEAN AND CANADIAN EQUATIONS, 1957–70

Dependent Variable	Independent Variables in Addition to P_{we}	Coefficient of P_{we}	Equation
DI_{we}	L, dO_{we}	−860 (5.42)	(22)
PE_{we}	L, dO_{we}	−291 (1.04)	(18)
DI_{we}	PE_{we}	−593 (2.28)	(2)
DI_c	dO_c, dO_{us-c}	+710 (4.79)	(23)
PE_c	dO_c, dO_{us-c}	+935 (5.71)	(19)
DI_c	PE_c, dO_{us-c}	+132 (.70)	(24)

coefficients of P in equations estimated for 1957–70. As DI_{we} falls, PE_{we} is little affected. The coefficient of P in (18) is just 291 with a t-value of but 1.04. Consistent with this is the large and significant negative coefficient of P in (2) that relates DI_{we} to PE_{we}. In contrast, PE_c is greatly affected by P with the relationship between DI_c and PE_c remaining substantially unchanged. P in (19) has a large and significant coefficient; in (24) it also has a positive coefficient, but it is small and insignificant.

These equations suggest that the decline in DI_{we} was largely matched by the acquisition of other funds by European affiliates. The U.S. funds released by this and by any borrowing by parent firms led to substantial increases in DI_c that did not displace Canadian funds but were combined with them in roughly the same proportions as previously to finance a greatly enlarged level of plant and equipment spending. If the coefficients are of roughly the correct magnitude, P had only a quite modest negative effect on DI to the two areas combined and had a substantial expansionary influence on PE.[37]

There are several reasons, however, to be tentative in accepting these results—especially those for Europe. They differ substantially from Herring and Willett's findings. Their three estimates of the shortfall in PE_{we} in 1968 due to P range from $532 to $624 million [11, pp. 66–67],[38] compared with the

37. For a discussion of some of the various possible indirect future effects on the U.S. balance of payments from the program via the influence of DI and PE on interest, dividend, and merchandise trade accounts, see [11, p. 69].

38. These estimates are based on equations for PE_{we} in which U.S. domestic plant and equipment expenditure is the principal independent variable. Herring and Willett during some earlier research found a close statistical relation between the two. They

$291 million difference in that year from equation (18). Moreover, the sizes of the coefficients of P in the European equations of the present study are sensitive to the length of the lag specified for dO_{we}. In equations for PE_{we}, 1957–70, if dO_{we} is unlagged, the coefficient of P is -548 (though with a t-value of only 1.61), which gives a 1968 shortfall similar to that found by Herring and Willett, whereas, if dO_{we} is lagged one year, the coefficient is positive ($+182$) and insignificant ($t = .80$). The coefficient for P in equations for DI_{we} for the same period is $-1,130$ ($t = 8.51$) with dO_{we} unlagged and -477 ($t = 2.15$) with it lagged a year.

SUMMARY AND CONCLUSIONS

This study considers the causes of U.S. direct investment in the two developed areas that have been the major recipients of these capital flows: Canada and Western Europe. The hypotheses tested are that these international financial flows are positively related to changes in the size of the foreign markets and to the amount of residual cash flowing to firms in the United States, and negatively related to changes in the size of the American market. The theory from which these hypotheses are derived is that developed by Duesenberry in which the marginal efficiency of capital and the marginal cost of funds determine the equilibrium level of real investment. It is further proposed that the relationship between U.S. investment abroad and these various determinants was affected by the formation of the EEC and by the U.S. direct investment control program that began in 1965. To test the hypotheses, regressions were run using annual data for 1955 to 1970. Separate calculations were made not only for Canada and Western Europe but also for several subdivisions of the latter: the United Kingdom, the EEC, and all of Western Europe except the United Kingdom.

The statistical results strongly support the hypothesis that changes in the foreign market are a determinant of U.S. direct investment. In the European equations the preferred measure of market change is $dGNP$; in that for Canada, the results are more satisfactory if market size is measured by annual changes in industrial production. For Europe the coefficients of these variables imply elasticities of the book value of U.S. investments to changes in the foreign market of approximately unity. For investment in Canada the implied elasticity is somewhat lower.

warn that these are basically "black box" estimates but argue for their use because they know of no satisfactory quantitative analyses of U.S. direct investment based on an adequate behavioral model [11, p. 62]. They do not analyze separately PE_c but examine total PE worldwide and tentatively conclude that most of the decrease in PE_{we} that they find is matched by an increase elsewhere in affiliate spending on plant and equipment [11, p. 68].

The influence of U.S. cash and of changes in the U.S. market appear to vary among the areas. The difference in market growth between the United States and Canada is a significant variable in the Canadian equation, but U.S. corporate cash is not. The evidence for Europe is harder to interpret. Because of collinearity, both cash and change in the U.S. market cannot be included in the equations. Cash serves as a proxy for both. It is insignificant in the British equation but has significant positive coefficients in the other European equations. These results suggest that any negative impact of U.S. growth on investment in continental Europe is overwhelmed by the positive influence of the cash flow, whereas for investment in the United Kingdom, the effects of the two roughly counterbalance. The implied elasticity of direct investment in continental Europe to the cash variable indeed appears high, which may mean that cash serves as a proxy for some other variable as well.

The dummy for the formation of the EEC is rejected as insignificant. All that it aims to measure, however, are the effects of the formation of the EEC because of its influence on relative production costs inside and outside the Community, and because of possible increases in knowledge about the area. The formation of the Community still may have had important influences on direct investment via $dGNP$ if, as is frequently suggested, the creation of the Common Market substantially affected the rate of economic growth.[39]

Evidence about the effect of the U.S. direct investment control program comes not only from equations for direct investment but also from equations for plant and equipment expenditures of affiliates, 1957–70. The statistical results support the hypothesis that there was a large negative impact on direct investment funds flowing to Europe, and they also indicate a substantial positive effect on direct investment in Canada. Furthermore, the evidence suggests that the decrease in direct investment in Europe had little effect on the plant and equipment expenditures of European affiliates, while in contrast the larger flows to Canada were associated with proportionate increases in plant and equipment spending there. The dummy to represent the control program is crude, and its coefficients in the European equations are sensitive to the lags in the market variable. These results, therefore, must be employed with caution. They are, however, most interesting, especially since there are few econometric investigations of the impacts of the program.

39. It may be noted that there are a number of empirical studies of the importance of the formation of the EEC for U.S. direct investment with great differences in the conclusions of their authors. For references and a brief summary of the literature, see [14].

References

1. V. N. Bandera and J. T. White, "U.S. Direct Investments and Domestic Markets in Europe," *Economia Internazionale,* February 1968, pp. 117–33.

2. R. David Belli, "Plant and Equipment Expenditures of U.S.-Owned Foreign Affiliates: Revised Estimates for 1972 and 1973," *Survey of Current Business,* March 1973, pp. 45–52.

3. ———, "Sales of Foreign Affiliates of U. S. Firms, 1961–65, 1967, and 1968," *Survey of Current Business,* October 1970, pp. 18–20.

4. Richard E. Caves and Grant L. Reuber, *Capital Transfers and Economic Policy, 1951–1962* (Cambridge, Massachusetts, 1971).

5. Frederick Cutler, "Benchmark Survey of U.S. Direct Investment Abroad, 1966," *Survey of Current Business,* August 1971, pp. 13–15, 44.

6. David T. Devlin, "The U.S. Balance of Payments: Revised Presentation," *Survey of Current Business,* June 1971, pp. 24–57, 64.

7. James S. Duesenberry, *Business Cycles and Economic Growth* (New York, 1958).

8. Michael K. Evans, *Macroeconomic Activity* (New York, 1969).

9. Julius N. Freidlin and Leonard A. Lupo, "U.S. Direct Investments Abroad in 1971," *Survey of Current Business,* November 1972, pp. 21–34.

10. John F. Helliwell, *Public Policies and Private Investment* (Oxford, 1968).

11. Richard Herring and Thomas D. Willett, "The Capital Control Program and U.S. Investment Activity Abroad," *Southern Economic Journal,* July 1972, pp. 58–71.

12. Lawrence B. Krause, *European Economic Integration and the United States* (Washington, D.C., 1968).

13. Anthony E. Scaperlanda and Laurence J. Mauer, "The Determinants of U.S. Direct Investment in the E.E.C.," *American Economic Review,* September 1969, pp. 558–68.

14. Andrew Schmitz and Jurg Bieri, "E.E.C. Tariffs and U.S. Direct Investment," *European Economic Review,* November 1972, pp. 259–70.

15. Erich Spitäller, "A Survey of Recent Quantitative Studies of Long-Term Capital Movements," *International Monetary Fund Staff Papers,* March 1971, pp. 189–220.

16. Canada, Dominion Bureau of Statistics, *Indexes of Real Domestic Product by Industry (1961 Base),* 1968.

17. Organization for European Cooperation and Development, *Main Economic Indicators* and *Historical Statistics.*

18. ———, *National Accounts of OECD Countries, 1953–1969,* n.d.

19. United Kingdom, Central Statistical Office, *National Income and Expenditure, 1972,* 1972.

20. United States, Department of Commerce, *Balance of Payments, Statistical Supplement*, rev. ed., 1963.

21. ———, *International Commerce*.

22. ———, *The National Income and Product Accounts of the United States, 1929–1965, Statistical Tables*, 1966.

23. ———, *Survey of Current Business*.

24. ———, *U.S. Direct Investment Abroad 1966. Part I: Balance of Payments Data*, 1971.

25. ———, *U.S. Direct Investments Abroad–1966. Part II: Investment Position, Financial and Operating Data: Group I, Preliminary Report on Foreign Affiliates of the U.S. Petroleum Industry*, 1971.

26. ———, *U.S. Direct Investments Abroad–1966. Part II: Investment Position, Financial and Operating Data. Group 2. Preliminary Report on Foreign Affiliates of U.S. Manufacturing Industries*, 1972.

27. United States, *Economic Report of the President*.

Norway: Twenty Years After
The Marshall Plan

Eivind Erichsen

Eivind Erichsen

POSTWAR NORWAY AND MARSHALL AID

To rebuild Norway's war-torn economy after World War II and to bring her back to prewar prosperity and beyond was no minor task. Alice Bourneuf described the situation as follows:

> Norway . . . was faced with the difficult job of rebuilding an economy both devastated and dislocated by long years of war and occupation. Its problems were similar to those of other European countries, but they were perhaps more intense.[1]

The policy designed to solve these problems had as its keystone an extraordinarily rapid rate of investment financed by high domestic savings and a deficit on the external current-account balance far beyond available foreign-exchange reserves and readily available loans. Private consumption was allowed to increase only very gradually. The Norwegian approach omitted any drastic attack on the highly inflationary domestic monetary and credit situation resulting from money-printing financing methods in occupied Norway. Norwegian policy-makers gave first priority to establishing an economic environment

---

1. Alice Bourneuf, *Norway, the Planned Revival* (Cambridge, Mass.: Harvard University Press, 1958), p. 198.

favorable to full-employment conditions and rapid recovery. They feared that a drastic monetary reform might hamper these objectives. The imbalanced monetary situation was corrected only very gradually. An extensive system of physical controls, rationing, and price controls constituted an important element in the economic policy for many years.

This policy approach involved obvious risks. It might lead to a serious foreign-exchange crisis and a breakdown in the investment program. It might also result in an inflationary explosion. The Norwegian electorate might demand a more rapid improvement in private consumption, jeopardizing the investment effort. American support in the form of Marshall aid played a crucial part in helping Norwegian policy-makers to avoid these pitfalls.

Any evaluation of Norway's postwar achievements is inevitably a matter of judgment. In concluding *The Planned Revival*, Alice Bourneuf determined that in the main policy was successfully implemented:

> . . . The early plans were essentially followed throughout the recovery period. The basic policy lines were the same in each successive long-term program and annual budget. Economic planning for resource availabilities and uses played a very important role. . . . the plans were quite successfully carried out. . . . output and exports increased in accordance with the planned targets. By 1952 the expansion of output over the prewar level was greater than in any other European country. Output and productivity increased at rates which must be considered satisfactory even when the very high rate of investment is taken into account.
>
> . . . The plans to restrict consumption were not realized . . . [but] scarce resources were not used to any substantial extent to permit rapid increases in consumption. (. . . direct controls were effective) both in limiting total investment and consumption and ensuring that the distribution of investment and consumption accorded with the plans.
>
> The unplanned increases in output of domestically produced consumer goods and services probably helped to eliminate inflationary pressures in the consumer-goods sphere.
>
> Norway's experience suggests that suppressed inflationary pressures combined with direct controls may tend to promote rather than to hinder a rapid rate of growth. . . .Norway's experience also suggests that economic planning and direct controls need not be accompanied by interference with political or civil liberties.[2]

Even observers who dispute some elements of this picture agree that, on the whole, economic achievements in early postwar Norway were reasonably satisfying.

2. Ibid., pp. 199–202.

But what have been the policies and achievements in Norway since 1953? What is the state of the economy twenty years later?

NORWAY TWENTY YEARS LATER

1. Political debate during the Marshall Plan years centered around the economic policies of the Labor government. The planned-economy approach, and in particular heavy reliance on direct controls, came under heavy fire from the four opposition parties to the right of the Labor party. But as the years went by, and as the government gradually reduced its direct controls, the attitude and strategy of the opposition parties changed. Instead of attacking economic planning per se, they claimed that they could do a better job of planning if only the voters would give them victory at the polls. This is because planning has received increasingly broader political support in Norway over the last two decades. This growing support has importantly affected economic policies and developments during these years.

This is affirmed by the policy approach adopted by the parties to the right of the Labor party in 1965 when they succeeded in forming a coalition government. They showed little inclination to dismantle the existing planning machinery. On the contrary, they made full use of it. Until they fell from power in March 1971 (when a minority Labor government took over), the coalition government strived to improve and to extend the planning machinery. The acceptable degree of planning differed between the parties, but the Conservative party in Norway favored economic planning to an extent that would seem almost leftist in many other Western countries, including the United States. Today a political party hostile to comprehensive economic planning would stand no chance at the polls in Norway.

2. The kind of general economic planning now prevailing in Norway is characterized by two main features. It is comprehensive, but not detailed.

Since 1945, Norway's policy-makers have considered it important that planning should take place within a system of national accounts covering the whole economy. A comprehensive framework ensures consistency within the plan. In the Marshall Plan period, the National Budget[3] was based on estimates and information that the coordinating ministry (first the Ministry of Commerce, later the Ministry of Finance) received from other ministries. These data were evaluated and put together by ad hoc methods, often through successive approximations. This method still plays a part, but today a disaggregated

---

3. In Norway, the annual economic plan is called the National Budget as distinct from the Government Fiscal Budget.

econometric model serves as the chief instrument for reconciling the various elements in the plan. This model results from many years of cooperative effort by the Central Bureau of Statistics, the Oslo University Economic Institute, and the Ministry of Finance.[4]

Since the dismantling of most postwar regulations, policy instruments have been general and indirect, with the market mechanism allowed to play a key role in resource allocation. The principal physical control is a limited system of "building licenses." This approach reflects Norway's mixed economy, in which the public sector is no larger than in most other Western countries. Since the war, the Labor party has not promulgated nationalization as a principle.

A comprehensive, but not detailed, planning approach means that the various magnitudes entering into the National Budget and Longer Term Programs have different significance for policy planning. Some magnitudes reflect important policy goals, including the growth rate of public and private consumption, the level of investment, and the number of dwellings to be constructed. Other magnitudes are influenced by government policy to a lesser degree, and some are forecasts rather than goals. It is important to understand, however, that the National Budget is not just a set of economic forecasts but a government plan that specifies targets, policy objectives, and policy instruments. The plan is submitted by the government to the Parliament, where it is considered by the Finance Committee and, later, by the Parliament in plenary session. This procedure has been followed since the time of the Marshall Plan.

3. In many countries separate planning machinery exists apart from, and parallel to, traditional patterns of administration. This often occurs where there is insufficient popular support for planning. In Norway, however, this support has been so strong that it was necessary to sneak planning in the back door. At the war's end the role of planning was put directly under the traditional

4. The model consists first of a comprehensive set of input-output relations. Coefficients of these relations are adjusted annually. Important demand categories, such as investment, exports and public consumption, are determined exogenously. Total demand generates production and imports. Production determines employment. Employment, together with expected earning rates and the proposed level of taxation, generate private disposable income, which forms the basis for private consumption. The model summarizes mutual interdependencies that exist in the economy. The model is sufficiently detailed that it is possible to utilize available statistical information very extensively.

The main variables determined by the model are private consumption, imports and production at both fixed and current prices, private and public incomes, and various price indexes. Information on these variables is available in great detail. In the computer print-outs, exogenous and endogenous variables for the plan years are arranged together in national-accounts tables. See, for instance, Per Sevaldson, "Modis II: A Macroeconomic Model for Short-Term Analysis and Planning," the Central Bureau of Statistics, Nr. 23, 1968.

government administration. The aim has been to convert traditional government administration into modern planning machinery, not to establish additional planning machinery alongside the old administration. This approach has been pursued consistently. The old administrative machinery is far from an efficient and modern planning machine, but reasonable progress has been made over the last two decades.

During the Marshall Plan years, the Ministry of Commerce was responsible for coordinating economic planning, and the Ministry of Finance controlled the chief instruments of economic policy, the fiscal and monetary instruments. Inter-ministerial cooperation and coordination reduced the obvious risk of frictions between a ministry preoccupied with the preparation of ambitious plans and another pursuing more conventional treasury lines.

In 1952 the responsibility for coordinating economic planning was transferred to the Ministry of Finance. In my view, this was a sensible move. First, it made it easier to balance the tendency of planners to make overambitious plans against the inclination of old-fashioned treasury officials to be too cautious. Second, it improved the chances for wholehearted implementation of the plans, since it gave the ministry responsible for the plans control over the chief instruments of policy. Third, macroeconomic planning is so closely linked to fiscal budgeting that they are better done together.

Some may object that the job of planning and budgeting is too big for one minister and that the arrangement makes him too powerful. The work load of the top command of the Ministry of Finance is certainly heavy. But the planning and budget process is extensively decentralized among the other ministries, and the Ministry of Finance is primarily a steering and coordinating body, with only 200 employees. Apprehension that too much power is vested in one minister has not been supported by experience. Through the fifteen-member Cabinet the balance of power is struck in such a way that, if anything, the minister of finance is too weak rather than too strong. Some subsequent sections of this paper strive to substantiate this proposition.

4. Since the war the fiscal budget has been looked upon as a tool of general economic policy, rather than as a mere instrument of government finance. This led to a major budgetary reform in 1961, when, among other things, the fiscal year was shifted to a calendar-year basis to ensure better coordination with the National Budget. Shifting the timing of the fiscal year was no minor operation. Because it implied a complete change in the working pattern of the Parliament, it required amending the Constitution. The reform of 1961 involved a number of other changes, including a new classification of the budget, that made it possible to integrate directly fiscal-budget data with the national-income accounts and the National Budget.

To improve the basis for decisions regarding annual fiscal budgets, the

Ministry of Finance now prepares provisional fiscal budgets by broad program categories for an additional three years, providing a rolling four-year fiscal-budget perspective. Steps have been taken to bring program-budgeting ideas more effectively into the budgeting process. Program budgeting is looked upon, not as a completely new form of budgeting, but as an improvement in the budgeting process to be introduced gradually over a number of years. This work is only in its early stages, but it will receive considerable attention in coming years, and it has broad political support. If anything, fiscal policy in Norway is receiving even greater attention today than it did during the Marshall Plan period twenty years ago.

5. Obviously, a rolling four-year fiscal budget necessitiates similar extensions of national budgeting. A four-year macroeconomic framework is now prepared each year. This in turn has made obsolete the traditional Four-Year Plans that had appeared every fourth year since 1948. Even so, the tradition of presenting a plan every fourth year will be maintained, but the nature of these plans will change significantly. In particular, longer-term perspectives beyond the four-year period will be highlighted; specifically, perspectives will reach to 1980, 1990, and 2000.

Uncertainty increases enormously as the perspective is carried beyond five or ten years. But given that an exponential rate of growth of, say, 4 to 5% implies far-reaching changes even over a decade or two, it is important to see where projected changes lead, and to consider whether it is desirable to alter the main course of development. Longer-term perspectives were presented for the first time in connection with the Four-Year Plan for 1970–73. A major step in the same direction will be taken in the 1973 plan.[5]

6. Whereas monetary and credit policies played a modest role during the Marshall Plan period, they are key factors in Norway's current arsenal of economic policy instruments. Excess liquidity existing after the war was gradually corrected through sizeable fiscal surpluses and import surpluses partly financed by Marshall Aid.[6] This provided a workable foundation for subsequent credit policy. However, modern credit-policy legislation was not available. Instead, monetary and credit policy based on agreements between the Bank and Insurance Associations, the Bank of Norway, and the Ministry of Finance developed in the middle of the 1950s. The agreements primarily

5. The longer-term perspective analysis is based on a multisectoral growth model developed by Leif Johansen. See, for instance, Leif Johansen, "A Multi-Sectoral Study of Economic Growth" (Amsterdam, 1960).

6. Marshall Plan counterpart funds were not used for specific Marshall Aid projects as in other countries, but were sterilized in the Bank of Norway. This was a particularly sensible element of the Marshall Aid policies in Norway in that prestige projects were not allowed to confuse regular fiscal-policy priorities.

stipulated ceilings on credits extended by the banks and insurance companies and on the interest rates that could be charged.

Opinions differ concerning the successes and failures of these agreements, but they helped all parties to understand each other's situation and problems. Also, the experience gained proved useful in formulating the modern monetary-and-credit policy legislation enacted in 1965, which sets the framework for current policies in this field.

The 1965 Credit Policy Act empowers the government to make use of a number of credit-policy tools, such as liquidity reserve requirements and minimum deposits at the Bank of Norway for private banks and savings banks, obligatory investments in bonds for banks, insurance companies and some other institutions, and capital-issue controls. The act also authorizes the government to fix maximum interest rates. This power has yet to be used, but some rates are regulated through common understanding between the government and the credit institutions. Long-term interest rates have been kept relatively low throughout the postwar period, whereas short-term rates have risen to levels comparable with foreign rates. Although the 1965 act has replaced the credit agreements, cooperation committees between the authorities and the credit institutions have proved useful in implementing the new legislation.

A significant institutional development in the credit field during the past twenty-five years is the increasing share of credit extended by the state banks, which are specialized credit institutions for the allocation of credit to certain sectors. Credit extended by these institutions now roughly equals credit extended by private banks and savings banks combined. The largest single bank is the Housing Bank, which finances some 75% of all new dwellings in Norway. Originally, the state banks were financed by individual bond issues, but since 1952–53 they have been financed mainly through funds raised by the government itself through bond issues and budget surpluses. Funds are also provided by postal credit institutions. Both the Postal Savings Bank and the Postal Giro System have developed rapidly over the last twenty years. These institutions render remarkable service to business and consumers through the vast network of post offices.

The combined effect of the Credit Policy Act of 1965, the state banks, and the postal institutions is to give the government powerful economic policy instruments with which to supplement fiscal policy. These domestic controls are reinforced by restrictions on capital movements to and from foreign countries. These controls seek to prevent capital flows from interfering with the achievement of the objectives of the domestic credit policies.

7. In 1967 a new national social security scheme was put in operation to cover the entire population. It expanded and merged previous schemes into one comprehensive compulsory insurance and pension system. This has had far-

reaching effects. An important element of the new scheme is the gradual introduction of old-age pensions that are tied to incomes actually earned by each individual while in active work. The idea behind this approach is that no pensioner should be forced to alter drastically his way of life when he leaves the working population.

Costs of the social security system are met by contributions from the individuals actively employed, by contributions from employers, and to a lesser degree by payments from the state and the municipalities. The contributions are related to the incomes and wages of the individuals.

A main objective in the arrangements for financing the scheme is to ensure sizable revenue surpluses for many years to increase the nation's total savings. This makes the new social security scheme an additional powerful instrument of financial policy. The goal is to broaden the financial base to support a high level of capital formation, and to make it possible to meet additional claims on resources that will stem from additional pensions later.

8. Although fiscal and credit instruments are strong, it is broadly recognized that they need to be supplemented by incomes policies. In the Marshall Plan period a special Wage Board possessed the power to decide on wages whenever collective bargaining broke down. Since 1952, however, only through an act of Parliament is it possible to empower a wage board to handle specific disputes. In general, wage settlements have been reached without compulsory arbitration.[7] The principle of free negotiation of wage settlements is deeply rooted and generally recognized. Wage settlements covering the main body of wage-earners in the private sector are negotiated between the nationwide Association of Employers and the Federation of Trade Unions. However, throughout the period under review a well-established system of compulsory mediation has existed. It is fair to say that the government continously entertained some kind of incomes policy to coordinate income determination for labor, business, agriculture, and fishing.

In 1962 a Contact Group was established consisting of the prime minister, the finance minister, and the minister of wages and prices on the one hand, and representatives of the unions, employers, farmers, and fishermen on the other. In this forum the government can exchange views and information with respective groups while income settlements are prepared or negotiated. Also the government may commit itself to the use of particular policy measures to help bring about proper settlements.

7. Professor Mark W. Leiserson, who was a senior economist with the Marshall Plan Mission in Norway in 1951–53, has analyzed the process of wage determination in Norway in his *Wages and Economic Control in Norway 1945–57* (Cambridge, Mass.: Harvard University Press, 1959).

Since 1966 the Contact Group has been assisted by a Technical Expert Group chaired by the director of research of the Central Bureau of Statistics and consisting of experts from the parties concerned. The Expert Group prepares estimates of likely effects of alternative settlements on prices, incomes, production, and so on. The group uses an econometric model derived from the larger model used in the preparation of the National Budget. The model distinguishes between industries exposed to foreign competition, in which prices are mainly determined in the international markets, and the more-sheltered sectors of the economy, in which domestic wage-increases rather easily lead to price advances.[8]

Fact-finding and forecasts based on alternative wage increases have introduced greater realism to deliberations preceding wage settlements. The parties concerned are much more aware of the consequences of their decisions. It must be recognized, however, that an incomes policy is more a political and public-relations question than a technical one. No incomes policy can succeed that is not considered fair and reasonable by public opinion and, in particular, by the union rank and file. (In Norway agreements between the negotiating bodies are subjected to referendums among their members.) Therefore, a successful incomes policy cannot be restricted to wages alone but has to cover other categories of incomes as well. Although this has been a guiding principle in Norway, it must be admitted that it is difficult to implement in practice.

9. The foregoing sections describe the development of Norway's policy instruments from the early postwar years. Now we consider what have been the policy goals and what have been the results.

It may be useful to turn to the Organization for Economic Co-operation and Development in Paris (OECD), which, as late as January 1972, analyzed longer-term trends and problems in Norway.[9]

> The broad objectives which have guided Norwegian economic policy during the post-war period have not been different from those pursued in other countries: full employment, rising living standards, social equity, balanced regional and sectoral development, external financial equilibrium and a reasonable degree of cost/price stability. But these general objectives have been supplemented by a wide range of much more specific policy aims expressing priority scales in various fields of economic and social life. Policies designed to raise the level and influence the composition of investment would in this respect seem to have produced the most far-reaching effects. (p. 5)

> Policies directed towards maintenance of social peace and high levels of demand

8. See Odd Aukrust, "PRIM I: A Model of the Price and Income Distribution Mechanism of an Open Economy," Central Bureau of Statistics, Norway, 1970.

9. OECD, *Economic Surveys, Norway* (Paris, January 1972).

and activity on a continuing basis have been important in creating a favorable investment climate. (p. 8)

Viewed against the background of the main policy objectives and considering the inherent tradeoffs between the various objectives the authorities can certainly claim to have had a large measure of success. (p.8)

The rate of growth of total output has not been spectacular by international standards, but it has been relatively steady and sufficiently high to keep output per employed and income per capita rising in line with developments in most other Member countries. Furthermore, since the beginning of the sixties there seems to have been an acceleration in the productivity trend probably related to the strong increase in capital endowments per employed person during the previous decade. Nevertheless the incremental capital-output ratio has remained significantly higher than in most other OECD countries implying that growth has been comparatively costly in terms of reduced consumption. (pp. 8–9)

The external financial position of Norway has been remarkably stable throughout the post-war period. Official foreign reserves have increased steadily not only in absolute terms but also in proportion to imports. (p. 14)

The OECD also recently reviewed Norway's incomes policies and price performance.[10] The main findings may be summarized as follows:

The general price level (GNP deflator) in Norway has increased at about the same pace, 3½ to 4 percent annually in the 1960's, as in other industrialized European OECD countries.

It is difficult for small countries, with large sectors of the economy open to external competition, to maintain a better price and nominal-wage performance than those of their trading partners.

The merit of the Norwegian incomes policy, besides being an instrument in income distribution, lies in the fact that it has enabled the Government to keep the use of productive resources on a very high level throughout post-war years. While the average increase in prices and production costs does not differ much from developments in most other countries, unemployment has usually been lower than the European average, and economic growth has been rapid and steady. With persistently strong pressures on resources, uncoordinated wage and incomes policies could easily have led to wage and price inflation.

Since this OECD evaluation was made, the Norwegian price performance has been less satisfactory, and the latest OECD survey on Norway[11] notes that "the last couple of years have seen some deterioration in Norway's remarkable

10. OECD, *Economic Surveys, Norway* (Paris, January 1971), p. 44.
11. OECD, *Economic Surveys, Norway* (Paris, January 1973).

post-war performance of combining reasonable price stability with high and steady levels of employment and a high degree of social peace.'' Fortunately, this development has most recently sparked a new and promising initiative to extend considerably the coordination of fiscal policies with incomes policies.

Norway's current external account has been in deficit most of the period because of large-scale imports of capital goods, in particular, of ships. The basic balance on current and long-term capital transactions has mostly been in surplus, since long-term borrowing on ships and other capital goods has exceeded the current deficit.

Norway has avoided the brief periods of recession occurring elsewhere, except in 1958 when the effects of a tax reform were miscalculated. The level of unemployment has been consistently very low, and the rate of investment has remained exceptionally high. In 1967–69 fixed investment amounted to 27.4%. Comparable figures are 20.5% for the OECD countries as a whole and 16.6 percent for the U.S.[12]

The financial foundation of this high investment rate has been a combination of high business savings and high savings from the fiscal budget and the social security system. In addition net imports from abroad have helped to finance the investment rate.

The substantial savings in the fiscal budget and the social security system stem from a high level of taxation and social-security charges. It is of interest to note here that the largest single source of revenue in Norway is a 20% value-added tax (VAT) levied on a broad range of goods and services, including food. It may seem surprising that a modern welfare state would include such a levy in its tax arsenal. How can this be socially acceptable? The answer is that it is the income-distribution effect of the tax system as a whole that matters and not the effect of a single tax. It is clear that over-all the Norwegian tax and subsidy system has a strong redistribution effect. Without a high VAT (or general sales tax) it would be difficult, perhaps even impossible, to shoulder the rapdily increasing public expenditures for such purchases as health, education, and communications and additionally to support the high investment level. In Sweden and Denmark the VAT is also a key element in the tax system.

During the Marshall Plan years Norway relied heavily on a general indirect tax on the retail level, usually amounting to 10 percent. In 1970 this sales tax was transformed into the value-added tax.

10. Over the last two decades current-dollar government expenditures

12. OECD, *Expenditure Trends in OECD Countries 1960–80* (Paris, 1971). The OECD countries are the Western European countries, plus Greece, Turkey, the United States, Canada, Japan, and Australia—23 countries in all. The rate for Norway in 1967–69 is somewhat higher than it was in 1950–52, but somewhat lower than in most years of the last two decades.

(goods and services plus transfers to the private sector) have risen faster than GNP in all industrialized countries. In Norway this trend has been stronger than in most other countries. Thus government expenditures in Norway rose from 28.3% of GNP in 1957–59 to 39.8% in 1967–69, compared with a rise in the OECD countries taken together from 27.0 to 32.5% and in the United States from 25.9 to 31.7%.[13] The main reason for this development is the rapidly increasing demand for services traditionally provided through the government and through social-security schemes. This development, of course, implies a need for higher taxes and social-security charges. Whereas total taxes in Norway amounted to 30.1% of GNP in 1957–59, the share rose to 38.7 in 1967–69.[14]

Since 1967–69 the percentage of GNP taken in taxes has continued to increase, and it will probably reach 45% in 1972. It appears that the share will push even higher in the years to come if already-committed extensions of government programs and social security services are to be matched. Clearly, these prospects present difficult policy problems. Although the general public and the business community press for more services through the government sector, their willingness to accept further tax increases is naturally less pronounced. At some stage the increase in taxes as a percentage of GNP has to stop, and this stage may not be far off. Some significant change in financing strategy must soon be devised. This may involve transferring certain financial obligations from the government to the private sector. This should be possible without creating social injustice, since wages and salaries are now at much higher levels than a decade or two ago. But such a policy will be difficult to carry out, because all parties are committed to increased government expenditures in most sectors.

11. Social security expenditures now comprise about one quarter of total wages and salaries in Norway. It is estimated that by 1980 they will increase to 40–45% even without any extension of the present services (beyond what has

13. Ibid.

14. Ibid. Corresponding figures for the OECD countries were 25.8 and 30.5%, and for the United States, 25.4 and 30.0%. It may be of interest to compare how different types of taxes have developed in Norway compared with the United States. The U.S. figures are in parentheses. Social security charges as a percentage of GNP increased from 3.0 (3.0) in 1957–59 to 9.1 (5.4) in 1967–69. Indirect taxes increased from 13.8 (8.4) to 15.6 (9.1), personal taxes from 10.4 (9.0) to 12.6 (11.0), and direct taxes on corporations went down from 3.0 (5.0) to 1.5 (4.4). In Norway the direct taxes on corporations are a remarkably low percentage of GNP. This is partly a consequence of the high rate of plowback into new investment. At the same time the social security contributions formally levied on corporations are high. These amount to some 15% of total wages paid by the corporations.

already been politically committed). This development is, of course, key to the problems discussed in the previous section. It also raises the question of the distribution of income between the working population on the one hand and the older generation (the pensioners) on the other.

Over the last two decades government policies have aimed at increasing the share of national income flowing to the older generation. This has now been achieved to such an extent that some rethinking is required. The young and the newly married are now unduly squeezed. It also seems that policies have paid too much attention to ensuring the older generation's financial resources while paying too little attention to facilities that are particularily valuable to the old people. Greater welfare for the old people probably could have been obtained with lesser claims on economic resources if the emphasis had been shifted somewhat from financial resources to improving certain services and facilities, a lesson that may prove useful to other countries. Therefore, the indicated shift of policy strategy may encompass such a change of emphasis in the care of the older generation.

12. In the Marshall Plan years nobody in Norway was really concerned with environmental problems. Today, twenty years later, the protection of the environment is a very topical question even in Norway with its large area and scattered population. School used to teach that Norway was a poor country with only 33 inhabitants per square mile, and only 3% tillable land, and that more than 70% of the country was "mere" mountains. Today we know that space is a precious commodity and that mountains and a scattered population are great assets.

Because of Norway's sparse population, she has not yet made many of the mistakes of other countries regarding congestion and land use. To ensure a sensible pattern of settlement in the future, a new and powerful law regulating the use of land has been put into operation. Regional policy is no longer looked upon as relevant only to the less-developed areas, but to the physical environment of the whole of Norway.

The land-use dimension of Norway's environment policy appears well in hand, but pollution problems may be more difficult to handle, partly because of airborne pollution from industries in England and on the Continent. Also, the oceans around Norway's long coastline are polluted by many countries. In addition Norway's rivers are polluted by her own industries, agriculture, and other sources. Norway is seeking to meet these problems through international cooperation and through a set of domestic measures. "Polluters pay" will be a guiding principle in Norway's policy in this field. In general the Norwegian approach, at least for the next decade, will be not to stop or to drastically reduce economic growth to protect the environment but to influence the composition of growth in a direction benign to environment. A Ministry for Environmental Protection was established in 1972 to promote environmental policies.

Norway has a special environmental problem resulting from its large-scale hydroelectric power installations. Because these installations divert great rivers from one valley to another, they raise important ecological questions. The government has recently proposed that a number of areas be exempted from hydroelectric power developments. At the same time, the allocation of hydroelectric power to industries heavily dependent upon power will be severely restricted. These are definitely new signals relative to the policy at the time of the Marshall Plan. It is fair to say that Norway hitherto has been far too willing to provide power to heavy industry at much too low a price.

13. The single most outstanding question in Norway during the entire period since the war has been whether the country should join the European Economic Community (EEC).

Norway has engaged actively in international economic cooperation throughout the postwar years, and she has benefited greatly from this. In particular one may mention the cooperation through the OEEC established in 1947 for the implementation of the Marshall Plan, and its successor, the OECD. Membership in the European Free Trade Area (EFTA) was also important to Norway. Participation in these organizations had broad support from all major parties and from the Norwegian people. However, the question of membership in the EEC split Norwegian public opinion more deeply than any policy question since the war. This is because EEC membership is different in kind from previous efforts at international cooperation—different economically, financially, socially, and politically.

According to Norway's Constitution, a decision to join an organization like the EEC requires a 75% majority in Parliament. However, the Parliament decided, quite extraordinarily, that before voting on the question, a consultative general referendum should be held on 25 September 1972.

Most of the political establishment in Norway campaigned energetically in favor of membership. Of the political parties represented in Parliament, only the Center party, previously the Farmers' party, was solidly against joining. The Liberal party and the Christian People's party were split. But the leadership of the Labor party, by far the biggest party with 74 of 150 seats in the Parliament, and that of the second-biggest party, the Conservatives, went all out in favor of membership. So also did the labor-union leadership, practically all of the business community, and most newspapers. The state-owned television and radio services naturally kept a neutral stand while giving broad coverage of the campaign issues. In the final stages of the campaign the Labor party government put extra pressure behind its drive for membership by announcing that the government would resign in case of a "No" from the people.

But in face of it all, a majority of the voters in fact decided to say, "No," implying that a large proportion of the traditional Labor party voters went against their own government. The government accepted the verdict, withdrew its proposition of membership, and resigned. A minority government of representatives from the Center party, the Liberal party and the Christian People's party was established in October 1972. Its parliamentary basis is narrow, and most observers expect that it will not last much longer than it takes to negotiate a free-trade agreement with the EEC, similar to that which Sweden has already obtained.

But the political repercussions of the EEC battle in Norway will be long-lived and far-reaching in just about every walk of life. Any effort to evaluate these repercussions would bring us down to the fundamental issues of the referendum campaign, a task too lengthy for this paper. As for the political parties, the EEC battle may have lasting effects on their relative strength. The block of floating votes, which hitherto has been extremely small, may increase. Thus, though in 1972 the political picture resembled that of twenty years earlier, we may experience important changes over the coming decade or two.

14. Another recent event that may prove of considerable importance to economic, social, and political development is the exploitation of oil and natural gas just beginning outside Norway's coastline. These natural resources may be considerable, and so they cannot fail greatly to influence life in Norway for good or ill.

15. Finally, looking back at the aspirations, hopes, apprehensions, and fears at the time of the Marshal Plan twenty to twenty-five years ago, and measuring them against the developments since, it seems justified to conclude that, for the most part, the aspirations and hopes have been vindicated, and the apprehensions and fears have been overcome. New apprehensions and fears exist today, but even so, twenty years later, we can safely predict that history will give high marks to the Marshall Plan contribution and efforts in Norway.

Inflation, Trade and **Taxes**

Taxation, Inflation, and Growth

Richard A. Musgrave

Until recently, economists have concerned themselves principally with the effects of taxation on the performance of the economy, including such matters as inflation and growth. Of late, however, concern has switched to the reverse side of the coin: to the effects of inflation and growth on the tax system. In line with this trend, this study treats this reverse aspect first.

NEUTRALIZING THE EFFECTS OF INFLATION ON THE TAX SYSTEM

Over the five years 1968 to 1972 annual inflation rates in Europe, the United States, Canada, and Japan have ranged from 4 to 7 percent, while Latin American countries have recorded rates between 40 and 70 percent. Whereas the traditional concern focused on compensating tax adjustments to retard inflation, the impact of this experience has turned the tables and raised the question of how to protect the tax system against inflation.[1]

More precisely, what are the hazards against which the tax system is to be "protected" or the effects that are to be "neutralized"? I shall here define neutrality as a situation where inflation affects neither (1) the level of revenue in real terms, i.e., leaves the government's share in total income unchanged, nor (2) the distribution of the tax burden by (real) income groups. These neutrality

1. For a recent survey of the problem see A. Prest, "Inflation and the Public Finances," *Three Bankers Review,* December 1972.

conditions would be met if we could assume (*a*) that inflation leaves relative prices unchanged, (*b*) that individuals do not hold claims or debt, (*c*) that taxes are imposed on an ad valorem basis, (*d*) that all tax rates are the same, and (*e*) that there are no assessment or collection lags. Obviously, these conditions are not met, so unneutralities arise.

Applications to Income Tax

For various reasons, inflation is of particular importance to income taxes, especially at the individual level. Issues arising in this context relate to both rate structure and the definition of taxable income.

Progressive rates. The progressive nature of the individual income tax—due to personal exemptions and rising bracket rates—means that an inflationary increase in money income moves taxpayers with given real income into higher rate brackets. As a result, the average rate of tax or ratio of revenue to taxable income rises. With prices rising at the same rate as income, revenue increases in real terms, the government's share in income is increased, and our first neutrality condition is not met. Moreover, the progressivity of the burden distribution is reduced, thus offending our second condition. This follows because the average (or effective) rate schedule flattens out as one moves up the income scale, due to the simple fact that there is an upper limit (usually set well below 100 percent) to marginal rates. Similarly, relative burdens tend to rise for large, as against small, families. Since multiple exemptions are allowed as the number of dependents increases, the declining real value of exemptions imposes a heavier burden on large family units.

In devising measures to neutralize these effects, two problems arise. The first is whether the adjustment should be made by lowering rates or by raising the nominal value of bracket limits. Either technique will do to offset gains in real revenue, but only the adjustment of bracket limits will also meet our second neutrality condition. An equal-percentage reduction of liabilities across the scale would not prevent a shift in relative liabilities toward reduced progression, with a complex pattern of rate adjustments needed to prevent this. Yet the objective is accomplished readily by raising bracket limits in line with consumer prices.

The second question is whether the adjustment should be automatic, say on an annual basis, or whether discretionary changes undertaken at an interval of, say, two or three years will suffice. At high rates of inflation the prompt response of automatic adjustment is helpful, but under conditions of moderate inflation discretionary adjustment when needed may be preferable. Since I doubt that total escalation is the solution to the inflation problem, precisely because it will hardly succeed in being total, automatic escalation may suggest too unconcerned a view of this problem.

Nevertheless, the current vogue is for automatic adjustment. Latin American countries such as Chile that have had the benefit of experience with high rates of inflation for a long time have made successful use of such devices for many years, and other countries (including the Swiss Confederation, Sweden, Netherlands, Denmark, Iceland, and most recently Canada) have now turned their attention in this direction. Technical problems arise in the implementation of index adjustments, such as the treatment of indirect taxes; but the general principle is straightforward, and I need not consider it further here.[2]

Changes in asset value. I now turn to a less-discussed but more difficult aspect of the income tax problem. This is the treatment of changes in asset value. I begin with two propositions that I believe to be inherent in the philosophy of the income tax as a personal tax, to be imposed in line with ability to pay. One is that income as a measure of taxable capacity must basically be thought of in real rather than in nominal terms. The other is that capital gains constitute an addition to a person's economic capacity and should be considered part of taxable income, along with wages, dividends, and other forms of accretion. Moreover, this should be the case whether such gains are realized or retained in accrued form. Although income tax statutes—even more so, I gather, in Europe than in the United States—do not satisfy these criteria, this only points to a universal need for income tax reform.

With this in mind, we note an important distinction in the impact of inflation on income flows such as wages or dividends and on income that takes the form of changes in asset value. This will be seen by assuming for a moment that the rate of income tax is proportional. In this case inflation does not affect the wage-earner's tax burden in real terms. As wages double in money terms, so does the tax. Assuming that prices rise in line with wages, all variables are unchanged in real terms. Inflation is tax neutral. But now consider the case of real assets. If prices rise, the value of the asset increases in nominal terms. Hence, a nominal capital gain is recorded, but the taxpayer's real net worth has not changed. To measure changes in net worth in real terms, an inflation adjustment must be applied so that a tax is paid only if a real gain is derived. Inflation thus requires an adjustment in the tax base even if proportional rates apply. In the case of current income flows no such adjustment is needed, the only problem posed by inflation being that which arises from progressive rates.

A similar problem arises with regard to claims and debt. As prices rise, holders of money and debt claims (creditors) suffer a real loss, just as debtors find their net worth increased in real terms. For a consistent application of the

2. For discussion of this problem see Lars Mathiessen, "Index-Tied Income Taxes and Economic Policy," *Swedish Journal of Economics,* March 1973; and Vito Tanzi, "A Proposal for a Dynamically Self-Adjusting Personal Income Tax," *Public Finance,* Vol. 21, No. 4 (1966).

tax to income in real terms, these changes in real net worth should be accounted for as well, i.e., debtors should record real gains and creditors should be permitted to claim real losses. Although the principle is clear, application of such adjustments on a universal basis would be very difficult; and such being the case, the question arises whether much is gained if an inflation adjustment is applied to capital gains on real assets only. Moreover, it is questionable whether an inflation adjustment for realized gains should be allowed as long as such gains are taxed at preferential rates, no interest is charged for the advantage of tax deferral until realization, and unrealized gains are permitted to remain entirely free of tax.[3]

Nevertheless, students of taxation who make much of the need for tax equity (including myself) should face up to the principle that equitable taxation relates to real gains and losses and that implementation of this principle under conditions of inflation imposes serious difficulties.

Depreciation. A related issue arises with the allowance for depreciation. If income is to be measured in real terms, there is a good case for permitting depreciation at replacement cost rather than original cost. By the same token, an inflation adjustment should be applied to the entire balance sheet including recognition of real gains due to a decline in the real value of net indebtedness. Moreover, such an adjustment is appropriate only if the timing of depreciation is in line with economic depreciation, i.e., at a rate in line with the income stream to be derived from the asset. If faster depreciation is permitted, and especially in the case of free depreciation, no such adjustment will be needed.

Timing of payments. It remains to note the great importance that the timing of tax collection assumes under inflationary conditions. Delay in tax payment is always to the taxpayer's advantage unless an adequate interest charge is imposed, but this advantage is increased if the real value of the tax debt erodes in the process of inflation. Depending on the rate of inflation, collection delays may significantly reduce the real value of revenue to the government, and differentials in delay may greatly affect the distribution of tax burdens among groups of taxpayers. Since taxes on wage and salary income are typically withheld whereas capital income enjoys an assessment lag, the net result is one to dampen the progressivity of the income tax structure.

Other Taxes

Although the impact of inflation is especially acute in the case of income taxes, other taxes are affected as well. In the case of excise taxes the distinction

3. On the interrelationship of these various effects see Roger Brinner, "Inflation Deferral and the Neutral Taxation of Capital Gains," *National Tax Journal,* December 1973.

between unit and ad valorem taxes becomes of major importance. As nominal yield stays constant under a unit tax, the real value of revenue declines. Ad valorem taxes in turn record rising nominal yield while maintaining constant real revenue. Since retail-sales and value-added taxes are general and of the ad valorem type, they tend to be inflation-neutral.

Taxes on real property, finally, are threatened by inflation due to assessment lags. Since such lags tend to be substantial, especially in developing countries that rely heavily on land taxation, inflation imposes a serious drain on public revenue. If inflation does not change the relative value of parcels, this might be compensated for by escalating assessment values in line with the rise in general prices; but where relative values change in the process, frequent assessment is the only satisfactory solution.

Effects on Tax Mix

Since the revenue response of various taxes to inflation differs—whether due to progressive rates, assessment lags, or concurrent changes in relative prices and the sizes of various tax bases—one may expect the inflationary process to shift the composition of the tax structure toward the more responsive taxes. This is to say, one would expect a shift from consumption (retail-sales or value-added) taxes toward progressive income taxes, with the behavior of profits-tax revenue depending upon the structure of the particular inflation. At the same time, one would expect the income tax to become less progressive. On balance it is difficult to predict the net effect of these opposing forces on the over-all progressivity of the tax structure.

Moreover, it is reasonable to expect that resulting changes in the composition and level of total revenue will call forth legislative changes and compensating adjustments. As observation of various countries shows, such changes have in fact tended to neutralize the effects of inflation on the composition of the tax structure in most countries. This is not surprising, especially where we deal with relatively moderate rates of inflation that permit plenty of time for legislative adjustments to be made.

Effects on Expenditures

We have argued before that an inflation-neutral system leaves revenue unchanged in real terms. It thus enables government to maintain a constant real level of expenditures. This, however, assumes that prices paid by government (including the wage rates of public employees) do not increase faster than do other prices. In many instances this assumption is optimistic. In the United States, for instance, the price index for government purchases rose 20 percent faster during the 1950s than did the cost of living and 50 percent faster during the 1960s. The latter was a reflection in considerable degree of rapid increases in the wage rates of public employees, a factor to be noted again when considering cost-push inflation. Given this lead in government prices, a rising ratio of revenue to GNP or revenue elasticity in excess of one is needed to maintain real government expenditures unchanged.

USING THE TAX SYSTEM TO RESTRAIN INFLATION

I now turn to the other side of the coin, i.e., the use of the tax system to restrain inflation. The worth of tax policy as an anti-inflation device depends on the nature of the inflationary process. In the case of excess-demand inflation, increases in tax rates are appropriate as an anti-inflation device; but the case is less obvious if inflation originates in the factor market and is of the cost-push variety.

Demand Inflation

In the simpler case of demand inflation, the inflationary gap would be reduced and inflation restrained if tax rates were increased and the collection lag shortened. A given increase in yield is more restrictive, the more it curtails the level of private expenditures. An increase in regressive taxes tends to be more potent in reducing consumption than a rise in progressive taxes, and an increase in consumption taxes tends to be more potent than an increase in income taxes, especially if consumers are subject to money illusion.[4] An increase in corporate taxation especially if in the form of reduced investment incentives (e.g., reduction in the investment credit) tends to be most effective in reducing investment and so forth. With the proper mix of tax increases, tax policy may thus affect the structure as well as the level of private expenditures, thereby directing the deflationary impact so as to meet the structural sources of the inflation pressure. Moreover, the effectiveness of tax increase in retarding inflation differs, depending on whether the revenue is used to retire debt or to reduce the money supply. According to the monetarist view of expenditure behavior, the latter use becomes of crucial importance for the restrictive effectiveness of tax increase; but I trust this controversy need not be aired here.

As an offset to demand inflation, a high degree of automatic response of revenue to inflation is to be welcomed, because it generates an inflation break and reduces the need for statutory rate increases. If the revenue elasticity in response to an inflationary rise in the money value of GNP is less than one, the tax system may be said to contribute to inflation, a coefficient of one may again be said to reflect a neutral system, and a coefficient above one renders the tax

4. See E. Cary Brown, "Analysis of Consumption Taxes in Terms of the Theory of Income Determination," *American Economic Review,* March 1950.

system an inflation-restraining factor. Thus, models of demand inflation may be rendered self-terminating by the presence of a progressive tax system with a revenue response in excess of one.

All this, of course, assumes that the increased revenue is applied to a reduction in deficit or an increase in surplus, i.e., that the rate of government expenditure is independent of its revenue. If we assume (as perhaps we should) that government expenditures rise with receipts, the deflationary power of built-in flexibility is reduced. Indeed, if the government's marginal propensity to spend out of increased revenue exceeds the taxpayer's, built-in flexibility accentuates rather than retards inflation; and so, for that matter, does an increase in tax rates.

Even where the existence of a progressive rate structure results in a high-revenue elasticity and thereby provides a check to inflation, it also generates an inequitable redistribution of the tax burden. Since there is little point in combating the inequities of inflation by increasing those of the tax system, reliance on built-in flexibility is not the best approach. If stabilization and equity objectives are to be reconciled, two policy instruments are needed, including (1) an index adjustment to raise bracket limits and (2) an across-the-board increase in tax rates more than sufficient to offset the revenue loss from (1). Built-in flexibility alone will not solve the problem and may, in fact, do more harm than good.

Incomes Inflation

Matters are more difficult in a setting where inflation originates in factor rather than in product markets. Consider an inflation model where various groups of income recipients demand incomes that valued at current prices exceed total output. Assume further that stabilization policy (including monetary and fiscal measures) is such as to underwrite whatever level of income is needed to sustain full employment. In such a situation continuous and (depending on the lags) cumulative inflation may result. Nothing can be done in this case to check inflation by demand restraint in the product market. Statutory increases in tax rates would create a fiscal drag and unemployment, without halting inflation. Given the shape of the Phillips curve, government may at best use fiscal measures to choose its point thereon; but other devices must be applied if inflation is to be constrained (the Phillips curve shifted) while high employment is maintained.

This then is the world of direct controls and incomes policy. All that tax policy can do is to minimize the damaging effects of inflation on tax equity by index adjustments in rate brackets. This, at least, will protect the distribution of the tax burden against the arbitrary effects of inflation. Other and stronger medicine is needed to tackle the inflation problem itself.

Mixed Inflation

Although this scenario is not totally unrealistic, it is nevertheless too bleak a view of the actual situation. A more realistic model would combine elements of initial demand or pull inflation with those of initial cost-push; and beyond this, it must allow for the feedback effects of price increases upon wage rates via escalator clauses, thus generating a cost-push process leading to further price rise and so forth. In this setting demand restraint may work to some extent, especially if it succeeds in tapering off the rate of inflation and thereby slowing down the escalating forces on the cost side. In any case, such is the hope of any policy package that tries to deal with the problem without including a more or less permanent resort to direct controls. Although such controls have not been strikingly successful, it can hardly be said that the deescalation strategy has done much better.

For our purposes it need be noted further that the escalation process may in fact be accentuated by the existence of an income tax with progressive bracket rates. Such is the case if the escalating process (i.e., the desire to compensate for rising prices so as to maintain real wages) relates to *after-tax* rather than before-tax income. In the absence of taxes the percentage increase in money wages needed to hold real wages constant equals the percentage rise in prices. The same holds for a proportional income tax. After-tax income remains constant in real terms if the percentage increase in before-tax income matches the rate of price increase. But the percentage increase in before-tax income must be larger than that of prices once progressive rates are allowed for.

The magnifying effect depends on the average rate of tax applicable to the initial income and the marginal rate of tax applicable to the increment. Thus, if the initial rate is 20 percent and the marginal rate is 30 percent, a 10 percent increase in prices calls for a 16 percent increase in money wages. If the marginal rate is 40 percent, the needed wage increase is 33 percent, and so forth. With an initial rate of 30 percent, marginal rates of 40 and 50 percent call for increases in money wages of 230 and 600 percent respectively. For this reason the cost-push process is magnified in situations (such as in Scandinavian countries) where incomes policy tends to apply the escalation principle to after-tax income.[5]

Indexing of tax brackets, it should be noted, would not solve this problem. Indeed, it would worsen it. By keeping taxpayers from sliding up into higher brackets (where the differential between average and marginal rates becomes less), the escalating effect would continue in full force as inflation proceeds.

5. To maintain post-tax wages constant in real terms, we must have

$$\frac{M_1(1 - t_1)}{P_1} = \frac{M_1(1 - t_1) + \Delta M(1 - t_m)}{P_2}$$

GROWTH EFFECTS ON TAXATION

It is interesting, finally, to compare these problems with those that arise when tax-base changes involve economic growth and expansion in *real* terms. The problem is once more two-directional, including both the effects of growth upon the tax structure and the effects of the tax structure upon growth.

Built-in Flexibility

In the case of the effects of growth upon the tax structure, issues of built-in flexibility are once more of primary importance for the income tax. The problem differs, depending on whether the growth occurs in per capita income or reflects population growth with a constant per capita income.

Growth in per capita income. We have argued that an inflation-induced upward shift of taxpayers into higher rate brackets is inequitable because it distorts the distribution of the tax burden across different levels of real income. Such is not the case if the increase in money income reflects real growth. In this case the rate of progression across different levels of real income remains unchanged. Yet, "effective progression"—defined as the ratio of the Gini coefficient for income after tax to that for income before tax—is reduced. Effective progression declines as rising per capita income pushes taxpayers up the income scale. Eventually all taxpayers occupy the top bracket, thus rendering the rate structure proportional.

Taking the long view, one may well argue that an equity-neutral income tax is one that maintains constant relative liabilities (or ratios of effective rates) between various points (say decile averages) in the income scale. This is accomplished by raising bracket limits in line with the percentage growth of per capita income, thus lowering the rate of tax at any given level of real income. Moreover, such growth indexing (calling for rising bracket limits in line with rising real income) might be combined with inflation indexing (calling for

---

where M_1 is the initial money income, P_1 and P_2 are the price indices for the initial and subsequent period, t_1 is the average tax rate applicable to M_1, and t_m is the marginal tax rate applicable to the required increase in money income. It follows that

$$\dot{M} = \dot{P} = \frac{(1 - t_1)}{(1 - t_m)}$$

where $\dot{M}$ is required percentage increase in pretax money income and $\dot{P}$ is the percentage increase in price level to which $\dot{M}$ is to be adjusted. See Mathiessen, "Index-Tied Income Taxes and Economic Policy." This tax-multiplier phenomenon was first discussed by E. Lundberg, *Business Cycles and Economic Policy* (London, 1957) (Swedish edition, 1953).

declining bracket limits with rising prices) so as to allow for both types of adjustment.[6]

Growth indexing, moreover, has the consequence of holding the revenue elasticity of a progressive income tax (in relation to the tax base) at unity. Although growth indexing still leaves a "fiscal dividend" in absolute terms as revenue rises, its magnitude is reduced. The question is whether this is an advantage or a disadvantage. Assuming constant population, increased revenue is not needed for the continued servicing of initial program levels. The dividend left with growth indexing will permit government expenditures to grow at the same rate as outlays in the private sector. A constant share of government expenditures in total outlays is maintained automatically, without requiring tax rate adjustments.

Those who believe that the public sector tends to be overexpanded would regard this as too much. In their view an absolute increase in program levels should be undertaken only at the cost of explicit voting to raise tax rates. The rules of the game would then call for growth indexing of rate brackets combined with rate reduction so as to offset the revenue effects of productivity growth. Others would argue that the windfall benefit of more-than-proportional revenue growth should be grasped so as to facilitate a more rapid growth of the public sector, based on the view that the political process tends to understate rather than to overstate its "proper" size.

Between these two extremes the constant share provided by growth indexing may prove a reasonable compromise, reflecting the presumption that the income elasticity of demand for public service will ordinarily be unity. Moreover, this approach tends to avoid fiscal drag as well as fiscal push, by neutralizing the net effect of built-in revenue and expenditure changes. It thereby produces a useful benchmark around which discretionary measures of stabilization policy may be applied, as called for by particular situations.

These considerations, as well as those noted in the inflation context, suggest that a high level of built-in elasticity is not necessarily a desirable feature, at least not in the context of longer-run fiscal policy. Cyclical flexibility is a different matter, but even here explicit formula flexibility may well be preferable to the more-or-less arbitrary formula embedded in a given tax base and a rate structure; beyond this final reliance has to be upon discretionary measures.[7]

6. For a proposal for combined indexing see Tanzi, "A Proposal for a Dynamically Self-Adjusting Personal Income Tax."

7. In a recent study of the Canadian experience, it was shown that built-in flexibility, if permitted to operate unbridled, may come into effect with a substantial lag as the price effects of an expansionary disturbance (which continue to call forth a built-in response) lag substantially behind real-output effects. Thus the restrictive effects of built-in flexibility come into play after real expansion has ceased and may then exert a deflationary influence on employment. See J. Bossons and T. A. Wilson, "Adjusting Tax Rates for Inflation," *Canadian Tax Journal,* 1973 (No. 3).

Population growth. These considerations are modified if the growth of real income reflects population growth rather than a higher per capita income. In this case growth indexing is inappropriate. Assuming the distribution of income to remain unchanged, the existence of progressive rates would not affect the elasticity of the revenue response to the tax base, this elasticity being unity whether rates are proportional or progressive. Moreover, the built-in revenue gain now performs the function of providing for the future financing of the initial service level. A system that combines productivity and population growth thus calls for indexing (i.e., bracket reductions) in line with productivity growth but not in line with population growth. What we have previously described somewhat loosely as growth indexing should thus more precisely be referred to as productivity indexing.

Revenue Mix

Similar considerations may be applied to other taxes. Because factor shares are relatively stable in the long run, the revenue mix between income taxes (assuming productivity indexing to apply) and profits taxes may be expected to remain fairly stable. Since the consumption share is also a fairly constant fraction of income, so will be the revenue mix between income and consumption taxes. Although the role of selective consumption taxes may be changed as a product moves from luxury to necessity status, over-all changes in the composition of the revenue structure may be expected to remain relatively slight. The only major exception is again the role of progressive income taxation in the absence of productivity indexing.

Incidence

Having viewed the effects of a given rate of growth upon tax revenue and burden distribution, we once more turn the tables and consider the effects of tax policy upon growth. These effects are important not only as a matter of growth policy but also in their bearing on tax incidence. This is the long-run aspect of the incidence problem that concerned classical economists such as Ricardo and that is now being reviewed by the application of neoclassical growth models to the incidence problem.[8]

Suppose that we replace a regressive income tax by a progressive one. The immediate effect is to redistribute the tax burden from lower-income to upper-income groups, thereby rendering the system more progressive. But suppose further that this redistribution of the tax burden results in a decline in the rate of

8. See M. Krzyzaniak, "The Long Run Burden of a General Tax on Profits in a Neoclassical World," *Finance Publique,* 1967; and M.S. Feldstein, "Tax Incidence in a Growing Society with Variable Factor Supplies," *Quarterly Journal of Economics,* November 1974.

saving and the rate of growth. This has further distributional effects, with the specific nature of these effects depending on the production function. If the share of capital income declines as the capital-labor ratio falls, this may accentuate the initial effect of making the tax structure more progressive, since capital income is distributed less equally than wage income. But even if factor shares do not change (as would occur with a Cobb-Douglas function), factor returns would be affected. With the relative scarcity of capital increased, the before-tax rate of return on capital would rise and that of labor would fall. This being the case, the after-tax income of high-income groups (a larger share of whose income is from capital) would not rise as much as it would otherwise.

Apart from resulting changes in factor shares and rates of return, the decline in the rate of growth would depress the absolute levels of net income for both capital and labor at any future time. In discussing the incidence problem, one must thus define just what is to be measured (e.g., changes in the size distribution of income, changes in factor shares, changes in rates of return, or changes in absolute levels of income), and one must allow for the fact that the pattern of incidence differs, depending on how much time is permitted to elapse.[9]

Once a longer period is allowed for, there thus exists a close interaction between considerations of incidence and tax equity on the one side and taxation effects on growth upon the other. Both factors must be allowed for and weighed against each other. The task is to minimize conflict by choosing whatever instruments of growth policy are least damaging to tax equity and vice versa. This applies to measures aimed at raising the rate of saving (an aspect of particular importance to developing countries) as well as to the choice of appropriate investment incentives (e.g., investment credits, grants, or acceler-ated depreciation). By judicious choice of instruments, the equity cost of growth policy can be reduced, thus avoiding a situation where the pursuit of growth targets becomes an excuse for disregarding equity objectives.

CONCLUSION

As is evident from these considerations, the "good tax structure" cannot be designed with reference to a stationary economy in which neither inflation nor

9. Economists, in their innate urge to obtain equilibrium solutions, have tended to focus on such results as will obtain after the economy has moved from one equilibrium growth-path to another. Although such comparisions are of interest, one should not forget that the equilibrating adjustment, even if it tends to occur, takes a long time. (See R. P. Sato, "Fiscal Policy in a Neo-classical Growth Model," *Review of Economic Studies,* February 1963.) Given an adjustment process that extends over decades, policy-makers may do well to be concerned with intermediate rather than terminal results.

growth take place. The tax base and its distribution are not fixed but subject to macroeconomic influences that affect both the equity and revenue performance of the tax structure.

All this is of particular importance with regard to the income tax. The existence of inflation causes problems with regard both to rate structure and to the way in which taxable income should be measured. With respect to rate structure, inflation may be neutralized by changing bracket limits in line with prices, but the measurement of taxable income in real terms encounters substantial difficulties. The bearing of real growth upon the income tax differs, depending on whether growth occurs in per capita income or the population grows with per capita incomes constant. Although per capita income growth leaves liabilities at given levels of real income unchanged, it reduces effective progression as measured by the ratio of liabilities between various points (say deciles) in the income scale. This problem may be avoided by productivity indexing, which also neutralizes the effects of growth upon revenue and results in a unit elasticity of revenue with respect to GNP. In all, inflation and growth complicate the role of progressive income taxation in the good tax structure, but the difficulties can be met and need not lead one to downgrade the importance of this tax.

Absolute Poverty and Macroeconomic Activity

Ann F. Friedlaender

I. INTRODUCTION

In assessing poverty there are two distinct, but related, concepts: absolute poverty and relative poverty. Absolute poverty refers to the number of families or individuals whose income lies below some specified level that is deemed adequate for a minimum acceptable standard of living, otherwise known as the "poverty line."[1] Relative poverty refers to the over-all income distribution and, specifically, to the degree of equality or inequality that exists in society. Thus it is concerned with where the poor (usually defined as the lowest quintile) stand relative to the rest of the population.

Although these two concepts are obviously related, they could give very different measures of the extent of poverty in a given economy. Consider, for example, two economies: one that is poor but egalitarian, and the other that is rich but with a very uneven income distribution. Let us assume that the poverty line is the same in both economies.[2] A family below, but near, the poverty line

1. In the United States the measures of the poverty line are based on the cost of basic food requirements, adjusted for family size, sex of family head, age of family members, and place of residence. For a good discussion of different measures of the poverty line, see Kershaw (1970).

2. Of course, the poverty line is itself relative. The first society would probably have a lower poverty line than the latter, consistent with its lower level of income.

in the first economy might have an income above the median, whereas a family above, but near, the poverty line in the second economy might lie in the lowest quintile. The family in the first economy would be poor in an absolute sense but not in a relative one, and the family in the second economy would be poor in a relative sense but not in an absolute one. In terms of absolute poverty the family in the first economy is worse off than the one in the second, but in terms of relative poverty it is better off than the one in the second.

The policy-maker is presumably interested in reducing poverty in both a relative and an absolute sense. There are, however, some conceptual problems associated with measuring poverty in a relative sense. First, measures of inequality are often not very reliable.[3] Second, unless income is distributed equally, there will always be some individuals who are in the lowest quintile and thus who are poor relative to the rest of the population. Although the policy-maker could measure the change in the median income of this lowest quintile or changes in the ratio of the median income of the lowest quintile to the median income of the population, such measures do not really tell how well-off the lowest quintile is in an absolute sense or how poor the poor really are.

In contrast, measures of absolute poverty are straightforward and have a certain operational simplicity. Once the poverty line has been established for given families or individuals,[4] the policy-maker can readily determine how many families and individuals fall under this line. The poverty line can be adjusted over time to reflect changes in income levels and prices, and the policy-maker can determine how the number of families and individuals falling below the poverty line has changed over time. But, just as measures of relative poverty fail to show the absolute level of poverty, measures of absolute poverty fail to show how badly off the poor are relative to the rest of society.

Thus in assessing the effect of policy or of economic activity upon the poor, it is necessary to consider poverty in both a relative and an absolute sense. In recent years a number of studies have analyzed the impact of macroeconomic activity and policy upon income distribution and poverty in a relative sense,[5]

---

3. The Gini coefficient, which measures the area under the Lorenz curve relative to the area under the line of equality, is usually taken as the global measure of equality. As long as one Lorenz curve lies within another, the Gini coefficient gives an unambiguous measure of the change in inequality. If, however, the Lorenz curves intersect, the Gini coefficient gives ambiguous measures of the change in inequality. For a good discussion of measures of inequality, see Atkinson (1970).

4. Of course, the determination of the poverty line involves several conceptual problems and is itself something of a relative concept. Kershaw (1970) has a good discussion of these issues.

5. See, for example, Metcalf (1969, 1972), Schultze (1969), and Thurow (1970).

but relatively few have analyzed their impact in an absolute sense.[6] Moreover, because of data limitations, these latter studies have had to use proxies for the number of families or individuals lying below the poverty line.[7] Thus relatively good information exists concerning the expected response of the over-all income distribution to changes in macroeconomic activity or macropolicy, but there is relatively little information concerning the responsiveness of the poor to macroeconomic activity or macropolicy.

Consequently, the focus in this paper will be on the responsiveness of absolute poverty to the level of macroeconomic activity. Currently, the lack of quantitative knowledge about the impact of macroeconomic activity upon the poor makes evaluation of anti-poverty measures difficult. This is particularly true with respect to the ''war on poverty,'' whose duration coincided with the boom accompanying the Vietnam War. Thus it is difficult to determine whether the changes in the number of poor that took place during the late 1960s and early 1970s reflected the effects of the war on poverty or the boom and subsequent recession.

To the extent that the incomes of the poor are responsive to macroeconomic activity, policies to maintain a high rate of growth and full employment will be effective means of reducing the absolute level of poverty. Moreover, to the extent that the incomes of the poor respond relatively more to macroeconomic activity than the incomes of other members of society, stabilization policies will be an effective means of reducing relative poverty. In this case the interests of the poor and the rest of society coincide, and direct redistributive measures could be aimed at the hard-core poor whose income does not respond to economic activity. But if the poor were generally unresponsive to economic activity, the reduction of poverty in both an absolute and a relative sense would be more difficult and require direct redistributive measures. Moreover, it is entirely possible that macroeconomic activity may reduce poverty in an absolute sense, but fail to reduce it in a relative sense if the incomes of the poor grow more slowly than those of the rest of society. In this case policies to maintain growth and full employment would reduce absolute poverty, but redistributive measures would be required to reduce relative poverty.

6. Hollister and Palmer (1969) analyze the impact of inflation upon the poor, and Perl and Solnick (1971) study the relationship between GNP growth and the number of families with income under $2,000 or $3,000. Mirer (1972) analyzes the impact of economic activity upon distributive shares, and Anderson (1964) considers the relationship between GNP growth and the median income of various groups that have traditionally had a low income (e.g., blacks, families with a female head, and so on).

7. Data on the number of families and individuals lying below a specified poverty line are published annually for the period since 1959. Thus the limited degrees of freedom have made time-series analysis of the relationship between the poor and macroeconomic activity difficult.

Obviously, the analysis of the interrelationships among absolute poverty, relative poverty, and macroeconomic activity is a major undertaking. The scope of this paper is considerably more modest. It is concerned with the incidence of absolute poverty and attempts to provide answers to two specific questions: First, how responsive are different categories of the poor to the level of macroeconomic activity? Second, did the war on poverty have a discernible impact upon different categories of the poor over and above that caused by economic activity?

Briefly this paper takes the following form. Section II considers the distribution of the poor among various categories of the population. Section III discusses the factors determining income levels and derives reduced-form equations that are used to estimate the relationship between the number of poor and economic activity, the war on poverty, the structure of the labor market, and so on. Section IV then summarizes the findings and discusses their policy implications.

II. THE POOR: AN OVERVIEW

As Anderson (1964) has indicated, the number of any given group that crosses over any given poverty line during a specific time period depends in large part upon the relationship between the income distribution of that group and the poverty line. Suppose, for example, there are three groups in the population, each of which has a log-normal income distribution,[8] as illustrated

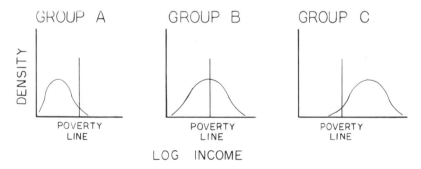

INCOME DISTRIBUTION BY CATEGORY OF POOR
FIGURE 1

8. Metcalf (1969, 1972) has argued that the income distribution of the entire population of the United States can be approximated by a displaced log-normal distribution. Of course, this need not imply that the income distribution of any given subgroup of the population is log-normal.

in figure 1. Group A is very poor with a median income well below the poverty line; Group B is moderately poor with its median income at the poverty line; Group C is relatively affluent with its median income well above the poverty line. Thus the bulk of population Group A lie below the poverty line; half of group B lies below the poverty line; and few of Group C lie below the poverty line. If the median income of each group shifts an equal absolute amount in response to economic growth, Group B will show the largest proportionate reduction in the number of poor, Group A the next largest, and Group C the least.

Of course, the responsiveness of the number of poor in any population group to economic activity depends upon a number of factors: the shape of the income distribution of that group; the relationship between the median (or mean) income level of that group and economic activity; and the relationship between the median (or mean) income level of that group and the poverty line. We therefore cannot simply predict the responsiveness of the number of poor in any given population group to economic activity by the percentage of that group which is poor. Nevertheless, by examining such data, we can probably make

TABLE 1

NUMBER OF POOR INDIVIDUALS BY CATEGORY OF POOR, 1971

Category of Poor	Number (Thousands)	% of Total Poor	% of Population Category
Persons in families and unrelated individuals, all	25,559	100.0	12.5
White head	17,780	69.6	9.9
Nonwhite head	7,780	30.4	30.9
Male head	14,151	55.4	8.1
Female head	11,409	44.6	38.0
Persons in families, all	20,405	79.8	10.8
White head	13,566	53.1	8.2
Nonwhite head	6,839	26.7	29.7
Male head	12,608	49.3	7.5
Female head	7,797	30.5	38.7
Unrelated individuals, all	5,154	20.2	31.6
White	4,214	16.5	29.6
Nonwhite	941	3.7	44.9
Male	1,543	6.4	23.9
Female	3,611	14.2	36.6
Over 65, all	2,563	10.0	42.3
White	2,222	8.7	40.2
Nonwhite	341	1.3	63.3
Male, all	445	1.7	32.6
White	338	1.3	28.8
Nonwhite	107	0.4	55.7
Female, all	2,118	8.3	45.1
White	1,884	7.4	43.3
Nonwhite	234	0.9	67.4

Source: Current Population Reports, Series P-60, Consumer Income, *Characteristics of the Low Income Population, 1971*, No. 86 (December 1972) tables 1, 21.

some inferences about the nature of poverty and its probable responsiveness to economic activity.

Table 1 gives the number of poor individuals (in families and unrelated) in 1971 for various categories of the population. It shows the percentage of each category that is classified as poor as well as the percentage of poor accounted for by each category. Table 2 gives similar data for the number of families. All other things being equal, groups with a substantial proportion of poor (say, 40 to 60%) should show a greater proportionate drop in the number of poor in response to economic activity than groups with a small proportion of poor (say, 10 to 15%).

Examination of tables 1 and 2 indicates that all population categories fall within Groups B or C. Moreover, the proportion of the following groups that is poor is always greater than that of its counterpart: nonwhites versus whites; females versus males; elderly versus nonelderly; families whose head is in the

TABLE 2

NUMBER OF POOR FAMILIES BY CATEGORY OF POOR, 1971

Category of Poor	Number (Thousands)	% Poor Families	% Population Category
Families, all	5,303	100.0	10.0
White	3,751	70.7	7.9
Nonwhite	1,552	29.3	28.8
Male	3,203	60.4	6.8
Female	2,100	39.6	33.9
Head and Service Worker, all	565	10.7	15.3
White	282	5.3	9.9
Nonwhite	283	5.4	30.2
Head other than Service Worker, all	2,244	42.3	5.5
White	1,720	32.4	4.6
Nonwhite	524	9.9	15.5
Head and Nonfarm Laborer, all	273	5.1	9.7
White	174	3.2	9.6
Nonwhite	99	1.9	18.3
Head other than a Nonfarm Laborer, all .	2,236	42.2	5.4
White	1,828	34.5	4.8
Nonwhite	408	7.7	13.3
Head under 65, all	4,243	80.0	9.3
White	2,909	54.9	7.7
Nonwhite	1,334	25.1	26.8
Head over 65, all	1,062	20.0	14.2
White	842	15.9	12.4
Nonwhite	220	4.1	33.4
Male, all	828	15.6	12.8
White	681	12.8	11.4
Nonwhite	147	2.8	29.7
Female, all	234	4.4	23.0
White	161	3.0	19.2
Nonwhite	73	1.4	43.6

Source: Current Population Reports, Series P-60, Consumer Income, *Characteristics of the Low Income Population, 1971,* No. 86 (December 1972), tables 4, 21, 25.

labor force versus families whose head is not in the labor force; unrelated individuals versus individuals in families. Thus to the extent that all groups share equally in economic growth, the following groups should show a greater proportionate decline in the number of poor than their counterpart in response to economic growth: nonwhites, females, the elderly, unrelated individuals, families whose head is not in the labor force. But these groups generally do not share in economic growth equally with other groups. A given increase in GNP will probably not shift the median income of these groups as much as that of their counterparts. Hence, even though a larger percentage of these groups than of their counterparts is poor, a given amount of economic growth may not reduce their numbers of poor proportionately more than in the case of their counterparts. Alternatively stated, a disproportionate share of these groups are poor precisely because they do not respond to economic growth.

It is important to remember, moreover, that the reduction of absolute poverty also depends upon the distribution of the poor among the various groups. If the bulk of the poor are concentrated in type-C population groups, a given rightward shift in the median income level in response to economic growth may lead to a large absolute decline in the number of poor even though it leads to a small decline in the proportion of that group which is poor. Tables 1 and 2 indicate that this may well be the case. Although 70% of all poor individuals are white, only 10% of all white individuals are poor. Similarly, although 63% of all elderly, nonwhite individuals are poor, only 1.3% of all poor individuals are elderly and nonwhite. Consequently, although a rightward shift in the income distribution of nonwhite elderly individuals could reduce their proportion of poor substantially, this would not have much impact on the over-all incidence of poverty. In contrast, although a rightward shift in the income distribution of white individuals would lead to a relatively small decline in their proportion of poor, it could have a substantial impact on the over-all incidence of poverty.

Clearly, the responsiveness of the incidence of absolute poverty to economic activity depends upon a great many factors and cannot be predicted by the data given in tables 1 and 2 alone. Thus we now turn to an analysis that relates the number of poor to the levels of economic activity and other relevant factors.

III. ANALYTICS AND ESTIMATION OF ABSOLUTE POVERTY

A. The Question of Group Heterogeneity

The previous discussion indicated that the poor are not a homogeneous group. Thus it is useful to consider whether the responses of the poor to economic activity differ among groups. The numbers of poor individuals are stratified by family status, sex, race, and age; the number of poor families are stratified by race, age, and occupation. Altogether table 1 contains 24 classifications of poor individuals, and table 2 contains 29 classifications of poor families. Because of the impact of discrimination, differences in the supply and demand responses, and differences in the relationship between earned and unearned income, it would be surprising if all of the groups of poor responded similarly to economic activity.

Because we are primarily interested in the response of the poor to economic activity in analyzing intergroup homogeneity, the number of poor are postulated to depend upon the level of economic activity alone; specifically they are postulated to depend upon the level of current GNP and the unemployment rate. Current GNP incorporates the effect of the growth of real income and inflationary price changes, and the unemployment rate captures the pressure on aggregate demand with respect to different categories of the labor force.[9] Thus in analyzing homogeneity of response, we concentrate on demand responses alone.

In analyzing intergroup homogeneity, slope and intercept dummy variables provide a straightforward way to compare the response of any two groups of the poor to economic behavior. A statistically significant dummy variable on GNP indicates that the response of the dummied groups with respect to GNP is different from that of the undummied group. Thus by using dummy variables, we can readily identify the sources of differential behavior, if any.[10] Consequently, to test for the similarity of response to economic activity between different groups of the poor, regression equations were run in the following form:

$$P_{ij} = \alpha_0 + \alpha_1 d_j + \alpha_2 GNP + \alpha_3 GNP \cdot d_j + \alpha_4 U + \alpha_5 U \cdot d_j + \varepsilon \quad (1)$$

where

P_{ij} = number of poor in category i and number of poor in category j

GNP = annual GNP in billions of current dollars

U = annual unemployment rate

d_j = 1 if poor in category j; otherwise 0

ε = error term

9. In developing a more extended regression analysis, we also made use of the GNP gap, which stresses the relationship between potential and aggregate output and hence the aggregate pressure in the labor market.

10. In contrast, simple covariance analysis permits us to determine whether the over-all behavior is heterogeneous between groups, but it does not let us determine the specific source of any observed heterogeneity.

Thus for category i the estimated response of the number of poor to economic activity is given by

$$P_i = \hat{\alpha}_0 + \hat{\alpha}_2 GNP + \hat{\alpha}_4 U , \qquad (2a)$$

while for category j the estimated response is given by

$$P_j = \hat{\alpha}_0 + \hat{\alpha}_1 + (\hat{\alpha}_2 + \hat{\alpha}_3)GNP + (\hat{\alpha}_4 + \hat{\alpha}_5)U \qquad (2b)$$

Hence if $\hat{\alpha}_3$ or $\hat{\alpha}_5$ is statistically significant, we can infer that the response of the poor in group j to GNP or the unemployment rate is different from the response of the poor in group i.

In running regressions in the form of equation (1), pairwise comparisons of opposites were made with respect to family status, age, sex, race, and occupation. In virtually all cases significant differences between groups were found to occur with respect to economic activity.[11] Thus we cannot combine, say, male- or female-headed households, since the responses of these households differ with respect to economic activity. The only cases where significant differences did not appear to exist were in the behavior of white and nonwhite families whose head was a service worker or a nonfarm laborer, or in the case of families whose head was an elderly male or female. Thus the response of the poor with respect to economic activity appears to be sufficiently heterogeneous that a significant aggregation is not possible.

B. Poverty and Economic Activity

Having established that the behavior of the various groups of poor differs with respect to economic activity, we now attempt to answer the following two questions: (1) To what extent do the number of poor in each group respond to macroeconomic activity? (2) To what extent did the war on poverty increase the responsiveness of the poor in each group to macroeconomic activity? To answer the first question we need to develop a simple model that will capture the demand and supply responses of each group to economic activity. To answer the second question we must formulate the analysis in such a way that it will capture the differential impact of the war on poverty.

In analyzing the income level of any group, it is useful to distinguish between unearned and earned income. The most important component of the poor's unearned income is probably government transfers, which show some evidence

11. The specific regressions in the form of equation (2) will be made available by the author upon request.

of moving in a countercyclical fashion.[12] The other source of unearned income, such as income from stocks or bonds and annuities, should move with economic activity. Except for the elderly, however, it is doubtful that these income sources would affect the number of poor.

The mean or median earned-income level of any given group should be determined by the interaction of the supply and demand for the labor provided by that group, which may or may not be relatively homogeneous.[13] According to the competitive model, the demand for a given type of labor is determined by the real wage and that labor's marginal product, which in turn depends upon output levels and the capital utilized by that type of labor or embodied in it through education. The supply of a given type of labor depends upon the real wage, the existing pool of that type of labor, and various institutional factors such as union rules.

Because of various market imperfections, however, the competitive model should fail to reflect adequately the relevant supply and demand responses. Of these, the three most important may be discrimination, the minimum-wage law, and geographic and sectoral labor immobility. Discrimination tends to shift the demand curve down for a given type of labor as well as limiting its ability to achieve its potential productivity. Thus the observed income differentials between nonwhites and whites (or females and males) undoubtedly reflects the direct effects of discrimination as well as the indirect effects that prevent nonwhites from achieving the same skills and education as whites. The minimum-wage law prevents certain markets from clearing at a low equilibrium wage and thus creates unemployment in those markets. While the employed members of that market may have a higher income than that implied by the competitive solution, the unemployed have a lower one. Labor immobility may be due to inadequate information, transfer costs, institutional barriers such as union rules, and so on. Its effect is to limit the labor-market adjustments and hence to increase the unemployment rate. This, of course, will lower incomes and increase the numbers of poor. In general, market imperfections should limit the income growth of the poor in response to any demand increases and thus reduce the responsiveness of the number of poor to macroeconomic activity.

The war on poverty represented a broadly based effort to reduce the incidence

12. See, for example, Fromm and Taubman (1969).

13. Strictly speaking, the supply and demand responses determine the wage rate, which in turn determines the income level in conjunction with the participation rate. Piore (1970) has indicated that the poor generally participate in the ''secondary'' labor market, which is characterized by low wages and irregular employment. Thus the low incomes received by the poor reflect a combination of low wages and irregular employment.

of poverty. Although the provision of subsidy programs such as Medicare, Medicaid, and Titles I and II of the Elementary and Secondary Education Act of 1965 should probably be included in the war on poverty,[14] its heart was doubtless contained in the programs emanating from the Office of Economic Opportunity (OEO). Most of these were aimed at increasing the education and skills of the disadvantaged, and thus their productivity.[15] The Job Corps and the Neighborhood Youth Corps were aimed at training people with little or no skills to enable them to move into the primary labor market. Head Start and Upward Bound attempted to raise the educational levels of preschool and school age children to enable them to enter the primary labor market directly. Although not a part of OEO, the government also instituted programs to reduce job discrimination in response to the Equal Opportunity Amendment.

Thus the immediate thrust of the war on poverty was to increase the productivity of the poor. This, coupled with efforts to equalize employment opportunities, should have increased the responsiveness of the poor to economic growth. Consequently, to the extent that the war on poverty was successful, we should observe a greater drop in the number of poor in response to economic activity during its existence.

C. The Regression Analysis

In analyzing the homogeneity of the response of the poor to economic activity, we concentrated on the simple demand relationships. But as we have pointed out in the preceding paragraphs, the number of poor in any population category depends upon a complex supply-demand response and the relationship between earned and unearned income. Unfortunately, since data on the number of poor by population category are only available annually since 1959, there are

14. Although Medicare was not primarily an anti-poverty measure, because the poor form a disproportionate share of the elderly and because medical bills form a disproportionate share of the elderly's budgets, Medicare should have a major impact on the elderly poor. Medicaid was established as a program to help the poor receive adequate medical care, with the federal government reimbursing the states for 50 percent of the program's cost. Titles I and II of the Elementary and Secondary Education acts included the provision of funds for special education programs and facilities to economically depressed areas.

15. Other programs were aimed at organizing the poor and increasing their effectiveness. Vista was envisaged as a kind of domestic Peace Corps that would send trained volunteers into neighborhoods to help develop various anti-poverty projects. The Community Action Program encouraged neighborhoods to organize themselves and to develop services and programs that could be coordinated with federal programs to alleviate poverty in the neighborhoods. Neither Vista nor the Community Action Program was aimed directly at increasing the skills of the poverty residents, but they hoped to increase the awareness of the poor and thus to move them out of the secondary labor market.

too few observations to build a structural model explaining the number of poor. Instead, we must be satisfied with using a more modest reduced-form equation that incorporates the relevant forces. Thus we can postulate a general relationship between the number of poor of any given population category ($i = 1, \ldots, n$) and its determinants as

$$P_i = P_i(Y, E_i, Pop_i, T_i, W) \quad (i = 1, \ldots, n) \tag{3}$$

where Y represents economic activity; E_i represents the education and skills attained by group i; Pop_i represents the population of group i; T_i represents government transfers to group i; and W represents the impact of the war on poverty. The first two variables reflect factors affecting the productivity of labor and hence its demand. The population variable reflects the supply of labor of a given group, and the transfer variable reflects the impact of unearned income upon the poor. Of course, the response of the poor to unearned income that is associated with economic activity should also be incorporated in the variable Y. The war-on-poverty variable, W, reflects the differential impact of economic activity on the poor during the war on poverty.

A priori, it is not clear which variable(s) are the best proxy for economic activity. The simple demand analysis described above utilized current GNP and the unemployment rate. Together, these variables probably give a reasonable representation of overall demand pressures. However, because the labor market may be segmented, it is desirable to relate the number of poor in a given population category to the unemployment rate in that category. Thus in considering the total number of poor families, we would use the aggregate unemployment rate; but in considering the number of poor nonwhite families, we would use the nonwhite unemployment rate.

The gap between potential and actual GNP provides a global measure of economic activity. Potential GNP is defined as that level of GNP the economy is capable of producing without inflationary pressures. Thus as actual GNP approaches or surpasses potential GNP, inflationary pressures should rise and unemployment should fall. Similarly, as the GNP gap widens, inflationary pressures should fall and unemployment should rise. Hence, the GNP gap probably incorporates the same forces as current GNP and the unemployment rate, and may provide the best single global measure of economic activity.

We previously postulated that the war on poverty affected the response of the poor with respect to economic activity by reducing market imperfections associated with the poor. To test this, we can introduce dummy variables in association with the variables that represent economic activity. To the extent that the war on poverty had a differential impact upon the response of the poor, these dummy variables should be statistically significant. However, they should probably be interpreted with caution. The war on poverty coincided with a major boom. Hence significant dummy variables for the war on poverty may reflect nonlinearities in the labor-market response to unskilled labor during a boom rather than the effect of the war on poverty per se.

The education variable represents the education and skill levels of the poor and thus their productivity. Two specific variables were used to represent the impact of education: the median-years schooling of a particular population group and the percentage of a given population group that is unskilled labor. The first variable is a specific proxy for education; the second, for skills. Together these variables should capture the effects of capital upon productivity. Again, because of the likelihood of differential labor-market responses among different population groups, these variables were classified to represent different population groups. Thus for poor nonwhite families, the median years of school of nonwhites was used, and so forth.

The population variable is used to reflect demographic forces and the supply of labor. To eliminate multicollinearity with the income variable and to abstract from trend effects, the population variable was expressed in first differences. Nevertheless, because annual population change tends to grow in absolute amounts, the population variable may still reflect some trend effects. Because of differences in population growth, the population variables were divided into population categories comparable to those of the poor.

Finally, where relevant, transfers were divided into subcategories. Thus social security payments were used with the elderly poor, unemployment benefits were used with poor families whose head was in the labor force, and so on.

Because the unemployment rate and the GNP gap are highly collinear, they were not used together as explanatory variables. Thus two regressions were run in the following form: the first using GNP and the unemployment rate as proxies for economic activity; the second using the GNP gap.[16]

$$P_i = \beta_1 W + \beta_1 W + \beta_2 GNP + \beta_3 GNP \cdot W + \beta_4 U_i + \beta_5 T_i$$
$$+ \beta_6 DPop_i + \beta_7 L_i + \beta_8 S_i + u_i \qquad (4a)$$

or

16. Regressions were also run in first differences and percentage changes. But the results were generally less satisfactory in terms of goodness-of-fit, F-statistics, and so on, than those given here. In a few cases the intercept appeared to be collinear with the population and/or the education or skill variables. In such cases the constant was dropped and the war-on-poverty dummy was introduced on those variables. Finally, in a few cases, lagged values of the dependent variables were introduced as independent variables.

$$P_i = \gamma_0 + \gamma_1 W + \gamma_2 Gap + \gamma_3 Gap \cdot W + \gamma_4 T_i$$
$$+ \gamma_5 DPop_i + \gamma_6 L_i + \gamma_7 S_i + v_i \tag{4b}$$

where

GNP = GNP in billions of current dollars
U_i = Unemployment rate for group i
　　　i = all, white, nonwhite, male, female
T_i = Transfer payments in billions of current dollars
　　　i = all, social security payments, unemployment benefits
$DPop_i$ = Changes in population for group i
　　　i = all, white, nonwhite, male, female
L_i = Percentage of unskilled workers in the labor force of group i
　　　i = all, white, nonwhite, male, female
S_i = Median years schooling of group i
　　　i = all, white, nonwhite, male, female
Gap = GNP gap in billions of 1958 dollars
W = Dummy for war on poverty; 1 for 1965, 66, 67, 68; otherwise 0
u_i, v_i = Error terms.

Because of the limited number of observations and problems of multicollinearity among the demographic and human-capital variables, all of the variables were not used simultaneously in analyzing the number of poor. Moreover, in a few areas lagged dependent variables were introduced. When OLS regressions were run, the Durbin-Watson statistic indicated a high degree of serial correlation in the residuals of a number of regressions. These were reestimated using the Cochrane-Orcutt transform. Nevertheless, a fairly high degree of serial correlation in residuals remained in several regressions. In view of the rather simplistic specifications of our reduced-form equation, however, it is quite possible that some important explanatory variables have been omitted.[17]

Since there are over fifty categories of poor, we give a representative sample of the estimated regressions. (A full tabulation of all regressions will be made available upon request to the author.) The regressions given in table 3 are illustrative of the estimated relationships, which we briefly discuss. In the following section we discuss the quantitative relationships between the number of poor and economic activity in some detail.

The regression analysis generally explains the number of poor individuals in families and the number of poor families quite well, but it is only moderately

17. Of these, the most important might be the relation of the minimum wage to the average wage and the labor-force participation rate for various groups of poor.

TABLE 3

REPRESENTATIVE REGRESSION EQUATIONS FOR POVERTY GROUPS

Group	Const	W	GNP	GNP·W	U
Persons in families male head (T, SM)[a]	50215.0 (5.781)[b]	....	....	....	....
Persons in families, female head	4799.48[c] (3.037)	....	....	....	....
Unrelated individuals, male (UM, T, DP)	280.609 (.316)	....	−.9067 (1.093)	......	87.598 (1.415)
Unrelated individuals, female (UF)	2519.015 (3.286)	....	.9804 (1.507)	......	80.069 (1.325)
Unrelated individuals, elderly, male, white (UW)	461.783 (5.304)	....	−.0771 (1.267)	......	16.238 (1.438)
Unrelated individuals, elderly, female, white (DP65, UW, TS)	....	....	3.389 (5.820)	−1.285 (1.309)	137.507 (4.375)
Families, all, white head (UW)	6083.62* (11.876)	....	−4.3491 (12.120)	......	421.625 (6.340)
Families, all, nonwhite head (UN, T)	1545.14* (5.588)	720.131 (2.865)	−.5465 (.726)	−.9097 (2.941)	89.448 (4.061)
Families, head a service worker (DP)	−130.247 (.630)	....	....	....	....
Families, head a nonfarm laborer (U)	1094.26 (6.777)	−639.572 (3.231)	−.8626 (8.971)	.6887 (2.662)	5.525 (.269)
Families, elderly head, male, white (UW)	1152.744 (5.648)	....	−.5854 (4.089)	......	72.912 (2.752)
Families, elderly head, male, nonwhite (UN)	71.616 (.447)	....	.050 (.315)	......	20.447 (1.389)

Group	Gap	T	DPop	W·DPop	S
Persons in families, male head (T, SM)	131.490 (18.252)	−263.937 (27.391)	....	....	−1658.38 (2.245)
Persons in families, female head	11.7373 (3.141)	....	....	....	....
Unrelated individuals, male (UM, T, DP)	....	14.287 (2.371)	.6158 (.205)	....	....
Unrelated individuals, female (UF)	....	....	......	......	....
Unrelated individuals, elderly, male, white (UW)	....	....	......	......	....
Unrelated individuals, elderly, female, white (DP65, UW, TS)	....	−41.379 (3.396)	−.4552 (1.088)	3.2957 (1.373)	......
Families, all, white head (UW)	....	....	......	......	......
Families, all, nonwhite head (UN, T)	....	3.0738 (.468)	....	....	....
Families, head a service worker (DP)	.1423 (.072)	....	.3197 (3.534)	....	....
Families, head a nonfarm laborer (U)	....	....	......	......	......
Families, elderly head, male, white (UW)	....	....	......	......	......
Families, elderly head, male, nonwhite (UN)	....	....	......	......	......

	Lagged Dep	R^2	F	Durbin-Watson
Persons in families, male head (T, SM)	. . . .	.9965	671.386	2.6728
Persons in families, female head	.3179 (1.442)	.6098	5.470	2.1454
Unrelated individuals, male (UM, T, DP)	. . . .	.9112	14.957	2.050
Unrelated individuals, female (UF)....................	. . . .	.2002	1.1407	2.718
Unrelated individuals, elderly, male, white (UW)..............	. . . .	.5973	5.932	2.375
Unrelated individuals, elderly, female, white (DP65, UW, TS)....	. . . .	.8231	5.584	2.424
Families, all, white head (UW)......................	. . . .	.9859	279.115	2.135
Families, all, nonwhite head (UN, T)	. . . .	.9893	92.551	2.704
Families, head a service worker (DP)	. . . .	.7874	16.470	1.969
Families, head a nonfarm laborer (U).....................	. . . .	.9783	79.019	2.438
Families, elderly head, male, white (UW)..............	. . . .	.9076	39.309	2.005
Families. elderly head, male, nonwhite (UN)	. . . .	.3277	2.214	1.523

[a]Symbols in parentheses indicate actual variables used when applicable; they are:
    TS–Social Security payments
    T–Total transfers
    SM–Median years of school, male
    DP Change in total population
    DP65–Change in elderly population
    U–Aggregate unemployment rate
    UW–White unemployment rate
    UN–Nonwhite unemployment rate
    UM–Male unemployment rate
    UF–Femalw unemployment rate
[b]Figures in parentheses reflcet *t*-statistics.
[c]Regression run using Cochrane-Orcutt transform.

successful in explaining the number of poor individuals in families headed by a female, by a service worker, or by an elderly female or elderly nonwhite male. Moreover, it generally fails to explain adequately the number of poor unrelated individuals. Since our reduced form equation generally stresses market forces, this implies that unrelated individuals are generally removed from these forces, and that families headed by females, service workers, or the elderly are only moderately responsive to market forces.

Table 3 indicates theat the GNP gap is generally the best proxy for economic activity with respect to poor individuals in families, whereas GNP and the unemployment rate are best with respect to unrelated individuals and families. It is interesting to note, however, that the response of the number of poor individuals is often perverse with respect to GNP. This indicates again that the behavior of poor unrelated individuals cannot be explained by obvious market forces. Table 3 also indicates that the dummy variable associated with the war on poverty was generally insignificant. This indicates that the war on poverty did not have a significant impact upon the poor. We discuss this point more fully in the next section.

The education and skill variables were not usually statistically significant and did not generally add to the explanatory power of the regression. In table 3 the equation for poor individuals in families with a male head is the only one that contains either the education or the skill variable, although this is moderately significant. The lack of power of these variables implies that, within the range of skills and education encompassed by the poor, these variables do not significantly affect the number of poor. Alternatively stated, the level of these variables is too low to have much differential impact upon the poor.

The behavior of transfers is rather puzzling. Table 3 shows that it takes on a negative sign for nonelderly families, but that it often takes on a positive sign for unrelated individuals and elderly families. To the extent that transfers reflect unearned income, a rise in transfers should create an increase in income of the poor and hence a fall in the numbers of poor; its sign should be negative. But, to the extent that transfers move in a countercyclical fashion, they should rise with the unemployment rate and hence with the number of poor; its sign should be positive. Thus we might expect a positive sign associated with transfers in the regressions for the poor that are associated with the labor market (families with a male head, and so on), and a negative sign associated with transfers in regressions for the poor that are not associated with the labor market. In fact, the opposite happened. This behavior is difficult to explain, but may indicate that transfers act as a proxy for other variables. Obviously more work needs to be done to unravel the full implications of this variable.

Table 3 indicates that the population variable did not generally contain sufficient explanatory power to warrant its inclusion in most regressions. When included, however, its sign was sometimes positive and sometimes negative. If the population variable reflects shifts in the labor supply, it should be positively correlated with the number of poor. If, however, it acts as a trend variable, it should be negatively correlated with the number of poor; the number of poor has fallen during the sample period, while the change in population has risen in absolute terms. In table 3 we can see that the population variable acts as both a supply and a trend proxy and that there does not seem to be a consistent pattern of behavior.

In sum, the simple reduced-form analysis that we developed appears to explain the behavior of poor in families reasonably well, but not the behavior of poor unrelated individuals. Its performance with respect to families with a female or an elderly head is mixed. Since our analysis was associated with simple market mechanisms of supply and demand, it should explain the behavior of the poor that are susceptible to market forces better than those that are not. From this we can infer that families, whatever the race, occupation, age, or sex of their heads, are more responsive to market forces than unrelated individuals. But, all other things equal, families with a female or an elderly head are less responsive to market forces than families with a male or a nonelderly head.

IV. ECONOMIC ACTIVITY AND POVERTY

Of course, even though a given category of poor may be related to market forces, it may not be particularly responsive to macroeconomic activity. As we indicated in Section II, the response of the poor to macroeconomic activity depends not only upon the behavior of the income level of that group but also upon the distribution of income in the group relative to the poverty line. Thus in this section we consider the estimated elasticities of the poor with respect to macroeconomic activity.

By calculating the elasticity of the number of poor with respect to the relevant macroeconomic variables, we can determine the percentage change in the number of poor in a given category in response to a given percentage change in macroeconomic activity, as measured by the unemployment rate, the GNP, the GNP gap, and government transfers.[18] By comparing the elasticities for the sample period as a whole with the elasticities for the period encompassing the war on poverty, we can determine the differential impact of the war on poverty upon the poor.

Table 4 gives the elasticities of poor individuals stratified by family status, sex, race, and age, and table 5 gives similar elasticities for poor families, stratified by race, age, and occupation. Intra- and inter-table comparisons are somewhat difficult, however, because some categories are related to the GNP gap and others to GNP and the unemployment rate. Nevertheless, from these tables we can draw the following conclusions about the impact of economic activity upon the poor.

1. The poor in families are more responsive to economic activity than poor unrelated individuals. Table 4 indicates that the elasticity of poor persons in families with respect to the GNP gap is .976, but the elasticity of poor unrelated individuals with respect to the GNP gap is .019. Since the poor in families represent 80% of all the poor this indicates that the bulk of the poor are quite responsive to economic activity.

Similarly, the poor in families are more responsive to transfers than are poor unrelated individuals. The elasticity of poor persons in families with respect to

18. These elasticities were calculated on the basis of 1970. Since they are point estimates, they are not reliable for large percentage changes.

TABLE 4

ELASTICITY OF NUMBER OF POOR INDIVIDUALS
WITH RESPECT TO ECONOMIC VARIABLES BY CATEGORY OF POOR

Category of Poor	ELASTICITY OF POOR WITH RESPECT TO:			
	GNP	Unemployment Rate	GNP Gap	Transfer Payments
Persons in families and unrelated individuals, all	....	....	.249	−1.080
White head	....	....	.205	− .837
Nonwhite head	....	....	.150	− .797
Male head	....	....	.307	−1.467
Female head	....	....	.037	....
Persons in families, all	....	....	.976	−4.414
White head	−3.322	.112	....	....
Nonwhite head	....	....	.025 (.224)[a]	− .662
Male head	....	....	.328	−1.632
Female head	....	....	.049	....
Unrelated individuals, all	....	....	.011	b
White..................	....	....	.032	b
Nonwhite..................	....	....	.065	b
Male..................	− .658	−.300	....	.795
Female..................	c	c	....	....
Over 65, all..................	1.664	.275	....	− .950
White..................	c	c	....	c
Nonwhite..................	1.580	.210	....	− .593
Male, all	c	....	....	c
White..................	− .165	.160	....	....
Nonwhite..................	c	....	....	c
Female, all	1.509 (.936)[a]	.302	....	− .729
White..................	1.607 (1.039)[a]	.302	....	− .850
Nonwhite..................	b	....	....	.543

[a]Elasticities in parentheses reflect elasticities during war on poverty.
[b]Insignificant coefficient.
[c]Insignificant F-statistic.

total transfers was −4.414, whereas that of poor individuals was not significantly different from zero.

2. For virtually any category the white poor are more responsive to economic activity than nonwhite poor. The elasticity of all poor white persons (related and unrelated) with respect to the GNP gap was .205, and that of nonwhites was .150; the elasticity of families with a white head with respect to GNP was −2.15, and that with a nonwhite head was −.35. It is interesting to note, however, that the elasticity of nonwhite individuals with respect to the GNP gap was greater than that of white individuals: .065 as opposed to .032. Both of these elasticities, however, indicate a low degree of responsiveness to economic activity. Nonwhite elderly families also appear to be more responsive to GNP than white families, with respective elasticities of −2.65 and −1.32. Finally, poor families headed by a nonwhite service worker have an elasticity of

TABLE 5

ELASTICITY OF NUMBER OF POOR FAMILIES
WITH RESPECT TO ECONOMIC VARIABLES BY CATEGORY OF POOR

Category of Poor	ELASTICITY OF POOR WITH RESPECT TO:			
	GNP	Unemployment Rate	GNP Gap	Transfer Payments
Families, all	−2.389	.189	....	....
White head	−2.145	.513	....	....
Nonwhite head	− .352	.485	....	b
	(− .937)[a]			
Head a service worker, all	....	....	b	....
White	....	....	b	....
Nonwhite	−3.432	.870	....	....
Head other than service worker, all	−1.160	.390	....	....
White	−1.282	.431	....	....
Nonwhite	− .707	.299	....	....
	(1.432)			
Head a nonfarm laborer, all	−2.821	b	....	....
White	−2.164	b	....	....
	(− .652)			
Nonwhite	−10.068	b	....	....
	(−4.872)			
Head other than a nonfarm laborer, all .	−1.027	.351	....	....
	(−1.443)			
White	− .882	b	....	....
Nonwhite	− .303	.290	....	....
	(− .958)			
Head under 65, all	− .995	.602	....	....
White	−1.155	.638	....	....
Nonwhite	− .981	.003	....	....
Head over 65, all	−2.594	....	....	−1.077
	(−3.210)			
White	−1.324	....	....	b
Nonwhite	−2.653	....	....	−1.370
Male, all	−1.040	.355	....	....
White	−2.328	.244	....	....
Nonwhite	c	c	....	....
Female, all	c	....	....	....
White	1.146	....	....	....
Nonwhite	b	1.015	....	....

[a]Figures in parentheses represent elasticities during war on poverty.
[b]Insignificant variable.
[c]Insignificant F-statistic.

−3.43 with respect to GNP, whereas those headed by a white service worker have an elasticity that is not significantly different from zero.

The behavior of the white and nonwhite poor with respect to the unemployment rate is similar to that with respect to GNP or the GNP gap. Thus while the elasticity of the number of white families with respect to the white unemployment rate was .513, the elasticity of the number of nonwhite families with respect to the nonwhite unemployment rate was .485. Similar differentials appear to exist with respect to transfers.

Our earlier discussion indicated that, *ceteris paribus*, groups with a large proportion of poor (40 to 60%) should show a greater proportionate reduction in the number of poor in response to economic activity than groups with a low proportion of poor (10 to 15%). Nonwhites generally fall in the first category, and whites fall in the second. Our findings therefore indicate that all other things are not generally equal and thus corroborate those studies specifically concerned with the economic impact of discrimination.[19] Whether due to discrimination, inadequate training, or both, honwhites do not generally share equally in economic growth with whites. In this connection it is interesting to note that two of the categories in which nonwhites appeared to be more responsive to economic activity than whites were unrelated individuals and elderly families, two groups that are not closely related to the labor market and thus less subject to the economic manifestations of discrimination.

3. For any given population category, females were less responsive to economic activity than males. The elasticity of persons in families with a male head with respect to the GNP gap was .328, but the elasticity of those with a female head was .049. Similarly, whereas the elasticity of male unrelated individuals with respect to the GNP gap was .065, no discernible relationship between female unrelated individuals and any of our variables could be found. Similar differentials exist with transfers.

Since any population group with a female head has a larger proportion of poor than a similar population group with a male head, *ceteris paribus*, we would expect those groups with a female head to be more responsive to economic activity than those with a male head. Thus just as with nonwhites, our findings indicate that females are the victims of inadequate training, discrimination, or both. They do not participate equally in economic growth with males.

4. The elderly poor in families appear to be quite responsive to economic growth, but the elderly unrelated individuals do not. The elasticity of elderly families with respect to GNP was −2.59, whereas, that of unrelated elderly individuals was 1.66. In virtually all cases the relationship of elderly unrelated individuals and GNP was perverse; an increase in GNP implies an increase in the number of poor unrelated individuals. However, the response of poor elderly families with respect to transfers was virtually identical to that of poor elderly unrelated individuals; the elasticity of the first group with respect to transfers was −1.077, and that of the second was −.950. Apparently, social security payments affect the related and unrelated elderly poor in a similar fashion.

5. With the exception of families headed by a service worker, the responses of families whose head is in the labor force are similar. Poor families whose head is a nonfarm laborer appear to be somewhat more responsive to economic

19. See, for example, Becker (1957) and Thurow (1969).

activity than poor families whose head is other than a nonfarm laborer or other than a service worker, but the differences are not substantial. It is interesting to note, however, that families whose head is a service worker are not generally responsive to economic activity, except those headed by a nonwhite. This may indicate that poor service workers are generally removed from market forces.

6. Finally, the dummy variables for the war on poverty were generally insignificant or did not add substantially to the explanatory power of the equations. Although they were generally significant in the case of poor families whose head was in the labor force, in the case of white families whose head was a nonfarm laborer the war on poverty apparently reduced the elasticity with respect to GNP rather than increased it. On balance, however, the war on poverty appears to have increased the responsiveness to economic activity of families whose head was already in the work force. It also increased the responsiveness of families with an elderly head. But it did not seem to affect specific groups of elderly families or the number of poor individuals.

Although somewhat tenuous, these findings indicate that the war on poverty primarily helped the poor that were already tied to market forces, and had little effect on those removed from these forces. Indeed, because the war on poverty coincided with a major boom, it is entirely possible that its observed positive effect reflects the differential impact of the boom rather than the war on poverty itself. Although it doubtless aided some of the poor, these are probably the poor who would have benefited from economic growth in any event. Thus the over-all impact of the war on poverty appears to be somewhat marginal.

In conclusion then, although they have widely differing degrees of responsiveness to economic activity, the bulk of the poor appear to be quite responsive to macroeconomic activity. The poor in families, the white poor, and the poor in families headed by a male all show high degrees of responsiveness to either GNP or the GNP gap. Since these groups represent respectively 80%, 70%, and 50% of all the poor, we can infer that most of the poor will cross the threshold of the poverty line if policies to maintain a high rate of growth of income and a low unemployment rate are followed.

Clearly, however, not all the poor are affected by economic growth. Poor unrelated individuals, the nonwhite poor, and the poor in families headed by a female do not generally respond to economic activity; neither do poor elderly unrelated individuals. The problem is compounded if a poor person shares these characterisitcs. Thus a poor elderly, unrelated, nonwhite female is apt to be totally removed from the impact of economic activity. It is interesting to note that the dummy variable for the war on poverty was not significant in these latter categories. This implies that these groups are also not susceptible to the kind of remedial actions encompassed in the war on poverty.

What, then, can we infer about the proper policies to follow with respect to absolute poverty? First, policies to maintain a high level of economic activity should substantially reduce the incidence of absolute poverty. Consequently, market-related antipoverty programs such as the war on poverty are probably unnecessary. Although they certainly increase the responsiveness of certain groups of poor to economic activity, these groups are generally responsive to economic activity and would probably cross the poverty threshold in the absence of these programs. Thus the poor who are not susceptible to economic growth pose the real policy problem. This group, which constitutes 20 to 30% of the poor, will remain poor unless direct redistributive measures are undertaken. Such measures are doubtless difficult to structure and to achieve general support, but without them it seems clear that we will always have poverty in an absolute sense as well as a relative one.

References

Anderson, W. H. Locke, "Trickling Down: The Relationship between Economic Growth and the Extent of Poverty among American Families," *Quarterly Journal of Economics* 77 (November 1964): 511–24.

Atkinson, A. B., "On the Measurement of Inequality," *Journal of Economic Theory* 2 (1970): 244–63.

Becker, Gary, *The Economics of Discrimination* (Chicago: University of Chicago Press, 1957).

Budd, E. C., "Postwar Change in the Size Distribution of Income in the United States," *American Economic Review* 60 (May 1970).

Budd, E. C., and D. E. Seiders, "Impact of Inflation on the Distribution of Income and Wealth," *American Economic Review* 61 (May 1971).

Fromm, Gary, and Paul Taubman, *Policy Simulations with an Econometric Model* (Washington, D.C.: Brookings Institution, 1968).

Hollister, R. G., and J. L. Palmer, "Impact of Inflation upon the Poor," Institute for Research in Poverty, University of Wisconsin, No. 40–69, 1964.

Kershaw, Joseph A., with the assistance of Paul M. Courant, *Government against Poverty* (Washington, D.C.: Brookings Institution, 1970).

Metcalf, Charles E., *An Econometric Model of the Income Distribution* (Chicago: Markham Publishing Co., 1972).

———, "The Size Distribution of Personal Income during the Business Cycle," *American Economic Review* 59 (September 1969).

Mirer, Thad W., "Effects of Macro Economic Fluctuations on the Distribution of Income," Institute for Research in Poverty, University of Wisconsin, No. 410–72, 1972.

Perl, L. J., and L. M. Solnick, "A Note on Trickling Down," *Quarterly Journal of Economics* 75 (1971).

Piore, Michael J., "Jobs and Training," in Samuel H. Beer and Richard E. Barringer, eds., *The State and the Poor* (Cambridge, Mass.: Winthrop, 1970).

Schultze, T. Paul, "Secular Trends and Cyclical Behavior of the Income Distribution in the United States, 1944–1965," in Soltow, ed., *Six Papers on the Size Distribution of Income,* NBER, Studies in Income and Wealth, No. 33 (New York, 1969).

Thurow, Lester, "Analyzing the American Income Distribution," *American Economic Review* 60 (May 1970).

———, *Poverty and Discrimination* (Washington, D.C.: Brookings Institution, 1969).

A Cross-Section Study of Tax Avoidance by Large Commercial Banks

Edward J. Kane

> Why should we break our backs
> Stupidly paying tax?
> Better get some
> Untaxed income:
> You've got to pick a pocket or two,
> Boys, you've got to pick a pocket or two.
>   (Fagin to the Pickpocket Chorus, *Oliver!*)

This paper deals with large U.S. banks' attempts to pay their taxes wisely, a task that depends only partly on their ability to seek out and utilize categories of untaxed income (i.e., exclusions). Wise taxpayers take advantage of deductions, deferrals, preferential tax rates, and tax credits too.

The author wishes to acknowledge the great contribution that Joanne Grolnic's research assistance has made to this paper. Thanks are also due to Burton Malkiel and Richard Musgrave for helpful criticism, to David Alperin, Ted Baker, Kris Branson, Donald Isaacs, Donald Kenny, and Walter Sullivan for compiling the data, and to the Federal Reserve Banks of Boston and the National Science Foundation for financial support.

Formally, we concentrate on income and balance-sheet characteristics that reduce or increase the exposure of a bank's net operating income to federal income taxation. To study this empirically, we construct and estimate a regression model designed to allocate *ex post* (as in statistical cost accounting) a bank's annual federal income-tax bill across each of several identifiable categories of statutory tax liability or tax relief. Our specific focus is the effects of portfolio size and structure on explicit provisions for income taxes reported by individual commercial banks. We make no effort to account for such implicit taxes and subsidies as reserve requirements, deposit insurance, Federal Reserve check-clearing, wire-transfer, and discount services, or the prohibition of demand-deposit interest. Nor do we measure a bank's implicit income. We merely investigate how in the sample years 1966 and 1967 a bank's income and balance-sheet configuration influenced its effective tax rate (defined as the ratio of explicit provisions for income taxes to net operating income).

I. A CRUDE THEORY OF INDIVIDUAL TAX AVOIDANCE

Just as any other economic activity, wisely paying one's taxes uses up resources, and an individual should devote resources to this activity up to the point where its marginal cost rises to equal its marginal benefit. In figure 1 we conceive of tax-avoidance activity as any act that allows a taxpayer legally to exclude one or more dollars of net income from his taxable-income base. We measure this activity by X, the reduction in taxable income it brings about. For each individual taxpayer, X reaches a maximum when taxable income has been driven down to zero. This distance X_{max} equals the taxpayer's maximum potential income. We focus on maximum *potential* income to recognize that some forms of tax avoidance reduce the taxpayer's reported flow of net income below what it would be if all receipts were taxable as ordinary income. For example, coupons on tax-exempt state and local securities lie below those on equivalent taxable issues. The difference in coupons equals the amount of taxes payable on taxable issues by investors whose marginal tax bracket would leave them indifferent between the two opportunities. In the diagram such reductions are subsumed under the category of avoidance costs. Investors in brackets higher than the marginal one are able to exclude additional dollars from their taxable-income base. At the expense of the Treasury, they can earn higher after-tax yields in tax-exempts than they can in taxable issues.

On the vertical axis we plot the marginal cost and marginal benefit of each dollar of X achieved. *MC* is drawn with an initial range coinciding with the X axis to reflect any tax exemptions and deductions that accrue to the taxpayer without special effort. We assume a monotonically increasing *MC*, and plot two alternative marginal-benefit schedules, *MB* and MB′. *MB* is drawn as a step function representing the current federal corporate-tax structure: 22% on

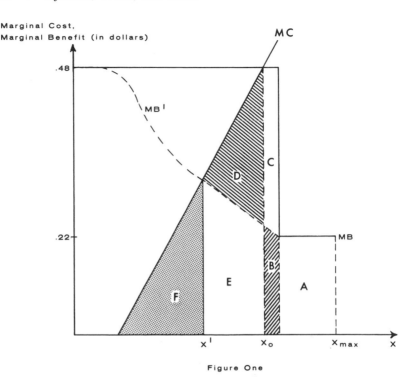

the first \$25,000 of taxable income and 48% on all higher amounts. This structure is often represented as essentially proportional, with the low first-bracket rate introduced to appease the small-business lobby. However, this manner of favoring small business affects the tax-avoidance incentives of larger taxpayers, particularly in industries such as banking that are taxed relatively lightly. MB' represents a "reform" schedule embodying a more smoothly progressive tax structure.

With the current tax structure the taxpayer would pay taxes equal to the sum of the areas labeled A, B, and C. He would also incur tax-avoidance costs equal to the sum of areas D, E, and F. From the point of view of the individual taxpayer (unless he gets special joy out of tax avoidance per se), tax-avoidance cost can be thought of as subjective tax payments that are received by someone other than the Treasury. Some of these subjective tax payments are intercepted and retained by the tax-avoidance industry, which consists primarily of tax lawyers, tax accountants, and their supporting staffs. In the national-income accounts these costs are income originating in this socially unproductive industry. Other costs, such as the taxes not collected from the *marginal investor* in tax-exempts, can be construed as incentive payments redirected by the Treasury either to subsidize state and local government expenditures or to encourage private investment or philanthropy.

If the "reform" tax structure, MB', were to be adopted, in place of MB, tax-avoidance activity would decrease to X' and tax-avoidance costs decrease to area F, freeing scarce resources for other uses but also reducing incentive payments for "merit" activities. The new tax bill would equal the sum of areas A, B, and E: an amount that will be less than, equal to, or greater than the alternative tax bill according to whether $E \lesseqgtr C$.

Even though this analysis omits a number of important details,[1] it has two important policy implications. First, it suggests, as our statistical study of the commercial-banking industry goes on to affirm, that under the current sharply discontinuous corporate income-tax structure a great deal of resources in a lightly taxed industry will be devoted to tax-avoidance activity. Second, it leads us to suspect that a more smoothly progressive structure could be designed to yield as much or more in federal income taxes (and, if desired, even in efficient incentive payments to promote *valid* social goals), while liberating both substantial amounts of resources (lawyers, accountants, data-processing machines, and so on) for other uses and substantial amounts of corporate income for investment or distribution to stockholders.

A. Tax-Avoidance Opportunities Open to Banks in 1966 and 1967

In general, an individual firm or household's effective tax rate is determined by two elements:
1. statutory tax rates on various categories of taxable income and property laid down in formal tax law; and
2. the extent to which the individual taxpayer can structure his accounts so as to shift income and property to categories that
   a. are not taxed at all (*exclusions* and *tax shelters*): depreciation, coupon income on state and local securities, transfers to tax-exempt reserves, charitable contributions;

---

1. These details include:
   a. the simple joy of outwitting a system of regulations;
   b. the reduction of reported net operating income by avoidance costs that have noncurrent or nonmonetary benefits:
      . (i) the overexpansion of tax-deductible promotional or directly enjoyable expenses;
      (ii) the ego gratification and professional advantages of becoming identified as a benefactor of one's alma mater or one's favorite cultural or philanthropic enterprises;
   c. the cost of acquiring useful avoidance information and the uncertainty surrounding the benefits such information ultimately confers.

b. are taxed at a lower marginal rate than ordinary income (*tax preferences*): capital gains, multiple surtax exemptions for holding-company affiliates;
c. provide tax relief in some other way: deferrals and tax credits.

Tax deferrals are accounting transactions that move the payment date of taxes due on accrued current income to a later year. These transactions either postpone the realization of taxable current income to a future year or convert future costs into tax-deductible current expenses. Chief among banks' tax-deferral opportunities are: (i) delaying the realization of capital gains and accrued discounts while taking capital losses in the year they occur; (ii) writing off capital expenditures as current costs whenever this is licit; and (iii) using accelerated-depreciation schedules (especially in connection with equipment-leasing) to generate tax deductions in excess of true capital consumption. Deferrals *avoid* as well as postpone taxes because they reduce the present value of the cumulated tax liability on implicit current economic income.

Tax credits can be viewed as deductions to which the IRS has attached a fixed marginal-tax-rate mutliplier. When the statutory multiplier exceeds the taxpayer's marginal tax rate (as, e.g., in the 100% credit for taxes paid to foreign governments on income earned abroad), the equivalent deduction emerges as a multiple of the eligible expense.

In 1966 and 1967 the major sources of tax relief available to both financial and nonfinancial firms were the lower tax rate on capital gains; the zero tax rate on coupon income from state and local securities; the deductibility of interest payments on debt, as long as the proceeds were not used to finance the holdings of tax-exempt securities; the deductibility of leasing fees and philanthropic contributions; the 7% investment tax credit; and opportunities for taking accelerated depreciation. With respect to the last two of these, the suspension and later reinstatement of the investment tax credit made the intrayear timing of the order and delivery of capital goods of crucial importance. During the period of suspension (for property constructed from 10 October 1966 through 9 March 1967), a tax credit was allowed for the first $20,000 of investment in equipment. In addition, only the first $50,000 in real-property investment whose construction was begun during the suspension period was eligible for accelerated depreciation. These limitations were dropped when the tax credit was restored, both for new investment and for the portion of *any* investment property acquired or constructed after 24 May 1967. A third important general feature of the federal tax code was the continuing implementation of 1964 rules designed to put corporate income-tax liabilities on a fully current (or ''pay-as-you-go'') basis by 1967. These rules required estimated tax payments during the year from any corporation that could ''reasonably be expected'' to accrue a federal income-tax liability of $100,000 or more. In 1966 such corporations were required to file estimated payments during the calendar year equal to 74% of the expected tax liability; for 1967 the applicable percentage increased to 100%. However, provisions regulating the assessment of penalties for under-payment of the final corporate tax liability make the enforceable estimated tax percentage considerably lower than the statutory percentage, especially in a growth context.

Compared with nonfinancial firms, commercial banks had several additional opportunities for reducing the explicit tax bite to which their earnings were subject. The three best-known and (by general agreement) most important of these strictly financial opportunities involve:

1. the privilege of investing borrowed funds (deposits and debentures) in tax-exempt securities without having to surrender the deductibility of interest paid on these funds (an exclusion);
2. transfer of earnings to nontaxable reserve funds[2] (an exclusion);
3. tax trading of open-market securities:
   a. when such trading established net capital gains, these gains were taxed at the *low capital-gains* rate;
   b. when such trading established net losses, these losses could be used *without limit* to *defer* taxes due on an equal amount of ordinary income.

House Committee hearings on tax reform conducted in 1968 and 1969 resulted in a Treasury Department submission [4] and a committee report [3] sharply critical of all three of these tax-avoidance opportunities. However, the Tax Reform Act passed in December 1969 left the tax exemption of state and local securities unchanged and merely lessened the amount of tax savings available under the other two opportunities.

B. Summary and Outline

This study attempts to estimate: (1) the effective tax rates on various categories of income; (2) the marginal tax savings associated with specific

2. Before 1965 a bank's *nontaxable* transfers were limited by its own loss experience either in the previous 20 years or in any 20 consecutive years after 1927. To provide more equal treatment of banks chartered after the depression, in 1965 banks were allowed at their option to use either the ceiling based on their own loss experience or an alternative ceiling equal to 2.4% of their outstanding loans at the close of the taxable year. The Tax Reform Act of 1969 reduced the alternative ceiling rate to 1.8%, with two further reductions staged at six-year intervals.

tax-avoidance activities; and (3) the distribution of tax savings among banks of different deposit size. Empirical evidence is compiled in two forms: (1) frequency distributions of the ratio of taxes to net operating income realized by approximately nine hundred of the nation's largest insured commercial banks in 1966 and 1967, and (2) regression equations seeking to explain the variation in this ratio among different banks in terms of the extent to which the individual banks took advantage of these three specifically financial tax-avoidance opportunities. The regression equations incorporate a set of explanatory variables designed to capture special features of the tax law and opporunties for tax avoidance. Our statistical findings allow us to summarize the average rate of loss in government revenue attributable to each of the three financial tax-avoidance opportunities and indicate that "economies of scale" exist in some types of tax avoidance. By "economies of scale" we mean that an average dollar of tax avoidance becomes cheaper for banks to produce as they grow in asset size. As banks become bigger, their managements become more tax-wise, They hire more and better tax lawyers and tax accountants, who give them better advice about a wider range of avoidance options. In terms of figure 1, economies of scale exist if as banks grow in asset size the *MC* curve shifts to the right.

Both forms of evidence combine to suggest that, for commercial banks at least, the two-tier progressivity built into the corporate tax structure is defeated by tax-avoidance activity. Of course, some of the "avoided" taxes can be viewed as subsidies collected and routed directly to state and local governments and to banks as an incentive to invest in new plant and equipment. However, it is generally agreed that these subsidies are not raised and disbursed efficiently. In particular, the 70 percent ratio of average yields on *Aaa* municipals to average yields on *Aaa* corporates observed in 1966 and 1967 suggests that the break-even marginal tax rate for investing in tax-exempts was approximately 30 percent. It may have been higher in short maturities and even lower in long-term issues. This means that banks subject to the surtax were inframarginal investers for whom the aggregate federal tax liability avoided through holding state and local securities exceeded the interest subsidy ultimately enjoyed by the state and local government authorities that issued them.

More generally, tax-avoidance activity distorts the allocation of taxpayer funds and factor services among competing uses and applies scarce resources to the socially unproductive problem of finding and exploiting tax loopholes. Because a less steeply progressive corporate tax structure (or even a flat proportional tax on net corporate income of about 25% to 30% that admitted no privileged or exempted categories of income) could be designed to raise approximately the same aggregate tax and implicit-subsidy revenue at appreciably lower social cost, the burden of proof should fall on opponents of tax simplification to prove that the distortions and direct resource costs attributable to corporate tax avoidance are counterbalanced by identifiable social benefits transmitted to small corporations.

II.   FREQUENCY DISTRIBUTIONS OF TAX RATES PAID ON OPERATING EARNINGS

Table 1 presents statistics for approximately nine hundred large U.S. commercial banks on the mean and standard deviation of t_y, the ratio of explicit provisions for income taxes to net operating earnings in 1966 and 1967. These statistics show limited progressivity in that banks with between $500 million and $1 billion in deposits show a slightly higher effective tax rate than smaller banks. We hypothesize (and test this hypothesis by regression techniques later) that this differential is to a large extent a threshold effect associated with a second discontinuity in the corporate tax structure: the requirement that a firm had to file estimated tax payments when its federal income tax liability on the current year's income could "reasonably be expected" to exceed $100,000. As compared with banks whose expected income-tax liability is short of the cutoff, this requirement directly limits a bank's ability to defer tax payments on this year's income to the date next spring when it must file its annual return. Moreover, estimated-tax banks should feel themselves more closely monitored by the IRS and less free to take chances on debatable deductions that could embroil them in a full-fledged IRS audit. It is generally believed that the odds of a taxpayer's being audited rise substantially with income and that for each class of deduction a threshold value exists that flags returns as candidates for possible audit.

TABLE 1

SUMMARY STATISTICS ON THE RATIO OF TAX PAYMENTS TO NET OPERATING EARNINGS AT LARGE U.S. COMMERCIAL BANKS IN 1966 AND 1967

	Mean	Standard Deviation	Maximum Value	Minimum Value
All Sample Banks				
1966 (N = 868)	20.4%	11.7%	75.3%	0.0%
1967 (N = 897)	20.7	11.8	65.6	0.0
Banks with deposits over				
$1 billion				
1966 (N = 41)	16.8	9.1	34.3	2.1
1967 (N = 41)	19.4	9.0	33.0	4.1
Banks with deposits between				
$200 million and $1 billion				
1966 (N = 162)	21.6	10.9	50.3	0.1
1967 (N = 163)	22.0	10.7	46.8	0.0
Banks with deposits between				
$10 million and $200 million				
1966 (N = 665)	20.3	12.0	75.3	0.0
1967 (N = 693)	20.6	12.1	65.6	0.0

Source: Individual commercial banks' annual income and dividend Reports

TABLE 2

Frequency Distribution of Operating Earnings Tax Rates Paid by Large U.S. Commercial Banks in 1966 and 1967

	PROVISIONS FOR INCOME TAXES DIVIDED BY NET OPERATING INCOME (IN PERCENT)									
	Less than 10	10–20	20–25	25–30	30–35	35–40	40–50	50–60	60–70	70–100
All Sample Banks										
1966 (N = 868)	200	213	143	132	87	60	25	6	1	1
Percentage of group	23.0	24.5	16.5	15.2	10.0	6.9	3.0	0.7	0.1	0.1
1967 (N = 897)	195	215	149	130	113	61	27	5	2	...
Percentage of group	21.7	23.9	16.6	14.5	12.6	6.8	3.0	0.7	0.2	0
Deposits over $1 billion										
1966 (N = 41)	11	13	9	4	4	...	...	...	...	...
Percentage of group	26.8	31.7	22.0	9.8	9.8	0	0	0	0	0
1967 (N = 41)	8	12	4	12	5	...	...	...	...	...
Percentage of group	19.5	29.3	9.8	29.3	12.2	0	0	0	0	0
Deposits $200 million–$1 billion										
1966 (N = 162)	31	34	27	35	22	7	6	1	...	...
Percentage of group	19.0	20.9	16.6	21.5	13.5	4.3	3.7	0.6	0	0
1967 (N = 163)	27	33	37	26	23	13	4	...	...	...
Percentage of group	16.5	20.1	22.6	15.9	14.0	7.9	2.4	0	0	0
Deposits $10 million–$200 million										
1966 (N = 665)	158	166	107	93	61	53	20	5	1	1
Percentage of group	23.8	25.0	16.1	14.0	9.2	3.0	8.0	3.0	0.2	0.2
1967 (N = 693)	160	170	108	92	85	48	23	5	2	...
Percentage of group	23.1	24.5	15.6	13.3	12.3	6.9	3.3	0.7	0.3	0

Source: Individual banks' annual income and dividend reports.

The data show an "inverted J" relation between effective tax rates and bank size. In both 1966 and 1967 banks with deposits in excess of $1 billion paid lower average rates of tax than banks in the other two classes. Moreover, the rate of tax varied less among banks in this class than among banks in other classes, probably due in part to a greater influence of errors in reporting tax payments at smaller banks. Table 2 suggests that this lower average rate and lesser variability occurred primarily because these very largest banks managed to avoid completely rates higher than 35%, whereas more than 10% of the banks in the other size classes were subject to rates of 35% or higher. Under the federal tax code in effect in 1966 and 1967, the first $25,000 of a bank's net taxable income was subject to a 22% (28% for holding-company affiliates[3]) marginal rate of federal taxation (as compared with a 48 percent rate that applied to higher amounts). Moreover, most sample banks were subject to state income taxes as well. Even though we subsequently produce evidence that only a minority of sample banks reported state income-tax payments on the Income and Dividend Reports we employ as our data source, it seems clear that all forty-one of the largest banks managed to counteract the progression built into the federal corporate-profits tax structure.

This rather remarkable finding raises the question of whether economies of scale exist that allow very large commercial banks to exploit opportunities for tax relief more effectively than smaller banks can. The hypothesis that scale economies exist in tax-avoidance activity can be formulated and investigated statistically in two alternative ways. First, the differences (*a*) in mean tax rates contained in table 1 and (*b*) in the frequency distributions contained in table 2 can be subjected to *t* and chi-squared tests, respectively. Such tests simply ask whether the pattern of observed inequalities in tax rates is too extensive to attribute to chance. Alternatively, we can attempt by multiple-regression techniques to control for sample banks' efforts to avail themselves of specific opportunities for tax avoidance. This approach allows us to estimate the average tax savings available from each avoidance opportunity and to ask whether, after allowing for these tax savings, there remains any evidence of residual scale economies in finding tax relief, presumably in the aggregate nonlinear effects of opportunities included in the linear model and/or in the use of avoidance opportunities on which we have no satisfactory data, such as charitable contributions, leasing arrangements, interest and contractual debt, the investment tax credit, and accelerated depreciation allowances.

Table 3 summarizes the results of performing the *t* and chi-squared tests envisaged in the first approach. The null hypothesis of a proportional or "flat" structure of *effective* rates cannot be rejected. None of the values shown is

---

3. This multiple surtax exemption was phased out under the Tax Reform Act of 1969.

TABLE 3

RESULTS OF t AND CHI-SQUARED TESTS

1. Difference in means between banks in three deposit-size classes:
   a. largest size minus intermediate size
      $t = -0.78$ for 1966
      $t = -1.46$ for 1967
   b. largest size minus smallest size
      $t = -0.56$ for 1966
      $t = -0.50$ for 1967
   c. intermediate size minus smallest size
      $t = +0.23$ for 1966
      $t = +1.64$ for 1967
2. Differences in frequency distributions among the three-size classes (for 18 degrees of freedom $\chi^2_{.05} = 28.9$):
   a. chi-square $= 18.3$ in 1966
   b. chi-square $= 22.4$ in 1967

statistically significant at 5%. However, four of the six t statistics conform in sign, *not* to the two-tier progressive pattern built into federal tax statutes, but to the hypothesis of regressivity due to scale economies in tax-avoidance activities.

III. REGRESSION STRATEGY AND EXPERIMENTS

A. *Family of Models Estimated*

Our regression equations can be justified as vehicles for performing a naïve variety of statistical "tax accounting." We use these models to allocate (as far as the collinearity among the regressors permits) a representative bank's aggregate income-tax bill across specifically identified categories of statutory tax liability and tax relief. Formally, we focus on a family of tax-payment models. Each of these models treats a bank's over-all income-tax liability as the sum of a number of component elements distinguished in the tax code. These components consist of: (1) taxes due on net operating income, Y, and on each of n other statutorily distinct categories of income or specific other categorical sources of differences in tax liability (e.g., requirements for estimated tax payments, holding-company status, state income taxes), Y_i; and (2) the tax relief provided by each of m specific opportunities for tax reduction (e.g., exclusions and deductions), O_j. Although each model differs in the particular Y_i and O_j included in the analysis, all may be subsumed under the following general form:

$$T = a + b_o Y + \sum_{i=1}^{n} b_i Y_i - \sum_{j=1}^{m} c_j O_j + u \ . \tag{1}$$

To allow (and to account for) the current realization of previously deferred income and the consistent underprovision for current taxes, lag terms are introduced in Y and T. Because of these lag terms, the slope coefficients, b_i and c_j, of current variables represent effective "impact" or first-round marginal rates of tax and tax relief respectively. Since lag terms allow tax disbursements and tax savings to accrue gradually through time, in the presence of lag variables these coefficients should lie below both statutory rates and effective stationary-state rates. The customary random-error term is given by u, and the intercept a captures the average amount (calibrated in hundreds of dollars) of tax payments across sample banks not accounted for by the variables included in the model. Where dummy variables are employed, we frequently allow a separate intercept to be estimated for different subsample groups.

Experience with cross-section data drawn from firms of very different size suggests that the variance of the error term in equation (1) may be expected to increase with net operating income, Y. To avoid problems associated with heteroskedasticity, we divide every term on both sides of equation (1) by Y and estimate the parameters of the model in the transformed version (2):

$$\frac{T}{Y} = a\left(\frac{1}{Y}\right) + b_o + \sum_{i=1}^{n} \frac{b_i Y_i}{Y} - \sum_{j=1}^{m} \frac{c_j O_j}{Y} + \frac{u}{Y} \ . \tag{2}$$

Using this model, the intercept a of model (1) emerges as the regression coefficient of the $1/Y$ term, while the effective tax rate on net operating income is found as an intercept estimate. If $\sigma^2_u = \sigma^2(Y^2)$ with σ^2 constant, our procedure would stabilize the variance of the random error in model (2).

Equations (1) and (2) each define a family (or general class) of tax-accounting models, the members of which differ in the specific tax regulations in effect in any year and in the number and identity of the categories of tax liability and tax relief explicitly introduced into the analysis. Table 4 lists the conceptual variables and symbols employed in the course of our regression experiments.

B. Regression Experiments

Our regression strategy is to incorporate as far as we can the subtleties in the Internal Revenue Code applicable to banks. Since our data proxy many of these subtleties only in a rough way, we focus specifically on the average benefits that accrue to individual banks from exploiting the three specifically financial opportunities for tax avoidance listed in section IA above. The regression experiments reported in tables 5 and 6 include a great many regressors. The

TABLE 4

LIST OF VARIABLES

T—Total income-tax payments.

Y—Net operating income.

S—Holdings of state and local securities as of the preceding December 31.

Z—Deposits plus capital accounts as of the preceding December 31.

NG—Net gains (losses, if negative) on securities sales.

d_{PL}—Dummy variable that equals unity for so-called "pure loss" banks, defined as those whose gross losses on securities sales is ten or more times gross gains on such sales, and is zero otherwise.

d_{ML}—Dummy variable that equals unity for so-called "mixed loss" banks, defined as banks other than pure-loss banks that show negative NG, and is zero otherwise.

d_{PG}—Dummy variable that equals unity for so-called "pure gains" banks, defined as those whose gross gains on securities sales is ten or more times gross losses on such sales, and is zero otherwise.

d_{MG}—Equals $(1 - d_{PL} - d_{ML} - d_{PG})$

UG—Unavoidable gains on coupon securities maturing in the first six months of the taxable year.

ΔIRS—Change in IRS-approved loan-loss reserves.

d_{100}—Dummy variable that equals unity for banks with less than $100 million in 1966 deposits and is zero otherwise.

$d_{100-500}$—Dummy variable that equals unity for banks with 1966 deposits between $100 million and $500 million and is zero otherwise.

$d_{500-1000}$—Dummy variable that equals unity for banks whose 1966 deposits fall between $500 million and $1 billion and is zero otherwise.

d_{1000+}—Dummy variable that equals unity for banks with 1966 deposits in excess of $1 billion and is zero otherwise.

r_s—Flat state tax rate on bank income in the state in which the bank is located.

d_E—Estimated-tax dummy variable that equals unity for all banks whose income-tax payments in any year are $100,000 or more and is zero otherwise.

d_{HC}—Dummy variable that equals unity for each bank that is a holding-company affiliate* and is zero otherwise.

ΔFA—Change in fixed assets during the calendar year.

---

*As indicated by the Federal Reserve Board's *Subsidiary Banks of Bank Holding Companies* published each December, listing banks registered pursuant to the Bank Holding Company Act of 1956.

variables in S, NG, and ΔIRS are meant to capture the tax savings generated by investment in tax-exempt securities, tax-trading, and transfers to loan-loss reserves respectively. The size variable Z is meant as a catch-all variable to mop up unallocated residual scale effects. Changes in fixed assets ΔFA are included in the (typically forlorn) hope of proxying the net benefits of any investment-tax-credit and accelerated depreciation opportunities that apply. The holding-company and estimated-tax dummies (the latter is unfortunately a source of some simultaneous-equations bias) let us measure in a rough way the effectiveness of already-mentioned statutory constraints on tax-avoidance opportunities.

The remaining variables (the previous year's income, the value of the state income tax rate, r_s, to which each bank's income is subject, and the value of

TABLE 5

Regression Equations Explaining the Ratio of Individual-Bank Tax Payments to Operating Income at Large U.S. Commercial Banks in 1966 and 1967

Year	Number of Observations	Intercept	$1/Y$	S/Y	Z/Y	$d_t \cdot \frac{NG}{Y}$	$(1-d_{t_1})\frac{NG}{Y}$	$\frac{Y_{-1}}{Y}$	$\frac{\Delta IRS}{Y}$	$d_{100} \cdot \frac{\Delta IRS}{Y}$
1966	757	.094 (5.30)	245.83 (6.61)	−.004 (5.86)	−.0002 (1.46)	.148 (6.40)	.337 (3.97)	.059 (3.72)	−.124 (3.08)	.117 (2.73)
1967	823	.1291 (7.97)	303.70 (9.47)	−.0054 (9.38)	−.0006 (5.15)	.1862 (5.39)	.1391 (4.75)	.0572 (3.81)	−.1074 (3.46)	.0534 (1.50)
1967	797	.1005 (6.20)	302.45 (9.12)	−.0043 (7.53)	−.0005 (4.70)	.1627 (4.69)	.1304 (4.59)	.0394 (2.64)	−.0799 (2.65)	.0346 (.99)
		$\frac{\Delta FA}{Y}$	d_{HC}	r_4	d_E	$\frac{d_E}{(T/Y)_{-1}}$	$(T/Y)_{-2}$	$\frac{d_E}{(T/Y)_{-2}}$	Standard Error of Estimate	R^2
1966		−.008 (.93)	−.006 (.69)	−.157 (1.87)	.069 (6.16)	.305 (8.87)	....	....	.070	.626
1967		−.0068 (1.00)	−.0043 (.66)	−.150 (2.09)	.0758 (8.61)	.2934 (10.79)	....	....	.064	.695
1967		−.0062 (.94)	−.0071 (1.10)	−.138 (1.96)	.0713 (1.59)	.2267 (7.64)	.1470 (4.09)	.0438 (.95)	.062	.710

Note: Figures in parentheses represent values of the t-statistics appropriate to the coefficient above them. Input data measured in hundreds of dollars.

TABLE 6

Regression Equations Parallel to Those in Table 5 But Introducing Dummy Variables to Test for Significant Differences in the Behavior of the Nation's Largest Commercial Banks

Year	Number of Observations	Intercept	I/Y	S/Y	Z/Y	$d_L \cdot \dfrac{NG}{Y}$	$(1-d_L)y\,\dfrac{NG}{Y}$	$\dfrac{Y_{-1}}{Y}$	$\dfrac{\Delta IRS}{Y}$	$\dfrac{d_{100}\cdot\Delta IRS}{Y}$
1966	757	.079 (4.21)	310.29 (6.28)	−.004 (5.72)	−.0002 (1.53)	.140 (6.06)	.332 (3.95)	.057 (3.57)	−.138 (3.33)	.143 (3.16)
1967	797	.091 (5.47)	368.79 (8.28)	−.0043 (7.46)	−.0006 (4.85)	.1574 (4.53)	.1302 (4.58)	.0393 (2.61)	−.0905 (2.93)	.0553 (1.53)
			$\dfrac{\Delta FA}{Y}$	d_{HC}	r_s	d_E	$\dfrac{d_E}{(T/Y)_{-1}}$	$(T/Y)_{-2}$	$\dfrac{d_E}{(T/Y)_{-2}}$	$\dfrac{d_{100-500}}{Y}$
1966			−.007 (.82)	−.004 (.46)	−.164 (1.96)	.074 (6.63)	.292 (8.43)	· · · · ·	· · · · ·	−172.25 (.95)
1967			−.007 (1.09)	−.006 (.90)	−.141 (2.01)	.0722 (6.59)	.2170 (7.20)	.1410 (3.92)	.0549 (1.19)	34.96 (.20)
			$\dfrac{d_{500-1000}}{Y}$	$\dfrac{d_{1000+}}{Y}$	$d_{100-500}$	$d_{500-1,000+}$	$d_{1,000+}$	Standard Error of Estimate	R^2	
1966			−9915.31 (2.96)	1532.44 (.31)	.031 (2.52)	.124 (3.09)	−.015 (.60)	.070	.637	
1967			−4358.6 (1.48)	−3413.3 (.92)	.0288 (1.47)	.0162 (1.54)	.0590 (1.85)	.064	.697	

See note to table 5.

T/Y in the previous year) are proxy variables that have overlapping interpretations. The first variable is included to recognize that provisions for taxes recorded on a bank's I and D Report include final payments in settlement of last year's tax liabilities and accruals and required payments on estimated tax due on income earned in the current year. The second and third variables attempt to control for differences in the extent to which banks are subject to direct state income taxes and other forms of state and local income taxation. Data on r_s were drawn from [1] and [2]. In addition, the Y_{-1} and lagged T/Y variables should capture some of the effects of habitual tax-avoidance activity, especially the net effects of any tax deferrals or loss-carry-overs that might apply.

In regressions not reported in this paper, we tried to include both $d_E(Y_{-1}/Y)$ and $(T/Y)_{-1}$ in the three runs shown in table 5, but these variables proved insignificant and were rejected in accord with the prior hypothesis that they should be collinear with $d_E(T/Y)_{-1}$ and (Y_{-1}/Y) respectively. For banks not required to file estimated tax payments, one-year deferrals are captured fully by the (Y_{-1}/Y) term. Estimated-tax banks show an additional deferral captured by the $d_E(T/Y)_{-1}$ variable. The insignificance of $d_E(T/Y)_{-2}$ in the second 1967 run suggests that two-year deferrals occur at roughly the same rate at both classes of banks. The a priori reason for expecting this lag pattern is that estimated-tax payments are formulated entirely with a one-year context, to prevent taxpayers from holding back their current tax payments until the official settlement date. In 1966 and 1967 corporate taxpayers were required to make current payments equal respectively to 74% and 100% of the tax liability expected to be generated by their current operations.

Covariance tests investigating differences in coefficient estimates among banks of different sizes uncovered one consistent economy of scale: in tax avoidance accomplished by transferring income to loan-loss reserves in 1966. However, other regression experiments indicate that, rather than capturing a scale economy, the coefficient reflects differential use made of this opportunity by holding-company banks.

Estimated-Tax-Payment Banks. The significant differences in the a and b_0 estimates for banks in the $500 million-to-$1 billion deposit class in 1966 also turn out to be difficult to interpret. As indicated in table 7, only three banks in this class were not also in the estimated-tax-payment group. Moreover, only $1/7$ of the banks in the $100 million-to-$500 million class (which shows a significantly higher a) were not subject to estimated-tax payments. Since the significant differences did not recur in 1967 for the $500 million-to-$1 billion class (all of which should have made estimated-tax payments in that year), we have reason to suspect that the significant 1966 size dummies were capturing differences in structure between estimated-tax and other banks. Because the obligation to make estimated tax payments restricts a bank's ability to defer tax

TABLE 7

BREAKDOWN OF SAMPLE BANKS REQUIRED AND NOT REQUIRED TO FILE
FEDERAL ESTIMATED TAX PAYMENTS IN 1966 AND 1967,
BY DEPOSIT-SIZE CLASS

	TOTAL YEAR-END DEPOSITS				
	Less than $100 million	$100–500 million	$500–1,000 million	Over $1 billion	Totals
Number of banks required to file federal estimated tax payments					
1966	281	232	45	38	596
1967	290	257	51	41	639
Number of banks not required to file federal estimated tax payments					
1966	248	39	3	. . . .	290
1967	230	42	. . . .	. . . .	272

Note: Totals are limited each year to the subset of 1,010 sample banks whose income and dividend reports supplied figures on both income-tax payments and net operating earnings.

payments on current income to next spring's reconciliation date, and because the $100,000 exemption was reduced to $5,500 in 1972 and is to be eliminated altogether in 1977, there is also good theoretical reason both to expect and to investigate more-detailed differences in structure than the difference in b_o allowed in tables 5 and 6. Hence, before trying to interpret the other coefficients, we want to take account of all such differences.

Equations parallel to the first and third regressions reported in table 5 are presented for the subsample of estimated-tax banks in table 8. Interesting differences emerge in b_o (as hypothesized and incorporated in our earlier regressions) and in the coefficients of $1/Y$, S/Y, $d_L \cdot NG/Y$, $\Delta IRS/Y$, and $(d_{100}) \cdot \Delta IRS/Y$. These differences are tested for significance by adding d_E times all but the last of these variables (which was eliminated to avoid collinearity) to the regressors of the first and third equations of table 5. The results are shown in table 9. In both years significant differences emerge in tax-trading by loss banks, in transfers to loan-loss reserves, and in the coefficient of tax-exempt securities.

Holding-Company Affiliates. Reputed to be among the advantage of organizing a bank holding company are the opportunities for tax avoidance this corporate form affords, particularly the opportunity to shelter banking income with losses or other tax deductions generated by affiliated firms. This notion derives broad support from the figures reported in table 10. For each of four deposit-size classes the table compares the mean value of T/Y at estimated-tax-payment banks with that at holding-company affiliates. Since the bulk of holding-company banks are required to make estimated tax payments, this is a more relevant comparison than comparing holding-company tax rates with those at other banks of all types.

TABLE 8

Regression Equations Explaining the Ratio of Individual-Bank Tax Payments to Operating Income at Large U.S. Commercial Banks Subject to Estimated Tax Payments in 1966 and 1967

Year	Number of Observations	Intercept	$1/Y$	S/Y	Z/Y	$d_L \cdot \frac{NG}{Y}$	$(1-d_L)\frac{NG}{Y}$	$\frac{Y_{-1}}{Y}$	$\frac{\Delta IRS}{Y}$	$d_{100} \cdot \frac{\Delta IRS}{Y}$
1966	526	.135 (5.86)	188.46 (3.20)	−.003 (3.05)	.0001 (.27)	.209 (6.67)	.315 (3.34)	.052 (2.23)	−.076 (1.54)	.202 (3.37)
1967	589	.206 (9.38)	282.97 (5.83)	−.006 (6.75)	−.0004 (2.54)	.246 (4.61)	.118 (3.22)	.032 (1.58)	.129 (3.19)	.032 (.60)

			$\frac{\Delta FA}{Y}$	d_{HC}	r_s	$d_E \cdot (T/Y)_{-1}$	$d_E \cdot (T/Y)_{-2}$	Standard Error of Estimate	R^2	
1966			−.006 (.40)	−.008 (.84)	−.168 (1.58)	.351 (8.64)	....	.073	.43	
1967			−.005 (.61)	−.008 (1.07)	−.257 (3.01)	.209 (6.52)	.167 (5.31)	.063	.54	

See note to table 5.

TABLE 9

REGRESSION EQUATIONS PARALLEL TO THOSE IN TABLE 5 BUT INTRODUCING DUMMY VARIABLES TO TEST FOR SIGNIFICANT DIFFERENCES IN THE BEHAVIOR OF BANKS MAKING ESTIMATED-TAX PAYMENTS

Year	Number of Observations	Intercept	$1/Y$	S/Y	Z/Y	$d_L \cdot \frac{NG}{Y}$	$(1-d_L)\frac{NG}{Y}$	$\frac{Y_{-1}}{Y}$	$\frac{\Delta IRS}{Y}$	$d_{100} \cdot \frac{\Delta IRS}{Y}$
1966	757	.124 (5.26)	209.68 (4.31)	−.005 (5.33)	−.0002 (1.36)	.063 (1.76)	.333 (3.99)	.039 (2.42)	−.248 (4.98)	.172 (3.73)
1967	797	.068 (3.60)	322.86 (6.91)	−.003 (4.26)	−.0005 (4.26)	.075 (1.71)	.129 (4.59)	.037 (2.48)	−.026 (.70)	.017 (.47)

	$\frac{\Delta FA}{Y}$	d_{HC}	$\frac{d_{HC}}{y}$	r_s	d_E	$d_E \cdot (T/Y)_{-1}$	$(T/Y)_{-2}$	$d_E \cdot (T/Y)_{-2}$
1966	−.010 (1.25)	−.019 (1.64)	173.49 (1.89)	−.162 (1.96)	.031 (1.29)	.356 (9.51)	....	....
1967	−.008 (1.18)	−.008 (.90)	12.36 (.18)	−.132 (1.89)	.130 (6.31)	.212 (6.96)	.153 (4.23)	.012 (.26)

	$\frac{d_E}{y}$	$d_E \cdot \frac{S}{Y}$	$d_E \cdot d_L \cdot NG/Y$	$d_E \cdot \frac{\Delta IRS}{Y}$	Standard Error of Estimate	R^2
1966	−16.60 (.24)	.003 (2.15)	.151 (3.29)	.195 (4.59)	.069	.645
1967	−24.95 (.42)	−.003 (2.58)	.161 (2.37)	−.095 (2.51)	.061	.716

See note to table 5.

TABLE 10

RATIO OF TAX PAYMENTS TO NET OPERATING EARNINGS IN 1966 AND 1967
AT ESTIMATED-TAX AND HOLDING-COMPANY BANKS, BY DEPOSIT-SIZE CLASS

	1966 DEPOSIT-SIZE CLASS			
	Less than $100 Million	$100–$500 Million	$500–$1,000 Million	Over $1 Billion
Banks required to file estimated tax payments				
1966	27.7%	24.2%	21.3%	16.7%
1967	28.7	23.8	21.4	19.4
Banks that are holding company affiliates				
1966	22.3	20.5	19.0	12.8
1967	22.3	19.7	17.0	17.4

As a proxy for taxes accrued, provisions for taxes may function particularly poorly at holding-company banks. Without notifying the bank's management, the parent company may plan before 31 December to transfer income and potential tax deductions among affiliates. However, if bank managers attempt to allow for these possibilities, no consistent bias should result.

To determine to what extent we can account for holding-company banks' lower rates by differences in the operation of the tax-avoidance variables included in our model, we ran regression experiments analogous to those reported in table 9 for 90 holding-company-affiliate banks in 1966 and 107 such banks in 1967. In each year these subsamples include all holding-company banks for which we had data on all variables in the model being estimated. As

TABLE 11

BREAKDOWN BY DEPOSIT-SIZE CLASS, NEED TO MAKE ESTIMATED-TAX PAYMENTS, AND
GAIN (LOSS)-YEAR DECISION OF THE SUBSAMPLE OF BANKS THAT
WERE HOLDING-COMPANY AFFILIATES IN 1966 AND 1967

	TOTAL YEAR-END DEPOSITS				
	Less than $100 Million	$100–$500 Million	$500–$1,000 Million	Over $1 Billion	Totals
1966					
Identifiable in toto	52	39	10	7	108
Were subject to filing estimated tax payments ($d_E = 1$)	36	35	9	7	87
Took a loss year ($d_L = 1$)	37	30	7	7	81
Took a gains year ($d_L = 0$)	10	7	2	0	19
1967					
Identifiable in toto	48	50	11	7	116
Were subject to filing estimated tax payments ($d_E = 1$)	32	42	11	7	92
Took a loss year ($d_L = 1$)	11	23	5	5	44
Took a gains year ($d_L = 0$)	34	26	6	2	68
Both d_E and d_L equal to 1	6	19	5	5	35

Note: Totals in each category are limited each year to the subset of 1,010 sample banks whose income and dividend reports supplied figures on the conditioning variables used to construct the table.

indicated in table 11, for these subsamples the estimated-tax and loss-year categories included much the same banks. This collinearity makes it unwise to apply gains, loss, and estimated-tax dummies to a single variable in any year, forcing us to delete the $d_E \cdot d_L \cdot NG/Y$ term from the models being estimated. We also eliminated the term in $d_E \cdot (T/Y)_{-2}$. To assure comparability between the two years, we introduced a dummy variable, d_{NHC}, for the seventeen banks in the 1967 sample that were absent from our 1966 runs.

Table 12 reports regression estimates of the amended models for the holding-company subsample in each year. From these estimates it appears that holding-company banks paid a generally higher impact rate of tax on current income in each year, but this effect is softened in both years by negative coefficients for lagged earnings and smaller coefficients for lagged T/Y terms. Along with similarly high benefit rates estimated for net securities gains at loss banks and the marked rise in the add-on rate for estimated-tax-payment banks observed between 1966 and 1967 associated with the sharp increase in the percentage of estimated tax due currently, this evidence suggests that holding-company banks feel greater pressure to soft-pedal deferral opportunities. Perhaps they believed that some of the tax advantages of deferral were offset by the favorable effect that showing greater growth and stability in reported earnings has upon the price-earning ratio of the parent company's stock.

Two other interesting coefficient differences emerge only in 1966: (1) the significance of the coefficient for change in fixed assets in 1966, suggesting that in this subsample ΔFA may be proxying new investments eligible for accelerated depreciation and the investment tax credit; and (2) the unaccountably high coefficients (relative to the estimated impact tax rate, b_o) estimated for loan-loss transfers and for securities gains at 1966 gains banks. The latter result appears to trace to collinearity introduced by the perfect correspondence between large holding-company banks that took gains in 1966 and those not required to file estimated tax payments in that year.

The coefficient differences just identified are tested for significance by introducing them into the model of table 9. Because a maximum of 25 regressors is accepted by the Federal Reserve Bank of Boston regression package, we had to delete d_E/Y and $d_E \cdot (T/Y)_{-2}$ from the table 9 model to make room for these variables. As shown in table 13, our tests employ nine d_{HC} variables in 1966 and ten d_{HC} variables in 1967. In these tests the estimated impact tax rate proves significantly different in both years from the parallel coefficient estimated for the sample as a whole. The effect of the higher impact rates at holding-company banks continues to be alleviated by a net negative coefficient on lagged income. Both findings support the notion that holding-company banks deliberately forgo tax advantages associated with deferrals to improve their current earnings statement.

TABLE 12
REGRESSION EQUATIONS PARALLEL TO THOSE IN TABLE 9
FOR SUBSAMPLE OF BANKS THAT WERE HOLDING-COMPANY AFFILIATES IN 1966 AND 1967

Year	Number of Observations	Intercept	$1/Y$	S/Y	Z/Y	$d_L \cdot \dfrac{NG}{Y}$	$(1-a_L)\cdot \dfrac{NG}{Y}$	$\dfrac{Y_{-1}}{Y}$	$\dfrac{\Delta IRS}{Y}$	$d_{100}\cdot\dfrac{\Delta IRS}{Y}$
1966	90	.312 (4.10)	135.63 (.87)	-.010 (3.13)	.0003 (1.12)	.381 (5.88)	1.124 (3.26)	-.055 (1.17)	-.707 (4.24)	.645 (5.86)
1967	107	.233 (4.09)	623.48 (4.01)	-.003 (.97)	-.0006 (1.84)	.236 (1.99)	.115 (.76)	-.136 (3.29)	-.054 (.45)	.007 (.07)

			$\dfrac{\Delta FA}{Y}$	d_{NHC}	$\dfrac{d_{NHC}}{Y}$	r_s	d_E	$d_E\cdot(T/Y)_{-1}$	$(T/Y)_{-2}$	$\dfrac{d_E}{Y}$
1966			-.057 (2.04)	....	....	-.135 (.89)	-.051 (.77)	.337 (3.33)	....	-88.53 (.50)
1967			.009 (.53)	-.009 (.29)	52.22 (.20)	-.137 (.97)	.196 (3.54)	.131 (1.92)	.066 (.91)	-237.9 (1.41)

			$d_E\cdot\dfrac{S}{Y}$	$d_E\cdot\dfrac{\Delta IRS}{Y}$	Standard Error of Estimate	R^2
1966			.002 (.51)	.486 (3.37)	.051	.830
1967			-.006 (1.54)	-.173 (1.61)	.051	.755

See note to table 5.

TABLE 13

Regressions Introducing a Number of Differences in Holding-Company Behavior Directly into the Equations of Table 9

Year	Number of Observations	Intercept	$1/Y$	S/Y	Z/Y	$d_L \cdot \frac{NG}{Y}$	$(1-d_L) \cdot \frac{NG}{Y}$	$\frac{Y_{-1}}{Y}$	$\frac{\Delta IRS}{Y}$	$d_{100} \cdot \frac{\Delta IRS}{Y}$	$\frac{\Delta FA}{Y}$	r_s
1966	757	.149 (8.56)	201.97 (4.78)	−.005 (6.94)	−.0003 (1.96)	.074 (2.14)	.342 (4.24)	.030 (1.85)	−.156 (3.06)	.054 (1.10)	−.013 (1.57)	−.078 (.97)
1967	797	.114 (6.96)	190.16 (4.41)	−.006 (8.69)	−.0005 (3.82)	.129 (2.75)	.139 (4.84)	.064 (3.91)	−.058 (1.53)	−.006 (.151)	−.010 (1.45)	−.116 (1.62)

			$d_E \cdot (T/Y)_{-1}$	d_E/Y	$d_E \cdot \frac{S}{Y}$	$d_E \cdot d_L \cdot NG/Y$	$d_E \cdot \Delta IRS/Y$	d_{HC}	$\frac{d_{HC}}{Y}$	$d_{HC} \cdot \frac{S}{Y}$	$d_{HC} \cdot d_L \cdot \frac{NG}{Y}$	$d_{HC} \cdot d_E$
1966			.396 (13.20)	52.08 (.83)	.004 (4.60)	.100 (2.33)	.052 (1.10)	.141 (1.98)	1.30 (.01)	−.003 (1.51)	.310 (3.72)	−.058 (1.88)
1967			.324 (11.84)	126.23 (2.28)	.002 (3.29)	.094 (1.30)	.011 (.286)	.163 (3.47)	204.89 (2.11)	−.002 (.792)	−.024 (.163)	.035 (1.03)

			$d_{HC} \cdot Y_{-1}/Y$	$d_{HC} \cdot d_{100} \cdot \Delta IRS/Y$	$d_E \cdot d_{HC} \cdot \Delta IRS/Y$	$d_{HC} \cdot \Delta FA/Y$	$(T/Y)_{-2}$	$\frac{d_{HC} \cdot d_E}{(T/Y)_{-2}}$	Standard Error of Estimate	R^2
1966			−.057 (.98)	.323 (2.98)	.110 (1.04)	−.020 (.57)	....	....	.067	.671
1967			−.169 (4.19)	....	−.168 (2.33)	.031 (1.54)	.169 (6.99)	−.115 (1.20)	.062	.708

See note to table 5.

Other significant coefficients in table 13 affirm that: (1) holding-company banks that developed security losses in 1966 derived a tax advantage in line with their high impact-tax rates; (2) holding-company banks required to file estimated tax payments in 1967 benefited at an appropriately high impact rate from transfers to loan-loss reserves; and (3) the lesser tax advantage from loan-loss transfers experienced in 1966 by banks with less than $100 million in deposits is concentrated among holding-company banks of this size.

C. Interpretation of Regression Results

Regression Coefficients Reported in Table 9. Our regression estimates contain a great deal of information both about the benefits and about the frequency of use of various categories of tax-avoiding portfolio adjustments. Moreover, through the size variable Z/Y, they even suggest something about the aggregate benefits of tax-avoidance activities that we were able to include in the model either imperfectly (such as accelerated depreciation and the investment tax credit) or not at all (such as lease arrangement, interest payments on bank debt, and philanthropic contributions). The negative coefficient awarded Z/Y in our preferred equations (tables 9 and 13)—and especially this coefficient's statistical significance in the 1967 runs—indicates that economies of scale exist in the many avenues of tax avoidance taken together, confirming the impression imparted by the average effective tax rates reported in table 1.

The other coefficients can be interpreted more straightforwardly and their relative magnitudes can be used to alert us to possible multicollinearity. The sum of the estimated intercept b_0 and (when the dummy variables do not equal zero) the coefficients of d_{HC} and d_E represents the *marginal impact rate of tax* on current income. In the dynamically more detailed model estimated for 1967, this rate is seen to be about 20% for banks subject to estimated tax payments but on the order of only 7% for other banks. Moreover, the sharp jump recorded in 1967 estimates of the d_E coefficient in table 9 suggests that the law requiring estimated tax payments up to the full amount of taxes due on current earnings substantially reduced these banks' previously successful deferral of tax payments to the date in the spring of the following year when corporate tax returns had to be filed.

By dividing these impact tax rates into the coefficients of S/Y in the same year, we can calculate average running yields on state and local securities. This provides a consistency check on the reliability of these estimates. For banks not required to make estimated tax payments, these values (calculated with figures more precise than those shown in the table) are 4.00% in 1966 amd 4.64% in 1967. However, for estimated-tax-payment banks, the more-complicated dynamic structure—or multicollinearity—results in unrealistically low values: 1.68% and 2.84% respectively. Whereas the first class of banks achieves the bulk of tax savings from tax-exempt income in the current year, for estimated-tax-payment banks these benefits either accrue gradually over time or may even be wasted in some way. Evidence on the importance of deferrals at estimated-tax-payment banks discussed in the next section affirms the common-sense view that the benefits are deferred rather than wasted.

That the $1/Y$ coefficients consistently exceed the value of 55.0 hundreds of dollars implied by the 22% tax rate on a bank's first $25,000 in taxable income indicates that sample banks were on the average operating well beyond the first-bracket level. The coefficient of $d_L \cdot NG/Y$ is within two standard errors of the values of the impact tax rate applicable to both estimated-tax-payment and other banks. The rate of tax on securities gains at gains banks is not significantly different from the 25% statutory rate in 1966, although it is significantly lower in 1967.

The dynamic structure of the equations proves consistent between the two years. The deferral effect captured by Y_{-1}/Y is virtually the same in each year. Moreover, the sum of the lagged T/Y coefficients for d_E banks in 1967 (.212 + .153 + .012 = .377) is almost identical to the 1966 coefficient of $d_E \cdot (T/Y)_{-1}$.

Benefits from transfers to IRS loan-loss reserves were much greater for estimated-tax-payment banks in 1967 than in 1966, whereas the reverse was the case for other banks. This may indicate that the availability of large securities losses in 1966 led the more profitable banks to make relatively little use of these transfer opportunities in 1966. In line with the predilected lock-in effect, making such transfers would have reduced a bank's margin for realizing securities losses without impairing the bank's reported income. Correspondingly, such of these banks that took a gains year in 1967 should have had more gains to realize and, in consequence, could have felt greater latitude to build up their loan-loss reserves then.

The values of the other coefficients in the model generally indicate that the variables they are associated with fail to capture the effects they were intended to proxy. The change-in-fixed-assets variable achieves the anticipated negative sign, but it seems clear that we would have to decompose this variable into its accounting components to separate out the effects of accelerated depreciation and the income-tax credit. Similarly, the bank-holding-company coefficients only weakly support the hypothesis that these banks' 6% higher first-bracket rate (imposed by statute) was not offset by other tax-avoidance opportunities available to holding-company banks. Finally, the rate of state income tax shows a perverse negative coefficient that flirts with significance. The similarity in magnitude with the impact tax rate suggests (and conversations with bank examiners support) the hypothesis that this negative sign occurs because the majority of banks improperly report only *federal* taxes on the Income and

Dividend Reports that serve as our data source. For such banks higher state rates of income tax imply higher federal deductions. We checked this conclusion further by using two alternative definitions of the state income-tax structure: one using effective rates of state income tax calculated by James Eckert as part of a study for Congress [5] and another making allowances via dummy variables for special features of individual state tax laws. In all cases the state-tax variables showed a negative and marginally significant impact.

Calculating Stationary-State Average Rates of Taxation. As mentioned earlier, the various parameter estimates achieved in our regression equations are "impact" coefficients that measure current-year (or "first-round") effects only. If we make a number of simplifying assumptions, we can calculate a vector, t^*, giving the stationary-state average rate of taxation at each class of bank we have distinguished.

The key simplification is to neglect the detailed structure of income flows. This is equivalent to postulating a severe simplification of the tax code such that all sources of net income would be treated symmetrically. Our calculations also neglect the coefficient of Z/Y. This can be justified on the hypothesis that thoroughgoing tax simplification would greatly reduce economies of scale in tax avoidance, but including these coefficients would reduce estimated t^*'s by only about $3/5$ of a percentage point.

The value of t^* proves different for various classes of banks. This occurs because t^* varies with: (1) the mean value of $1/Y$ for each class; (2) the coefficient of any applicable dummy-variable terms of the form d_i and d_i/Y; and (3) the coefficients of lagged terms in T/Y, $d_i(T/Y)_{-1}$ and $d_i(T/Y)_{-2}$. Using i as the index of the various classes of banks we wish to distinguish, t_i^* can be found as the solution to the following equation:

$$(1\text{-coefficients of lagged } (T/Y) - \text{sum of coefficients of applicable } d_i$$
$$\cdot \text{lagged } (T/Y) \text{ } values) \text{ t}_i^* = b_i + (\text{coefficient of applicable } d_i) \cdot$$
$$+ (\text{coefficient of } (Y_{-1}/Y) + (a + \text{coefficient of applicable } d_i/Y)$$
$$(\text{mean } (1/Y)) . \tag{3}$$

Using coefficient estimates of table 9, table 14 presents estimated of t^* for 1966 and 1967. Values are calculated each year for four deposit-size classes and according to whether or not the banks generate enough taxable income to be required to file estimated tax payments. These calculations show: (1) an increase in Treasury "tax effectiveness" from 1966 to 1967, and (2) broad progressivity between estimated-tax-payment and other (in some cases only temporarily less-profitable) banks. However, within the classes of estimated-tax-payment and other banks, stationary-state average tax rates decline with bank size.

TABLE 14

ESTIMATED STATIONARY-STATE AVERAGE TAX RATES FOR
VARIOUS CATEGORIES OF U.S. COMMERCIAL BANKS CALCULATED FROM
THE EQUATION FOR 1967 REPORTED IN TABLE 9
(Neglecting the Z effect)

	DEPOSIT-SIZE CLASS			
	Less than $100 Million	$100–$500 Million	$500–$1,000 Million	Over $1 Billion
Banks required to file estimated tax payments				
1966......................	33.4%	30.6%	29.5%	29.4%
1967......................	44.6	38.4	38.2	37.9
Banks not required to file estimated tax payments				
1966......................	18.5	16.0	....	....
1967......................	22.4	19.2	....	....

Concentrating on the estimated-tax-payment banks, we find that stationary-state rates lie far closer to statutory tax rates than either the average rates reported in table 1 or the impact rates estimated in our various regression equations. This suggests that tax deferrals are an important device by which the largest and most profitable banks keep their effective average tax rates on current income as low as they do. The benefits of deferring taxes are conceptually equivalent to those from negotiating an interest-free loan from the government. The tax liability involved must eventually be discharged with future dollars whose value is reduced by discounting and eroded by inflation. In the meantime the bank retains use of the funds.

The class of tax deferrals is very wide, including any action that either brings future ''charges against income'' forward in time (e.g., accelerated depreciation) or postpones the realization of current income (e.g., accrued capital gains). Our estimates imply that even if a severe tax simplification were enacted, unless growth in bank income and capital investment were to level off and interest-rate fluctuations to cease, the nation's largest banks would still manage to keep their average rates of tax on current income far below statutory rates.

Measuring Avoidance Effects in Percentage Points. A final way to interpret the information contained in our regression equations is to calculate the average effect *in percentage points* of various status and balance-sheet variables on the effective tax rates paid by sample banks in 1966 and 1967. Using the coefficients reported in table 9 and concentrating on the major avoidance activities, table 15 summarizes differences in values calculated for banks of different status.

This table brings out much the same points as our earlier analysis with one important exception. By portraying holding-company banks as subject to a

Notes on the Contributors

David A. Belsley is professor of economics at Boston College and senior research associate at the National Bureau of Economic Research.

Richard A. Caves is professor of economics at Harvard University.

Eivind Erichsen is secretary general to the Norwegian Ministry of Finance.

Frances Esposito is associate professor of economics at Southeastern Massachusetts University.

Louis Esposito is associate professor of economics at the University of Massachusetts–Boston.

Ann F. Friedlaender is professor of economics and civil engineering at M.I.T.

Randall Hinshaw is professor of economics at the Claremont Graduate School in California.

Edward J. Kane is Everett D. Resse Professor of Banking and Monetary Economics at the Ohio State University.

Abba P. Lerner is professor of economics at Queens College, City University of New York.

Sarah Montgomery is professor of economics at Mt. Holyoke College.

Richard A. Musgrave is H. H. Burbank Professor of Political Economy at Harvard University.

Paul A. Samuelson is professor of economics and Institute Professor at M.I.T. and is the first American to be awarded the Nobel Prize in Economics.

Robert M. Solow is professor of economics and Institute Professor at M.I.T.

Robert Triffin is master of Berkeley College and Frederick W. Beinecke Professor of Economics at Yale University.

lower basic effective rate of tax than other banks, the table emphasizes that our model has not incorporated the specific devices with which holding-company banks control their tax payments. Banks required to make estimated tax payments emerge as handicapped on two ways: (1) by being subject to an especially high basic rate and (2) by having previously deferred income add 13 points to their effective rate instead of the 4 points added by deferrals at other banks.

Holdings of tax-exempts and bank size reduce average effective rates at all banks by between 2 and 5 percentage points. Tax trading appears to have lowered a bank's effective rate by about a point in loss years and to have raised the rate by roughly the same amount in gain years. Transfers to loan-loss reserves save up to 1.8 points, while the other variables show only a negligible effect.

References

1. Commerce Clearinghouse, Inc., *State Tax Handbook* (Chicago, 1967).
2. Tax Foundation, Inc., *Facts and Figures on Government Finance,* 14th biennial ed. (New York, 1967).
3. U.S. House of Representatives, Committee on Ways and Means, *Tax Reform Act of 1969,* 2 August 1969.
4. U.S. House of Representatives, Committee on Ways and Means, and U.S. Senate, Committee on Finance, *Tax Reform Studies and Proposals: U.S. Treasury Department,* 5 February 1969, part 3, pp. 458–75.
5. U.S. Senate, Committee on Banking, Housing, and Urban Affairs, *State and Local Taxation of Banks,* parts 1 and 2, Report of a Study under Public Law 91–56 Prepared by the Federal Reserve System, May 1971, and part 3, Appendices to the Report Prepared by the Board of Governors of the Federal Reserve System, December 1971.

TABLE 15

IMPACT OF SELECTED AVOIDANCE ACTIVITIES ON SAMPLE BANKS' EFFECTIVE 1966 AND 1967 TAX RATES, AS IMPLIED BY THE COEFFICIENT ESTIMATES IN TABLE 9

(In percentage rates on tax)

Class of Bank	Year	Basic Rate $[E_D + a(1/Y)]$	Realization of Previously Deferred Income	S	Z	$d_L \cdot NG$	$(1 - d_L) \cdot NG$	ΔIRS	ΔFA	r_s
All banks	1966	15.1	+3.9	-4.8	-1.7	-0.8	+0.9	-1.8	-0.1	-0.01
	1967	11.1	+3.7	-3.4	-4.6	-0.7	+0.7	-0.03	-0.1	-0.03
Banks required to file estimated tax payments	1966	17.4	+13.4	-1.5	....	-1.4	....	-0.4	....	....
	1967	22.8	+13.1	-4.9	....	-1.6	....	-0.8	....	....
Holding-company affiliates	1966	14.3	....	....	....	....	....	....	....	....
	1967	10.2	....	....	....	....	....	....	....	....
Banks with less than $100 million deposits	1966	....	....	....	....	....	....	-0.7	....	....
	1967	....	....	....	....	....	....	-0.1	....	....

Note: Unless a separate figure is supplied, the estimate for "All banks" applies to other classes of banks as well.

Index